NASARA

DISPATCHES FROM A DISTRICT HOSPITAL IN CHAD

JAMES APPEL, MD

All proceeds from the sale of this book will be used for improving
medical care in the Republic of Chad

To donate to the work going on at the Béré Adventist Hospital visit
www.adventisthealthinternational.org

Scriptures quoted are from the World English Bible, which is a public domain,
modern English Bible based on the American Standard Version.
For more information visit www.ebible.org

You can obtain additional copies of this book by visiting
www.createspace.com/3586897

To get a copy of the documentary *Unto the Ends*
about the Béré Adventist Hospital visit
www.untotheends.com

Cover photos courtesy of Jabel Busl

Cover design by James Appel, MD

Contact the author at NasaraBook@gmail.com

FOR SARAH GRY

"THE PERSON WHO RISKS NOTHING,
DOES NOTHING, HAS NOTHING, IS
NOTHING…"

SØREN KIRKEGAARD

CONTENTS

PREFACE

This book is a compilation of a series of email newsletters and blogs that I sent out to an ever-increasing number of subscribers over a three-year period from January 2004 through December 2006. I mostly wrote as an outlet to express the extraordinary things I was experiencing as a young doctor fresh out of Family Practice Residency training thrown into being medical director and only physician in a small district hospital in the Republic of *Tchad*. I saw so many tragedies, performed so many surgeries and other procedures I was not qualified to do, and saw so much death, especially in the form of small children, that in order to survive psychologically, I needed a release.

To my great surprise, many people in completely different circumstances found my writing inspiring. Over the years, some have asked if I was ever going to write a book. This shocked me since writing a book had never seriously crossed my mind. I resisted for many years, but finally came to the conclusion that maybe the world did need to see a more balanced picture of what it is like to work in such conditions.

Many people have this romantic idea of what it is to be a humanitarian aide worker. It seems exciting and adventurous. The travel logs of itinerant explorers are filled with enriching cultural experiences colored by short interactions with indigenous peoples. They often live entirely in the "honeymoon" period before the reality of long-term commitment sets in. You can go to Africa for a few weeks or months and delude yourself that you are making a difference without really touching the lives of those you are supposed to help. And the hope is to come away as a hero, a compassionate foreign benefactor helping the suffering poor.

However, the reality is often filled with mistakes, depression, frustration, anger, regrets, misery, and premature death. There is uncertainty, costly errors, poor decisions, gross cultural bumbling, hurt feelings, irreconcilable differences and a lack of appreciation for local customs.

No one seems to want to write about his own failures, he would rather present himself in a positive light, gloss over his inconsistencies and give excuses for the poor outcomes rather than face his own human weakness.

I am guilty of all of the above. Yet somehow, sometimes, when pushed to the limit, I was so far gone that I didn't care. In those times, the truth would sneak out through some hastily written email in the early morning hours before the cock crowed and the muezzin shouted out the call for prayer.

This book is a collection of some of those moments.

ACKNOWLEDGMENTS

To Dr. Richard Hart and the staff of Adventist Health International for their continued support of the Béré Adventist Hospital and other outpost medical centers throughout the developing world.

To my grandparents, Alva and Wilma, for inspiring me to work in far-off places through hearing their stories of growing up and living in China, India, and Sri Lanka.

To my parents, Jim and Gladys, for always encouraging me to do my best no matter what it was.

To all my professors and attending physicians at Loma Linda University for their excellent medical training and introduction to whole person care.

To my attending physicians at the Ventura County Medical Center for the best residency training available on the planet.

To the many surgeons who took me under their wing at Ventura County Medical Center teaching me the skills that have allowed me to save so many lives in *Tchad* despite not being a surgeon.

To Dr. Warren Dekraay for helping me refine my surgical skills.

To Drs. Effie Jean and Sam Ketting for handing me the scalpel and sharing with me their vast reservoir of surgical knowledge while I was doing an elective rotation in Nigeria.

To Greg and Audrey Shank for their mentoring, collaboration and friendship at the Koza Adventist Hospital in Northern Cameroon.

To Dr. Fatchou for taking me under his wing when I arrived in *Tchad*.

To Paul Kim whose documentary *Unto the Ends* unveiled to many the reality of working in a district hospital in Africa.

To Dee Reed for her invaluable advice and editing help.

To the hundreds of volunteers from around the world who've inspired us over the years with their courage and hard work

To the countless others who've encouraged and inspired me with their emails, calls, and letters during my time in *Tchad*.

INTRODUCTION

I first heard about the Béré Adventist Hospital from Monita Burtch, then health director for the Central African Union. I was trying to figure out what I was going to do after finishing my residency in Family Medicine when I was called to meet with the founder of Adventist Health International, Dr. Dick Hart. After discussing some of the possibilities for work in Africa, Monita spoke up:

"…And then there's this small hospital in *Tchad.*"

Little did I realize when I heard those words how much my life was about to drastically change. I could have hardly imagined that a few months later I would leave everything familiar behind and find myself working in obscurity in a run-down bush hospital in sub-Saharan Africa in the Republic of *Tchad.* How could I know that despite all I would give up, I would gain infinitely more professionally, socially, culturally, linguistically and spiritually.

Of course, I gave up electricity, running water, paved roads, solid infrastructure, reliable communications, modern medical facilities, proximity to family and friends, my mother tongue, a familiar culture and paradigm and all else that I had grown up feeling was normal.

But I gained a whole lot more than I sacrificed.

As a simple, unproven family physician straight out of residency I found myself immersed in an environment completely lacking in surgical care. This forced me to go through my own sort of surgical training program by trial and error, often with an open surgical text guiding me step by step in the operating room as I performed life-saving major operations. As the most qualified and often only physician present, I found myself pushed to the limits many times, and yet, often the outcomes were surprisingly positive. I was stretched often to the extremes of adaptability and, in the process, became a better doctor.

I've lived and worked with volunteers from Romania, Germany, Hungary, Switzerland, Portugal, Denmark, Norway, France, Belgium,

Niger, Cameroon, Nigeria, Togo, Congo, Puerto Rico, Canada, the United States of America, Argentina, Brazil and Peru. I've made friends at the hospital, in the local village and across the country. I've learned the rich benefits of generosity and hospitality, as modeled by my *Tchadian* colleagues.

I've raced horses in festivals, eaten millet paste and dried fish okra sauce, drank tea and *gahwa* on Arabic *tapis*, swam in hippo infested rivers, ridden horses with just a rope tied around the nose, and castrated two male cats, a male and a female dog and five horses. I've learned the proper technique for eating with one's fingers, how to use an intermediary in conflict resolution, become both a *patron* and a *client*, fix a radiator with gum and a faucet with a bicycle inner tube, play the tom-tom, prepare proper curry dishes, shake an important person's hand with the other hand touching the elbow of the shaking hand, to touch my chest with the fingers after greeting an Arab, how to bargain, how to get out of police tickets, how to cross road barriers without bribing, the importance of relationships, how to say "no" without using the actual word, how to determine if someone is really poor when they all look indigent and countless other cultural details of daily life in sub-Saharan Africa.

I've mastered French with an African accent. I can communicate in basic *Tchadian* Arabic. I can ask someone if they've vomited and other key hospital phrases in *Nangjeré*. I can even read, write and speak a few words of Danish. My brain has learned to not panic when I don't understand everything a person is saying, but to just try and get the gist and in the process, communicate.

I've been pushed to re-evaluate all that I learned growing up as a conservative Christian in a western land. I've been drawn into a fascination with Islam. I've discovered that all I consider true may be mostly couched in cultural traditions, yet at its core I've come to believe in it stronger than ever.

I've preached in Christian churches, discussed the Koran with Imams, watched pagan harvest festivals, been surrounded by fetishes and charms, exorcised demons, prayed *Al-Fatiha* with Muslim patients, tried to fast during Ramadan, baptized people in a muddy stream, and read the New Testament through twice and all of the Qur'an. In the end, I've come to the conclusion that most of what divides us religiously is tradition while somewhere underneath, very close by, is a truth too good to be true, and yet, somehow is bigger and better than any of us have ever thought possible.

So, when I heard those words, "…and then there's this small hospital in *Tchad*…" I didn't know where that would lead me, but I instantly knew it was where I was supposed to go.

This feeling was reinforced to me on my first landing in the N'Djamena airport when I stepped onto the tarmac with the *harmatan* blowing over the dim lights and the shadowy forms of robed Arabs striding purposefully and yet casually into the distance. I breathed in that cool desert air mixed with jet fuel fumes and I knew I was in the right place.

Finally, my decision was confirmed on a warm, tropical day in southern Cameroon when I turned around to the white-bearded man in the back seat of the old Nissan Patrol taking us to the airport from some Adventist Health International meetings and said:

"Hey, Dick, I think I'm going to go to *Tchad*."

Opening one sleepy eye, Dick looked me over for a few seconds, as years of experience in Africa seemed to flash before him. Then, replying with a half-smile he said, "If I was your age…that's what I'd do too."

If only I'd known what I was getting myself into…

NOTE:

Because of it's ubiquitousness in *Tchad,* its insidious nature, and its devastating consequences for children and pregnant women, I have chosen to capitalize the word *Malaria* in order to emphasize it's impact on life in Africa.

2004

01 JANUARY 2004
NEW YEAR'S EVE GREETINGS

This is it, my last night in the USA. I have mixed feelings.

First of all, I'm scared. Moving permanently to a new country is a new experience. It's not easy preparing physically or mentally. But ready or not, here I come.

Second of all, I'm excited. My whole life, God has been preparing me for this. From hearing stories of my dad and grandpa growing up in China and India, to living a year in Ecuador and Brazil, to getting into medical school at the last possible minute, to being accepted to a residency in Family Practice that in three years gave me the best training possible for working in a country like *Tchad*, to countless other small things along the way. I feel this was meant to be. This is the beginning.

What will the future hold over there? There are so many unknowns. All I know is I'll be challenged like never before in my life: professionally, culturally, linguistically, mentally, socially, spiritually, surflessly …

But I'll also have the adventure of a lifetime. I know that no matter what happens to me, my life will have been lived the way it was supposed to be lived. And I have a future beyond all this, waiting for me at the end. I'm ready for my mission.

07 JANUARY 2004
FIRST CHALLENGES

After a snowy, four-hour delay in Paris, I arrive in *Tchad*. As I step off the plane and breathe the cool, dusty night air of N'Djamena, I know I'm in the right place. Since then, I haven't been so sure. It has been a whirlwind of meetings with various authorities, much shaking of hands, and long formalities in French.

I've had many ups and downs already. It looks like many of my responsibilities will be in the area of administration. I'll spend a lot of time working with the Ministry of Health on a World Bank project for the development of our district hospital in Béré. This is very discouraging because I'd envisioned escaping paperwork and bureaucracy by coming here! I'm starting to see though, that this area may be where I can make the biggest contribution.

After my installation ceremony as Chief of Staff and Hospital Administrator, I settle in to my one room accorded me in the staff housing block. That evening, the staff calls me in to the hospital to do a hernia repair. I feel I'm ready. I read up on hernia repairs in my surgery textbook to refresh my memory. As I stand outside the OR staring across the courtyard lit by small cooking fires, I see the full moon rising against the black *Tchadian* sky.

I feel it's a good omen, until I start to operate. I can't seem to recognize any of the anatomy, much less the hernia sac. A half hour surgery quickly turns into a marathon. Finally, thanks to the help of Samedi, my *Tchadian* assistant, we excise the hernia and repair the defect.

I'm devastated. A million excuses come to my mind as to why I had trouble. The worst thing was that I had such high expectations of being able to help, but in the end it was a nurse with no official training who bailed me out on a simple case.

I think maybe I need all my dreams to be crushed so that I can turn to God. He knows what he wants me to do here in *Tchad*. Maybe it's not as a great surgeon like I imagined, but rather as an administrator or something else.

Sarah, the volunteer nurse from Denmark, has been a great ally. She's been here three months already and understands better than I do the specific issues here at the hospital. Along with our accountant, André, Sarah has agreed to help with the administration.

So far it has been a rich experience. It seems like I've been here forever already. So much happens in one day. Things are challenging in so many ways. It's not really what I expected. I anticipated such problems as lack of electricity and running water, but these were resolved before my arrival. We have a generator for electricity at night while a water tower provides good running water all the time.

14 JANUARY 2004
TRAVELS

I'm doing pretty well. I got a little diarrhea but not bad. I'm surprised I haven't really fallen sick yet. I've been running back a forth between Béré and N'Djamena. I've eaten at a lot of sketchy places along the side of the road. I'm now in Cameroon. I came here with the ex-administrator to see him off. He's heading home to Yaoundé, leaving us alone to struggle with the hospital administration. I'm going today to see the Koza Adventist Hospital.

Sarah and I are getting along great. She really is a remarkable woman. She's not only learned French these last three months, but has also started learning Arabic and a local dialect, *Nangjeré*. She came with me to N'Djamena and we've been hanging out quite a bit.

She has adapted tremendously and knows the city and the markets well. She has been a great person to strategize with about what we can do to get the hospital where we want it. The Ministry of Health has actually developed a great health care system on paper. We just need to find out how to make it a reality.

The challenges are huge but this is what I wanted. I'll just be happy to get back to Béré, settle in and get started. I also can't wait to see where this friendship with Sarah will lead.

17 JANUARY 2004
FRACTURE

Today, I see a four-year-old boy named Djimé in clinic. He fell off an ox and broke both bones of his left lower leg. The wound is open down to bone. It happened 11 days ago. The tibia still sticks out surrounded by pus. I take him to the operating room, clean out the wound, and try to set the bones. The leg is shortened by over two centimeters. The surrounding tissues have already shrunk down and attached to the bones. I can't reduce it.

I try and try. In desperation, I pray. I continue trying. After pulling bending, twisting and prying with the help of Samedi, I finally get the bones back in place. I am able to cover most of the bone with muscle and skin. I cast the boy's leg and prescribe antibiotics. He needs a miracle for it to heal.

Djimé wouldn't have had a chance if we hadn't been able to reduce the fracture. We don't have an x-ray machine, though, and neither do the two closest hospitals. I don't know how we're going to monitor his progress. We just have to pray, wait and see.

18 JANUARY 2004
SALAAM

I sit in the bare, cement block church. The paint is peeling off the walls. A few wooden benches without backs line the cracked, concrete floor. The warm dust filters the sunlight as it creeps in through a couple of fiberglass skylights and the narrow windows. Ants crawl along the fissures in the floor. Flies swarm before being casually swatted away. Large hornets buzz noisily around the sheet metal roof.

About 15 of us sit around in a circle on four of the wooden benches as André leads the discussion in French. "Paul says in Galatians 3:28 that there is neither Jew nor Greek, slave nor free, male nor female. In other words, there is neither Chadian nor American (looking at me) nor Danish (looking at Sarah) nor *Nangjeré* (looking at the locals from Béré)."

My mind drifts to some of the thoughts I've been having recently about being here in *Tchad*. I know I'm where I am supposed to be. I don't know exactly why or what I'm supposed to do or how I'll do it. All my expectations have come crashing down around me.

Instead of getting away from paperwork and focusing on clinical medicine, I find myself as hospital administrator trying to reverse the trend of a downward spiraling mission hospital. We are just trying to survive as a district hospital in the budding health care system of *Tchad*.

My clinical duties so far have been minimal. We only have five inpatients and about ten chronic TB patients. They are here for two months of directly observed therapy before being set loose on the population. Supposedly, they will finish their six months of treatment as an outpatient.

Instead of facing the expected lack of electricity and running water, I find myself wondering how the hospital can survive financially. We only make about $40 a day from patient revenue. At the same time, we have a debt of $8,000 to Social Security for what the hospital hasn't paid since 1995.

I have been told that the goal for the Béré Adventist Hospital is to make it a financially independent institution. That has made us feel incredibly

alone and abandoned out here in the bush of the poorest country in the world. Every other hospital in *Tchad* is supported either by the government or an outside entity. Yet somehow, we here in Béré are supposed to be self-sufficient.

We provide the only health care to not only our district of 140,000 people, but also to the adjacent counties. Yet we have hardly any suture, no autoclave, no x-ray or ultrasound and minimal lab facilities. Our buildings are falling down and most of the hospital beds have neither mattresses nor mosquito nets. Yet, patients still come to us from all over the country. We are making a difference in our own small way.

19 JANUARY 2004
FOOD

Sarah and I bought a huge bag of dried beans in Cameroon when we visited the hospital in Koza. In the market here in Béré, we can get rice, tomatoes, garlic, onions, carrots and lettuce. There are some roots I ate last night that are starchy like potatoes. Forty kilometers away in Kélo, we can buy peppers, bananas, papayas and mangos.

Sarah makes great crepes. For breakfast we have oatmeal and eggs. I'm really eating quite well. There's a dark red tea called *jus d'osai* that is made from some dried flowers. It's wonderful and supposed to have some medicinal properties.

Sarah is much more than I could have hoped for in a partner out here. She is phlegmatic and has a way of just smoothing things out. All the villagers, especially the kids, just love her. They are so impressed when she speaks in *Nangjeré* or Arabic. It's so important for me to have someone to strategize with, complain to, eat with, joke with and share with.

In the evening, we go to eat with Julie, one of Sarah's *Tchadian* friends. The house is made of mud bricks but is so clean and organized you could almost eat off the floor. The only light comes from a window whose sheet metal cover is propped open with a stick. We start off with a bowl of home cooked, glazed peanuts and Cokes. Then, Julie brings a plastic *sacand* and basin to wash our hands.

Digging into the pot of cooked pasta with our fingers, we eat large servings of boiled rooster in a red savory sauce. The chicken is cooked to perfection, almost melting off the bones. Afterwards, we sit around and talk. Julie wants to continue her education in Moundou, *Tchad's* second largest city. She is unusual for a *Tchadian* girl. Already 22-years-old, she is still single with no children. Instead, she prizes an education above all.

As the sun slowly sets and the shadows lengthen, Julie tells us stories of traditional medicine and how it has cured a lot of people here in Béré. It is especially good for poisonings, which they have a lot of here. There are a lot of venomous plants, fish and animals in the African bush. That's why the hospital is not very busy.

As I recline there in the cool of the evening listening to Julie and Sarah talk quietly, I can't help but think how strange it is that I'm here. It is a special moment in a crazy place.

24 JANUARY 2004
NEXT

I've just finished rounds. Dimanche, our obstetrical nurse, comes running to tell me about a patient. A woman just came in after trying unsuccessfully to deliver a baby at home. I examine the woman and see the baby's hand hanging out from between her legs. I call Samedi and we rush the woman into surgery for a C-section. We have the baby out in just a few minutes. I hand the baby off to Dimanche to be resuscitated and finish off the case cleanly and quickly.

As I unscrub, Dimanche informs me the baby is dead. I crash from the heights of accomplishment to the depths of wondering what if, if only and was it really worth it? Of course, it was worth it. The first objective here is always to save the mother as many women still die during childbirth. The mother goes home four days later without complications.

The next morning, I'm told in morning report that a critical patient came in yesterday. He was run over by his ox cart a three days ago. The nurse put in a nasogastric tube last night. Since it made the patient feel much better, the nurse didn't think I needed to see the man urgently.

I go to see him first thing on rounds. He complains of severe right upper abdominal pain. His belly is tense and he jumps at the slightest touch. These are signs of what is called a surgical abdomen. I put a needle into his belly and aspirate a syringe full of dark blood. The man probably has a liver injury.

I decide the man should be transferred urgently to a better-equipped hospital. André calls for the District Medical Officer to help with the transfer. But he's taken the ambulance out to supervise a national immunization program so there's no way to evacuate the patient. So, we decide to operate.

Am I scared? Yes. I'm not a surgeon and I've only seen a liver injury operated on once. I was holding a retractor. I look up liver trauma quickly in a Surgical Atlas and pray a lot. After the anesthesia settles in, I cut his abdomen open in a midline incision. A pool of dark blood wells out. I suction it up quickly and find three tears in the liver.

Working without electrocautery, with a surgical light that has only one of four bulbs working and without deep retractor, I do my best. Suddenly, things seem to slow down. I don't have much surgical experience and have never been this deep in a case. I also can't tie sutures with my left hand but as I reach in for the deepest laceration, I have no other choice. I go for it and I find myself doing it effortlessly. I somehow manage to close all the lacerations and stop the bleeding. Examining the rest of the abdominal cavity, I find no other obvious internal injuries.

After closing up the belly, I reflect on what just happened. I found myself doing things I was incapable of doing. I know that God was operating through me, there's no other rational explanation. I pull off my gloves and step outside of the muggy OR.

Seven days later the man goes home, completely recovered.

26 JANUARY 2004
STRANGULATED

There is yet another urgent surgical case. A woman with an irreducible femoral hernia comes in vomiting. She tells us part of the intestine is trapped inside. I've never seen a femoral hernia before much less operated on one. The memory of my first, less complicated hernia surgery on my first day here crowds my thoughts. That one was a disaster. But I know the woman can die if we don't do anything.

So I decide to operate. There is just one little problem: our autoclave is broken. As a result, we have only one sterile gown that we use as a surgical drape. The unsterilized instruments we prepare for surgery by pouring rubbing alcohol on them and setting them on fire. Worse yet, my surgery book isn't very clear on what to do. Amazingly, I am able to find the hernia, reduce the intestines and close the defect. The result is ugly, but effective. She recovers completely.

All week, I've been caring for an end-stage AIDS patient with diarrhea and cough. With no x-ray or sputum test I have no confirmed diagnosis. I have him covered with broad-spectrum antibiotics. He's just getting worse. In Béré, like in many parts of Africa, no one really wants to know if they have AIDS. If the family hears about it, they will abandon them. So I can't really talk openly about his prognosis.

Friday morning, first thing, the *garde* tells me is that the patient is in critical condition. I walk to his bed and know instantly he is dying. I tell the family. They want to take him home. I feel that medically, we have failed; we've done nothing to help him. But the family seems satisfied. It seems they've known the prognosis all along and were only waiting for us to be honest with them.

27 JANUARY 2004
ROLLER COASTER RIDE

A pregnant woman comes in with two baby feet hanging out from her crotch. It all started this morning. At the same time, a guy is brought in who's been thrown from a truck. He landed on his head. Now, he's combative and unconscious. A large gash on his forehead is the only other physical finding. Fortunately, the district medical officer is the one to bring the man in so he takes care of him while I go to see the pregnant woman.

We still have no sterile materials. Instead of a C-section, I'm forced to do a pubic symphysiotomy. I have no scalpel holder for the blade. But with the help of an orthopedic osteotome, I manage to open the pelvis a little to give more room in the birth canal. Then I grab the baby's feet and pull.

The baby starts to slide out. I reach in and sweep out the arm on top. Then I rotate the baby and deliver the other arm. Sticking a finger in the baby's mouth to flex the head I tug the head out. The newborn is not breathing but has a heart beat. I begin mouth to mouth.

As I'm breathing for the child, Sarah cries out that there is another one! Twins! The baby I was resuscitating begins to breathe. He finally has better muscle tone and isn't so floppy. The second twin comes out headfirst easily. Both are somewhat premature but seem to be doing well. I feel a special warmth run over me. I myself am a twin.

I wonder if I did the right thing. What kind of life have I brought these babies into? Poverty? Hunger? Malnutrition? An early death from Malaria or dehydration? Cerebral palsy from prolonged time in the birth canal with lack of oxygen?

But when I see the twins breathing and looking around, I feel such joy I know I've done the right thing. However, without any neonatal intensive care equipment, the first twin is dead the next morning. The other baby is dehydrated, hasn't been able to feed and is lying on the bed across from the mother. I touch him. He is cold. I feel betrayed.

Just two years ago, I lost my twin in a car accident. Here I thought I'd saved a twin, but now one is dead and the other is dying. I leave the scene. I can't take it. A few hours later I come back with Sarah and the baby is somehow still alive. We take him home to Sarah's apartment.

Sarah hooks him up to subcutaneous IV fluids to rehydrate him and give him glucose. I warm him up with a hot bath. He perks right up and even starts wanting to suckle. Maybe he'll be able to breastfeed. We eat supper with him sitting in the middle of the table. Then we take him back to his family.

We try to get the mother to breastfeed. Her milk has come down, but she'll have nothing to do with the baby. We leave him knowing tomorrow he'll almost surely be dead. These are the decisions we are faced with all the time. Was it a waste? Was there more we could have done? Maybe we gave his life some meaning by allowing ourselves to love him briefly and allowing him to touch our lives a little. In the end, I fall back on the hope I have. Maybe I'll see him again some day.

02 FEBRUARY 2004
THE RHYTHM OF AFRICA

The drum beats pound loud and long into the night. It is the rhythm of the plain. It is the rhythm of *Tchad*. The rhythm of Africa. The young dance in tune around the drums and small fires, their twisting bodies keeping perfect timing and allowing a temporary joy in an otherwise desperate life. The rhythm flows through all here. The generator that gives me power and light pounds out its cadence. It is everywhere. The turbans flowing, the robes churning the pedals up and down, up and down, keep its rhythm.

The pattering of chickens' feet. The bleating of goats. The crowing of roosters. The buzzing of flies. The hum of mosquitoes. The crying of Sarah's cat when left indoors. All the animal kingdom keeps time with the rhythm of this place.

The rumbling of intestinal sounds. The fast paced breathing of the severe Malaria or chronic tuberculosis patient. The pounding heart of the dehydrated infant. The short grunting squeals of the five-month-old in the midst of a seizure due to meningitis. The sucking of the premature twin—now breastfeeding well—having survived against all odds. The popping of fluid filled lungs of a child about to succumb to severe Falciparum Malaria. My own stomach demanding its own rhythmic ritual of purging as I call for the car to stop just as we're about to leave N'Djamena. The fish and sesame seed balls come up in the rhythm of vomiting as my body tries to adjust to the rhythm here. Fortunately, it only happens ten times more over the next hour or so and then my body has found contentment in the local cadence. All sickness, death, healing and life march in tune with the pounding out of this rhythm flowing in and through all here.

The lilting chant of Lazare, the maintenance man, singing hymns in *Nangjeré* with a rhythm unrecognizable to the western mind but in harmony with all things *Tchadian*. The rise and fall of *Tchadian* Arabic shouted out from the open-air markets all the way to the Mosque where Classical Arabic of the Koran is taught to the people in a dialect they can understand. The washing of feet, hands and head systematically with a small plastic pot on the side of any road or in front of any shop prior to the hour of prayer. Hundreds of synchronized forms rising and bowing and touching the forehead to the ground facing Mecca five times a day. The erect, proud stride of the turbaned *Tchadian* with robes flowing as he goes about his business. The beat runs through all.

You can try to fight; it doesn't work. Show up at seven as promised—but that is Western rhythm—move on. Do what you can and come back, then come back again. Work with the rhythm. All we can do is take the rhythm that is here but sing our own song to it, one that doesn't disrupt the fundamental heart of *Tchad*, and that doesn't interrupt the soul and the rhythm of Africa. That rhythm has been placed here by God, by Allah, and it goes on and on and on. Boom batta boom boom battata boom.

09 FEBRUARY 2004
TWINS AND HIPPO BITES

I'm sitting in Sarah's living room enjoying a nice quiet supper of carrot and tomato goulash, stale French bread and hibiscus tea. I finally get to relax after a busy day. There's a knock on the door. It's the night watchman. He has a note from the nurse saying there is a pediatric emergency.

I slip on my sandals to complement my professional attire of dusty shorts, T-shirt, headlamp, and stethoscope draped haphazardly around my neck. I walk under the light of the full moon, through the metal gate hanging crazily on almost broken hinges, past the church eerily lit with a single outdoor fluorescent bulb, over the sandy trail, close to the outdoor baptistery filled with plastic and other trash, under the mango trees, up the steps and around the corner, into the dark hallway of the administrative block and through the first door to the left into the emergency room or *Salle de Garde*.

Lit with another fluorescent bulb high on one wall and a kerosene lamp in the corner, the room is dim to say the least. I find myself face to face with an eight-day-old girl whose arms flex and twitch. She has a grimace on her face as if she tastes lemon for the first time, quick respirations and a desperate cry coming like clockwork between clenched teeth. Her parents have put some local remedies on the umbilical cord to help it fall off.

I quickly give her a shot of Valium and start searching for an IV so I can give some more medications to calm the spasms. She has tetanus, 90% fatal in newborns. The nurse tells me that the IV I'd started on the kid with Malaria was already bad. I tell him to bring the kid to the ER while I continue to search in vain for an IV on this tiny arm.

When the girl with Malaria arrives, I look over and see that the area around the IV catheter is swollen proving that the vein is blown. I take the plastic catheter out and then look up to see her right arm start moving rhythmically and her eyes kind of loll right as she starts to seize. Great. One of the kids is in the corner grimacing and shaking her fists, and the other is just kind of rolling her right hand along while her eyes gaze off into the mattress. These are not good things to be happening, much less at the same time.

Meanwhile, Anatole from the lab has arrived to get the anti-tetanus serum from the locked fridge and André is coming to get us some antibiotics from the pharmacy. Just as André arrives, a loud group of Arabs tries to push through the ER door.

André starts yelling at them that they can't come in right now since the ER is already full with two critically ill kids. He helps them out the door toward the waiting area when, suddenly, I hear the terrifying sounds of yelling in Arabic, pushing, shoving, things and people falling, things and people hitting the wall, benches, and each other, and the other obvious signs of an angry fight.

I quickly close the handle-less door and secure it "safely" with a rickety little metal bar you push across into a wimpy slot that's supposed to lock things from the inside. The parents of the two kids are scared out of their wits. One father tries to see what's happening by peering out the window into the darkness. I'm afraid the Arabs have attacked André. I consider going out to help, but am terribly frightened. I tried to occupy myself with continuing to care for the kids.

> SUDDENLY, I HEAR THE TERRIFYING SOUNDS OF YELLING IN ARABIC

The sounds quiet down and I hear André's voice at the window. "Doctor, get out of there. They have knives and a gun."

I go to the door and just as I pull open the lock, the fight breaks out again. I quickly close the door and go back to the grimacing, shaking, seizing, eye-lolling girls. I can't help but think how truly bizarre this is. I suddenly feel like either laughing or crying. Things finally quiet down. I get the IVs going on the two girls and go outside.

There is blood all along the floor of the hallway in front of my office. Anatole tells me Nassourrou, the charge nurse, is in the operating theater with one of the wounded Arabs. I go to see how things are going.

"Fine, doc," says Nassourrou, "no problem."

There are some large gashes across the man's left back, deltoid and chest and a puncture wound in his right lower belly. I tell Nassourrou to make sure to inspect that last wound carefully as it may have gone deep and hurt something internally. His belly is soft and non-tender.

The next morning, I find that Nassourrou was up till 2:30 a.m., opened up the patient's abdomen, and sutured a punctured intestine. Unfortunately, both little girls are dead. It is Friday. At 1 p.m. they bring in a young woman with convulsions. She has some weird signs, like eyes that roll toward wherever I open them. When I lift the upper lids, the eyes move up. When I open the lower lids, the eyes move down. I order a Malaria smear and it's very positive. I start her on Quinine.

Later that afternoon, as I sit by the river watching some fisherman toss nets from a leaky wooden canoe and an old man bathe naked in front of me, I can't help but think of the young girl with Malaria. Something's weird, not right, even if she does have Malaria.

Sarah is swimming in the river. When she finishes, we sit and talk on the riverbank for a while. Before we head home, I ask Sarah if we can pray for the girl with Malaria. She agrees. It just feels right. I don't waste time trying to be eloquent.

"I'm not sure exactly what's going on with this girl, God, but you do. Make up for our inadequacies and help her. Amen."

Sarah and I then bike lazily back to Béré as the sun goes down behind us and a cool breeze picks up. People all along the way greet us with the typical *Ca va?* Or *Lapia, lapia-ei?*

When we arrive home, I go to find out how the patient is doing. She's awake! I ask when she'd come to. The family says it was 90 minutes ago, the exact time we'd prayed for her! Okay, so maybe it was the Quinine we used to treat her Malaria, or maybe it wasn't. But it certainly didn't hurt to pray. She is discharged several days later.

That same Friday night, Jabel, Caleb and Jared arrive from N'Djamena to visit. David and Abraham, their *Tchadian* translators, accompany them. These are the guys from Frontier Builders who are here to build six schools in *Tchad*. They've lived in Africa most of their lives. We stay up late eating Sarah's crepes, drinking hibiscus tea and listening to their tall tales.

After church the next day, the boys and I drive out to the Logone River by Lai for a swim. The river is wide with steep banks on our side that are perfect for jumping. The current is pretty fast, the water clear and cool, and the river has a sweet sandbar about three feet under the surface in the middle.

Caleb, Jared and I jump in quickly and swim out to the sandbar. Just then, we hear Jabel cry for help. David has jumped in too, but doesn't know how to swim. Apparently he thrashed around for a while. Jabel at first mistook it for crude swimming. But then, David went limp with just his arm hanging up on the surface. That's when Jabel cried for help and jumped in after David. Jared and I dive off the sandbar and swim toward where Jabel is. Jabel surfaces with David and we help drag him to shore. Fortunately, David is fine, but we tease him the rest of the day. We tell him that he can truly testify that there is life after death!

Unfortunately, David isn't alone in his near death experience. Abraham convinces Jared he can swim good enough to get to the sandbar with a little help. Jabel, Caleb and I have waded almost clear across the sandbar when we hear another scream for help. We turn and see Jared about 500 feet away struggling to keep Abraham afloat. We dash back across the sandbar, but before we get there Jared manages to reach shallower water where they can touch down.

Unfortunately, David and Abraham aren't alone in their near death experiences that day. We get back to the hospital just in time to welcome a young man named Marty who's been bit by a hippo. Apparently he was casting his fishing net too close to a female hippo and her young and when the net landed on the baby hippo's head the mom went ballistic. She reared out of the water and as Marty desperately tried to untie the net from his wrist the hippo attacked and bit him on his buttocks.

The poor man then somehow managed to swim to shore and stumble about 50 feet before falling. Some other fisherman hauled him up to solid ground and then came looking for the ambulance. Unfortunately, our district medical officer needed it for personal reasons in Kélo so it wasn't there. So they commandeered an ox cart and pulled it three miles to where the victim lay and started to bring him to the hospital. Finally the

HIPPO

ambulance showed up on its way back from Kélo. He arrived at the hospital four hours after being bitten.

His rear is slashed open from the left side of the top of his pelvis down the middle over his lower spine and down to his tailbone through his anus, detaching his rectum, and cutting under to his scrotum revealing, but not damaging his testicle. The gluteus muscles are opened deep, almost to bone. I put my gloved hand in and lift it up the muscle to make a foot wide opening. I'm able to insert my hand on the superior surface under the muscle almost to his abdomen. The ligaments across the back left of the pelvis are in tatters, the tip of one of the pelvic bones is broken and exposed, and the muscles are shredded and bleeding. Fortunately, no major vessels are severed. His blood pressure is barely measurable, his feet and hands are like ice and his heart rate is fast. Amazingly, Marty is still conscious.

We rush him to the operating block, start two IVs and then go in search of blood. Outside, literally hundreds of relatives and people from his village are available and we hope several will match his blood type for a transfusion. There are about 50 bikes parked against the far side of the surgical suite. The crowd is so large, I have to fight through to get back into the operating room.

I sew his rectum and anus back together, reattach the ligaments, suture the muscles together in layers and give him a diverting colostomy so the stool will come out his abdominal wall temporarily and allow things below to heal. Six and half hours and a lot of prayer later, at 2:30 a.m., we finish the surgery.

22 FEBRUARY 2004
SOMEBODY SLAP ME

Thursday evening, Sarah is working the *garde* shift and a woman comes in to deliver her first infant. She's had no prenatal care. This is the first time she's been seen by a health care professional and it is her first pregnancy. Sarah escorts her into our bare cement floor delivery room equipped with three beds and two mattresses. Each mattress is covered with a haphazardly cut piece of thick plastic.

Twelve female family members accompany her into the room to help with the delivery. There's also a drunk guy who no one seems to know but who has plenty of advice for everyone until he is escorted from the room. Since it is her first pregnancy, she feels a lot of pain and doesn't know really what to do or what to expect. Fortunately for her, the 12 women are very experienced and compassionately help her through the process.

They start by violently grabbing her legs and pinning her to the bed while several others slap her silly every time she screams in birth pains. As Sarah tries to help without accidentally getting slapped, the woman manages to thrust a new life onto the world.

Sarah clamps and cuts the umbilical cord and hands the baby off to the waiting Neonatal Intensive Care Unit team waiting to the side. The team is equipped with fresh oxygen, clean blankets and a cute little cap woven by some elderly woman from the community…not exactly. Here the baby is handed off to the Twelve to be wrapped in a dirty piece of cloth and eventually weighed, maybe. Sarah then notices the woman is bleeding from a small tear during the otherwise peaceful delivery. So she calls me.

I arrive and find a tiny laceration. After injecting some local anesthetic, I look up to notice about 50 faces peering through the slatted windows. Apparently, the sight of two *Nasaras* at once is better than a movie and way cheaper! I shoo them away, grab a couple two-fingered cervical exam gloves and somehow manage to suture and tie using only two fingers on each hand with some instruments from the dark ages, borrowed from a museum somewhere, no doubt.

The next morning, I am about to start rounds when one of the nurses, Lona comes running in to tell me that he needs the key to the delivery room. The wife of our newly hired pharmacy tech, Koumabas, is about to deliver. I quickly go to open the door but fortunately, when we arrive, we see there isn't much for us to do.

The woman is sitting on the ground leaning against the door to the maternity ward in a pool of blood while a friend holds a bloody, pasty newborn. The umbilical cord is still attached to Mommy as the newborn girl begins to scream her fury at the rude welcome she has received. I quickly open the door and grab two instruments to clamp and cut the cord. I notice, however, that the scissors from the night before still haven't been sterilized. I quickly run to dunk them in some bleach at least before cutting the cord. Finally, we move mom to an actual bed, dry off baby with the traditional bright colored sheet the family provides, weigh our 3600-gram baby and hand her off to mom. *Il n'y a pas de problème.*

After that, I make little packages of scissors, clamps, needle drivers, and forceps and autoclave them in our tiny stovetop pressure cooker so we'll have sterile instruments available for deliveries. I found the instruments just last week on a shelf in the pharmacy. Who knows how long they'd been there. I'm talking bunches of scissors, clamps and forceps. And here we've been using the same set over and over. There's just so much to do here. One step at a time.

Marty, the man bit by the hippo is doing better. His wounds got really infected, but are starting to look really clean with our diluted bleach dressings. We pull the edges of the wound a little closer together today with some sutures, leaving some sections open so the infection can drain. That way we can continue to change the dressings and rinse the infection out every day. I think he'll make it, but recovery is going to be slow.

> IN THE EVENING, A WOMAN COMES IN WHO'S BEEN GORED BY A BULL

Djimé, the boy with the fractured leg who's been here almost as long as I have, is doing well. The wound is starting to close and I hope the bone will be covered soon and be able to heal. He has youth in his favor. Sarah entertains him almost daily with coloring, balloons or just little games that he loves to play, like pretending to feed her and then pulling it away at the last minute. When I come to examine him he lifts up his shirt so I can listen to his heart and automatically wiggles his toes so I can see that the cast isn't too tight and that his foot is fine.

In the evening, a woman comes in who's been gored by a bull between her legs. The cart they brought her in is covered with blood. Her body is covered with dried blood matted everywhere. I'm scared. It's dusk, so we try to start up the generator and it sort of works. There is light, but the fluorescent bulbs keep flickering on and off while I'm trying to do a gynecologic exam to see the extent of her injuries. The wound is only about a centimeter on the outer labia and I suture it easily, even though by now the generator has gone up in smoke and I'm working by flashlight. The horn must have hit a small artery or something because I have to put in more and more sutures until it finally stops bleeding.

The generator is noisy, expensive to run and maintain, and gives us electricity only from 6 p.m. until 10 p.m. unless there's an emergency. That means our hospital and lab has to function all day without power. After 10 p.m. the *garde* has to examine and care for all the hospitalized patients by the light of a kerosene lamp!

So, now we've had no electricity for two days. I wonder how much longer the water will last since there's a hole in the tank. Without the generator the water pump doesn't work. All we have is what's left in the water tower.

03 MARCH 2004
WEAKNESS

I am weak. As I lie here on the first carpet I've felt in two months with a welcome fan whirring overhead to chase the suffocating heat away; as I lie here without the ever-present dust suffocating and making it hard to breathe; as I lie here having eaten more than I should for consecutive meals for the first time in a long time; as I lie here having chosen to lie here over going to church; as I lie here, I have time to truly think and reflect for an extended period of time...and I am afraid.

An uncontrollable fear descends on me. I think of where I am and I want to be elsewhere. I think of what I have done, not done and what I face and I know I cannot face it alone. As you have heard so many tales of excitement, adventure, sorrow and joy you may have been tempted to think that somehow you couldn't do that. Let me tell you that's exactly what I think: I can't do that. I know that everything in my nature rebels against what I am doing, where I am doing it and why I am doing it. But when I do it, somehow the strength is there and everyday in some unexpected way there is joy as well.

I think of the young man, Ferdinand, who consistently approaches me about work. He is about 18 years old, married with a couple of kids.

"I'd like to help you with plant a garden."

"*Merci,*" I reply. "We'd like a garden, but without a fence the goats and pigs will destroy it. Come back when we have a wall built."

He keeps coming back anyway, "just to make a social visit." He brings tomatoes and lettuce from his own garden. They are impressive. He comes one time with the smell of alcohol on him. After he's gone, our Muslim chauffeur, Bichara, shrugs in disgust.

"Alcohol, *c'est pas bon.* It's no good."

Later, Ferdinand approaches me after a long day of work.

BICHARA

"I haven't eaten in five days. Everyone says I'm not man enough to provide for my wife and I shouldn't have gotten married yet. I've looked elsewhere for work. I can't find any. Don't you have any work for me?"

"I needed someone to do laundry, but I've already given that work to someone else, to Bruno."

"I asked you first about work, gardening or laundry."

"It could be true," I confess. Honestly, I can't' remember. "My French is pretty bad, so maybe I didn't understand you."

"Bruno has other work already." It's true. Our other physician, Dr. Claver, who has been assigned to the hospital by the United Nations Development Project pays Bruno 20,000 francs CFA (about $40) a month to clean, guard, and cook for him.

"How much are you paying Bruno to do your laundry?"

"500 francs."

"I'll do it for 250 francs. I'm desperate. I've been coming to church. Aren't Christians supposed to help each other?"

"True," I acknowledge. Inside I feel he only comes to church because he thinks it will help his cause. But I don't want to judge. "I'll talk to Bruno and see if he's willing to give it up the laundry work." He's not.

That night I happen to come to the hospital and Ferdinand is in the ER with his wife who has a cut over her left eye.

"What happened?" I ask.

"She fell," Ferdinand replies.

I'm accompanied by a Catholic nun who whispers in my ear. "She didn't fall. He hit her. " I don't know what to believe.

When I next see Ferdinand, he gets me at a busy time. I'm annoyed. It seems like I have no way out and I'm tired of being bothered. I tell him so. I haven't seen him since.

Did I do the right thing? Maybe he is a drunk. Maybe he beats his wife. Maybe he comes to church just to get some work (he hasn't been back since.) So logically I did the right thing. Then I read about Jesus and think what he would've done and this guy is exactly who Jesus welcomed, hung out with, healed, and served.

If I start helping too many people everyone will start to crowd around thinking the rich white man is the answer. It will never end if I start. Then I read that Jesus also was bothered. When he started healing people crowded around and never would let him have a moment's peace. Even when he tried to have some quiet time with his disciples they found him. What did Jesus do? He had pity on them. What did this guy ask of me? To have pity on him.

These are the difficult things I am faced with all the time. It's not just the medical work or administration or finances that is challenging. It is the myth that the white man is always rich and a source of gifts, handouts, money and work. I want to break that tradition. I want them to recognize me as someone who has come to work with them side by side as their equal not as just some magician or philanthropist. How do I do that and yet still not ignore their cries for help when I CAN help them? Where do I draw the line? These are not easy questions. Expectations are high. The myth is deeply rooted.

Later, a woman pregnant with twins comes in with a kidney infection. We hospitalize her and place her on antibiotics. She gets up one evening to use the hospital latrine and discovers a small foot sticking out below. She tells one of the nurses, Felix, who runs to tell me. We get things ready for an emergency C-section.

Someone runs to borrow the small generator from UNICEF while we go ahead and get started. It's pitch black, but fortunately I have my trusty headlamp. Sarah assists me and does very well except for the brief moment when she almost faints due to dehydration. She's been suffering from amebic dysentery. But she sucks it up and keeps going!

As I open the uterus I realize how nice it would be to have suction. A huge gush of amniotic fluid rushes out to join all the blood already in the operating field. I reach in the bloody puddle and find the first baby. I pull the leg out of the vagina and into the uterus and then do a breech extraction. She is fine.

I then break the other bag of water. The second twin is also breech. This delivery is a little more difficult, but he finally comes out and screams almost immediately. I then try to see what's going on down in the uterus with all that fluid and blood. Somehow God helps me to sew it together so that the bleeding stops and we finish the surgery. All three patients are doing well.. As I'm about to close the skin the generator shows up and roars to life.

Another day, I get called in to see a young man who had been hospitalized in December. He had been stabbed in the upper right chest and treated with a drainage bag for blood around the lung. Now he has right upper abdominal pain, a large tender liver, a rapid pulse, and bulging veins on his right abdomen, chest and neck. I think this has to be something different since the upper chest wound happened so long ago and looks healed. I do a quick but not complete exam, give him IV fluids, hospitalize him and go home.

I see him the next day and the right side of his face is swollen up. As I listen to his heart, I notice it is really displaced to the left and has a massive heart murmur that sounds like mitral regurgitation. I think maybe he has heart failure from rheumatic heart disease or something worse. Fortunately, however, God helps even stupid and blind physicians like me to make the right diagnosis eventually so that they can actually help their patients.

I listen to his lungs and find that there are no lung sounds over his right chest and it is dull to percussion with my fingers. I have the family buy a syringe and needle and stick it into his chest withdrawing brownish liquid. I send it to the lab. The results tell me it is almost all white blood cells indicating infection.

> IMMEDIATELY, COFFEE-COLORED FLUID SHOOTS OUT ACROSS THE ROOM

Since we have no proper chest tubes, I find a piece of rubber tubing about the right size (large) and cut small holes in the sides. I take him to surgery, put him to sleep, slice a hole over a rib, and poke a clamp over the rib and through the muscles into the chest cavity. Immediately, coffee-colored fluid shoots out across the room under a lot of pressure. I put in the tube and then slowly take off about four liters of liquid as I watch his heart rate return to normal, the swelling in his face go down, and his engorged veins flatten out. Not having the appropriate equipment for putting the tube to suction or water seal I tried to rig something. I end up just sticking the end in a huge jar of water so fluid and air can escape but air can't get back in. He's doing fine now.

05 MARCH 2004
MALARIA

I wake up feeling sick. Last night, Sarah and I had an important talk about trust. We are learning little by little to trust each other by sharing some very personal things. Unfortunately, we talked late. So I attribute my tiredness and soreness to that. Also, it has been very hot here, over 120 degrees. That must be why I've been sweating so much the past few days.

At morning report, the *garde*, Jean Bendé, tells us about several cases. He continues to prescribe inadequate treatments despite the fact that we've discussed the appropriate remedies many times before. Then, he mentions a child with severe Malaria that should have been hospitalized, but was sent home. Finally, he presents another case that he put on "observation" because, as he said, only the *médecin* can hospitalize.

That's the last straw. I explode. I tear into him. I tell him that they've been hospitalizing patients for years without me.

"How many patients did you personally hospitalized yesterday?" I ask the charge nurse.

"*Trois*," he responds. I continue my harangue until Jean speaks up in a very hurt voice.

"I know you're not happy with my work," he says. "But I've worked virtually all night without sleep. If you don't think I belong here, I'll just go back to the district medical offices and not work at the hospital any more."

"We're all tired," I reply. "You should go home and get some rest. We'll talk later."

That afternoon I do a mastectomy on a man with a mass on his chest. During the surgery all my muscles begin to ache. I feel nauseated. My head begins to kill me. I have a strange premonition I am passing through a certain rite of passage. I finish the surgery and go straight to the lab.

One of the lab techs, Mathieu, pricks my finger taking a small drop of blood he smears on a slide. After looking at it under a microscope he confirms that there are small parasites in my red blood cells of a certain familiar size and shape. I finally have Malaria. I'm kind of excited even though it means I've lost a bet with Sarah as to who would get it first. I now owe her my last bar of dark Swiss chocolate.

I get some Fansidar and Quinine from the Pharmacy and head home to rest. I feel like I've been run over by a train. As I crash onto my pillow the sleep comes quickly and is oh, so sweet. Aside from not being able to hear well and the worsening of my pounding headache from the side effects of Quinine, I feel alright. It is the first time in a long time I get a good, long sleep.

The next morning I feel wonderful, but still can't hear well. It's like having old earplugs in or listening underwater. At morning report we pray together and then I get up and apologize to Jean Bendé. He reports that he too had thought about it a lot and he didn't know what to do. So he was very glad to accept my apology. Today turns into the most relaxed day I've had since arriving in *Tchad* with the best interactions among the staff that I've seen. It's like everyone let out a long sigh that has lasted all day long.

14 MARCH 2004
BORING

It's a quiet Friday morning. Sarah isn't here because she's scheduled to start the *garde* shift at noon. So I finish consultations early and sit down to finish some paperwork right as Sarah comes to work. Suddenly, a couple comes racing in holding an eight-day-old baby in their arms. They are sweating and panting for breath.

Apparently, the baby was fine until that morning when she awoke with severe stomach pain and swelling. I examine the infant's belly and it's bloated and hollow-sounding without intestinal sounds. The baby also has a fever. Just to be a 100% sure—you have to always rule out Malaria here —we do a blood smear. Sarah starts an IV, puts a nasogastric tube down, and we start treatment with Quinine.

When the Malaria smear comes back negative, we stop the Quinine and give a bolus of IV fluids. I find Dr. Claver and ask him to come and see the baby. I need to confirm my suspicions that there is an intestinal obstruction that if not operated on could eventually lead to gangrene and death.

As I return to the hospital after notifying Dr. Claver, I see the ambulance from Kélo has just arrived. They have a two-day old with an imperforate anus. That means there is no way for the baby to poop. This baby's belly is also distended. This child has been sent from Kélo because the nurses are still on strike and refuse to do anything beyond the treatment of simple Malaria.

Nassourrou puts the first baby to sleep. As he's injecting the anesthetic, I ask how much he gives to babies.

"One to two milligrams per kilo."

"How much does the baby weigh?"

"Three kilos."

"Have you diluted the Ketamine?"

"No."

"Then you've already given 25 milligrams. It's too much. Do the math."

As we're speaking, the baby quits breathing so we wait for five minutes while Nassourrou breathes for the child using a bag-valve-mask. Finally, she starts breathing on her own again. We pray as we do before all surgeries and get started. We open her from sternum to pelvis in the midline of her abdomen and bloated intestines pop out. Sure enough, part of the intestine has twisted on itself.

We free a trapped portion of the colon and try to close the abdomen over the bloated intestines. As we try to force the bloated intestine inside, one part bursts spilling stool outside of the abdominal cavity. So we take the opportunity to empty the intestines of air and stool and then suture the tiny hole closed.

Meanwhile, halfway through the surgery, Sarah comes in to tell us that two more patients have arrived.

"They were lying on their mats in their huts when a tornado came through destroying the house," she says. "Some large bricks cascaded onto their heads. One is an adult female and the other iss a four-year-old boy who is semi-conscious, somewhat combative and has a fixed and dilated right pupil."

So after finishing with the little baby girl, I go out immediately to see the kid while Nassourrou prepares the infant without an anus for surgery. The kid with the head trauma's pupil is "blown" all right and as I feel his skull I find that where the brick has hit is a depressed skull fracture. I feel he is a priority, so we take him directly to surgery, the infant with imperforate anus can wait.

The boy's head is already shaved in the local style. Since we can't give him Ketamine because of his increased intracranial pressure and since we don't have any other general anesthetics we try a different tactic. We administer some antibiotics, give him some Valium and inject his scalp with a lot of local anesthetic.

I cut a C-shaped incision down to the skull and peel back the fibrous covering of the bone to reveal the depressed skull fracture. Using whatever I can find in the general instrument tray, after several tries I manage to wedge the pieces back up to their normal position. Then I lift one up to let out the blood that's compressing his

> I PEEL BACK THE FIBROUS COVERING TO REVEAL THE DEPRESSED SKULL FRACTURE

brain. I leave in a drain so the bleeding can't build up pressure again and sew up the scalp. He also has a broken lower leg that I set and place in a long splint.

I unscrub and go to the next room to see the infant we will operate on next. She's dead. She's been left there without anyone to observe her. She was overloaded with IV fluids. She should not have died. All we needed to do was a quick colostomy (bring out the intestine through the abdominal wall so she could poop) and that's it. She was the least critical, so we saved her for last. She was the one who had the least chance of dying, yet she was the one who died. One has to make hard decisions here sometimes. It's another example of how life here is such a roller coaster; you're up way high, then you come crashing down.

The next day, the little girl we operated on for the intestinal obstruction has a normal bowel movement and starts back breastfeeding. She's doing remarkably well. The boy hit with the brick is more awake and drinking some water.

I continue my rounds. Marty, the man bit by the hippo, is doing well and his wounds are starting to close. Djimé gets sent home with his dad. The wound has closed over the bone and his dad will continue dressing changes at home until the skin heals. Then he's supposed to go to Moundou and get an x-ray before coming back to see us. It's not ideal but the dad has run out of money and insists on leaving.

19 MARCH 2004
HURRY AND WAIT

I'm in N'Djamena again. I'm waiting as usual. I've come to the Central Market where one can buy everything from dried beans to pharmaceuticals to door locks to plastic pitchers to dried flowers for making Hibiscus tea to axes to radios to turbans to cloth to shoes and countless other useful and useless products.

I'm here buy cloth to make surgical gowns and drapes, but the owners of the fabric stall have run off somewhere. A boy passes by wearing the long flowing Muslim robes with a small bowl balanced perfectly on his head. Bichara is sitting next to me with his legs crossed contemplating the passersby. He orders a glass of red tea from a turbaned vendor and then buys a glass for me as well. A pair of Arab women with brightly colored wraps and shawls pass by giggling in Arabic as I try to balance the teacup in my hand without burning myself on the hot glass, Bichara, laughing as well, translates the women's joke, "So, *Nasara,* you drink tea, too?" Ha, ha, ha.

Several Arabs across the street start the ritual washing for prayer. The prayer mats are rolled out and ablutions begin. Taking a small plastic pitcher, they carefully wash first the hands and forearms, then the face, and lastly the feet and ankles rotating them flawlessly onto the mat when finished. All is done with a fluidity and grace that comes from doing this five times a day for who knows how many years. It is a communal event. An old man will be joined by a merchant who'll be joined by a passing youth and they will all stand together facing east. They will bow together. They will pray together, shoulder to shoulder. Finally, the man comes back with the thick green cloth I've been looking for. I move on through the souk and back to the truck.

Next, I find myself at the bureau of the State Police. I came here yesterday to have a paper signed authorizing Paul Kim to film his documentary of us in Béré. Two other offices had already signed the authorization. This was the last signature. I was told to come back at 9:30 a.m. today. I came back and at 10 a.m. was told to come back at noon. It's now 2 p.m.. The office is sparse with three desks. Behind one works the secretary, a wiry man with a little gray streaking his close-cropped head. He seems purposeful in his movements, always coming and going, bringing in and taking out papers, but I'm not sure if he really does anything with them.

It's hot but a little breeze comes in the doorway right where I'm sitting next to a large woman reading the Bible in French. I make small talk and she doesn't seem to mind being interrupted. The man comes back and says he can't find my paper among the visa requests. I say that's because it's a request for authorization to film.

"Oh that shouldn't have taken any time at all," he replies. "I thought it was a visa request." He comes back in two minutes with the paper signed and stamped with the all-important *cachet*.

The *cachet* or rubber stamp is very important here. One cannot survive in *Tchad* without it. I'm just beginning to discover its secret powers. Paul and I go to register him with National Security. He fills out a small form and we wait. Then the guy starts to ask me some questions. He seems suspicious. What is he doing here? Where will he stay? Who's responsible? Give me the address. I write down my name and the PO box of the hospital. He still has a scowl of disapproval on his face.

Then, thinking quickly, I reach for my secret weapon. To the untrained eye it is simply a piece of wood with some carved rubber pasted on the end. To the one who has wisdom, it is power. I place the rubber stamp in the ink and stamp it down forcefully on the paper leaving an official looking seal in purple ink. The man's face lights up. He smiles approvingly and shows me a stack of similar papers all with a variety of stamped ink seals. He returns in a couple minutes with the document approved having placed his own stamp in Paul's passport.

Later, I go to the General Hospital. I'm dressed in cargo pants, a t-shirt and tennis shoes with uncombed scraggly hair. At the gate, I inform the guard that I'm the Medical Director of the Béré Adventist Hospital. For some reason he doesn't believe me and asks for my credentials. I start to panic. I don't have any. They've all believed me before because I'm a foreigner. I have an appointment with the director of Women's Health that I'd like to keep. Then, I remember my secret weapon. I pull out my *cachet* and present it reverently to the guard. He nods knowingly allowing me to enter.

22 MARCH 2004
PREGNANCY

It's so good to be back in Béré. The first day back I discharge 13 people from the hospital. No one had bothered with rounds for almost a week and there were patients who had been ready to leave for several days. Unfortunately, the baby I'd operated on just before leaving for N'Djamena has died. However, the boy with the skull fracture and brain swelling is awake and eating. He won't see out of his right eye, though, and his eyelid has a permanent droop. I had put a cast on his lower leg fracture and it seems to be holding the bones in a good position.

Sunday, I do rounds and head to clinic while Dr. Claver, does a C-section. No big deal. Then around noon, three women come in at the same time, all in active labor. One is tiny with a huge baby whose head is too large for the pelvic opening.

I have the nurse place a urinary catheter while I shave the front of the pelvis and prep it with Betadine for a symphysiotomy. I inject some local anesthetic and slice through the skin, fat and cartilage with a large scalpel. The two nurses holding the woman's legs then rotate them out while pulling them apart. I feel and hear the pelvis open. I pack the wound with gauze and wait for the baby. It is still a difficult delivery and the baby comes out floppy and not breathing.

I suck out the gunk clogging up the airway and try to breathe for the newborn with a tiny bag attached to a face mask. The heartbeat is slow and weak. Sarah listens to the chest with a stethoscope and reports that there is no air movement. I adjust the mask and finally air starts going in. The baby is limp and blue. We continue our resuscitation efforts and finally, the heartbeat picks up. Then, the baby opens its eyes and coughs a few times. Some of the ever-present onlookers murmur "it's a miracle."

After cleaning up, I go home to eat. I'm talking with Sarah outside her apartment in the early evening when the *garde* comes to tell me about a pregnant woman who's just arrived with the baby's arm sticking out between her legs. I hurry over to the hospital to examine the woman. As the woman pulls up her sheet the baby let's us know he's okay by waving his hand!

We hurry her off to surgery as the *garde* calls in the OR team. Things go smoothly at first. After a bit of a struggle I deliver a healthy, screaming baby girl and I start to suture up the uterus. As I place the first suture in the uterus, I nick the uterine artery, which starts to spurt blood into the field. I quickly press on the artery with a surgical sponge and try to calm my panic. I ask for another suture hoping my voice won't crack, revealing my inexperience and fear. I place a figure of eight stitch and am able to control it without much blood loss.

As I pull off my bloody gloves, the *garde* approaches to tell me about another woman in labor who hasn't been progressing normally. I enter the delivery room and find the woman has adequate contractions but also has an inadequate pelvic opening. I prepare her as well for a symphysiotomy, which goes off without a hitch. She pushes twice and the baby starts screaming almost before it hits the mattress. By then it is almost midnight and I go home to catch a few hours of sleep.

The next morning at morning report, I find out about a woman who came in after midnight with a retained placenta. They didn't think it was urgent. I quickly get up and go see her. Fortunately, with a little steady pulling on the umbilical cord and some medicine to make the uterus contract, the placenta comes out easily without much bleeding. I prescribe some antibiotics and start rounds. In the middle of rounds, another woman comes in by oxcart from one of the outlying health clinics for a breech presentation. Thankfully, this C-section goes smoothly, delivering another screaming baby into a harsh world.

2 APRIL 2004
A TYPICAL FRIDAY

5:51 a.m.: The crow of a rooster breaks through the peaceful sleep provided by my earplugs. I realize I'm drenched in sweat as I lie on my *Tchadian* mattress. The foam has become compressed into a central crater that sucks me into it no matter what position I may start the night's sleep in. My sheet has come undone and has also been drawn irresistibly to the center. The dried, cracked skin on my heels has stuck to the mosquito net, drawing it in as well. Trying to untangle myself from my self-made spider web, I turn over onto my sweat-soaked pillow and fall back asleep.

6:10 a.m.: The sunlight pouring in my window wakes me with a start. I fear I might have overslept. When I realize it's only 6:10 a.m., I fall back onto the mattress. I try to pray but can only worry about the upcoming day. I grab my pocket New Testament and open to Revelation 4 where I left off yesterday. It describes what I long for: the next life. I close the Bible and get ready for work.

6:28 a.m.: I walk down the hallway to the bathroom where I take a shower. Halfway through, the water slows to a trickle. Nassourou has turned on the faucet just outside the window which sucks all the water from my shower. I try to wait patiently while my subconscious wants to yell out, "Why can't you just wait one more minute and I'll at least have the soap off my face!"

6:49 a.m.: I prepare to go next door, but am accosted by Dr. Claver who has slept outside. He's still "sick" with Malaria, although he has sat inside watching his car battery-powered TV all day since Tuesday while I handle all the work. He suddenly wants to discuss the housing situation. "What are we going to do when my wife and kids come in June? I think we should kick out André." That's funny, last night André told me we should boot out Claver. Just what I was hoping to solve right before breakfast.

7:26 a.m.: I go next door to Sarah's and sit down to breakfast: rice fried in peanut oil with eggs, onions and tomatoes. A plastic bottle of cool Hibiscus flower tea made just yesterday washes it all down nicely.

7:44 a.m.: I'm late for worship and they're in the middle of prayer. I wait outside the clinic until they're done. Then, I enter the waiting room and take my usual place on the front row of crude wooden benches. It's time for the *rapport du garde* when the night-duty nurse tells us all that's happened overnight. He describes a few patients admitted with Malaria and a woman with a headache who got Paracetamol and was told to come back today for a Malaria smear. He ends his report by telling us about a young boy who was trying to get a few mangoes before school, fell out of the tree and "seems pretty bad." Lona closes with prayer. As usual, no matter who prays, I am amazed by the awe, reverence, and depth with which they speak to God.

8:17 a.m.: I see the boy who fell from the mango tree. His femur is obviously broken near the knee with an open wound over it but no bone sticking out now. The parents inform me that the traditional bonesetter has already fixed it so I don't need to worry about it. I point to the leg shortened by six inches and the obvious deformity just above the knee and say that it still needs to be worked on. He's also having trouble breathing with some gurgling coming from his throat. His jaw is swollen on both sides and recessed. He never lost consciousness and is currently alert. However, his jaw appears to be broken in three places making it hard to breathe. I pull the family aside and say I think it's best to evacuate him to N'Djamena to be treated. They say that will be impossible. They beg me to do what I can.

> HIS JAW APPEARS TO BE
> BROKEN IN THREE PLACES
> MAKING IT HARD TO BREATHE

8:45 a.m.: I'm in the minor procedure room. Samedi has just started an IV on the boy.. I inject some Valium and Ketamine to put him to sleep. I then pull his leg and push on the displaced bone to reduce the fracture.

While our visiting medical student, Jonathan holds traction to maintain the reduction, I wash out the wound liberally with diluted bleach and suture it closed. Then I wrap the leg in cotton and place a plaster cast from thigh to mid-calf. It's the best we can do.

9:22 a.m.: What to do now about the boy's jaw? I watched a surgeon wire a jaw together once back in California. I remember that Nassourou told me a couple weeks ago that he found some wire suture in the garage. I walk over and open the door. The garage's oil-drenched floors are covered with odds and ends of machines, pieces of metal, old bed frames, broken down wheelchairs and scraps of lumber. Over in the corner, I see a stack of sterile, plastic-wrapped wire sutures. I return to the OR.

With the help of Samedi and Jonathan, I get started. The boy is missing a lot of teeth. I choose matching molars on top and bottom on each side and get to work. I wrap the suture around the base and use a needle-holder to tighten it down. The front four teeth on top and bottom at first appear pretty solid, at least until I tighten the wires which pulls two of them out of their sockets. I undo the wires and stick the two escapees back in place. Maybe they'll reattach themselves.

I find two matching molars on the other side and repeat the process. The mandible shifts forward into place. Then I pull the front jaw fragment forward and fix it in place using the two top and bottom teeth that are solid. The reduction is not perfect, but it's the best I can do.

11:28 a.m.: I go to see the hospitalized patients. I do rounds quickly, discharging six patients and writing notes and orders on the rest.

11:53 a.m.: I start clinic. I diagnose and treat two men with gonorrhea. I admit two children with Malaria. I see several other patients with various complaints and send them off for lab work. Sarah brings me a metal pot of ice-cold lemonade. I feel the refreshing liquid go all the way down!

2:40 p.m.: I go home only to be called back immediately by Anatole. The Mayor was in an automobile accident. I hurry back. There is a crowd gathered already. The Mayor is in the minor procedure room moaning and groaning but otherwise conscious. He's covered with dirt. His left face is swollen and his left eye can barely be opened. Pupils are normal. He has a small scrape on his forehead but no lacerations or obvious fractures. His left knee has an abrasion. Anatole starts an IV. The Mayor keeps writhing and groaning and holding his left wrist. It's obviously broken but appears to be a simple, closed fracture.

His wife comes in, a large woman dressed in bright yellow and orange. She falls to her knees moaning and groaning With difficulty she is escorted out. We clean up the scrapes and prepare to splint the broken bone.

A man tries to force himself in, tears streaming down his face. He is forcefully ejected. He repeats this at least three times as we try to work. We stabilize the broken wrist. The Mayor insists on going home. I offer to take him in the hospital's vehicle after he suggests driving himself home on his motorcycle!

4:22 p.m.: The mayor stumbles weakly to the truck and takes the passenger seat. Four close relatives including his large wife squeeze in the rear seat. 20 other people quickly fill up the bed of the pickup. We drive through the dirt roads of Béré past mango trees, mud brick huts, a soccer match in full swing, a small school, and a few roadside stands until we arrive at the gate of the Mayor's house.

They've prepared a mattress for him in the courtyard with a nice colorful rug on top. There are about 50 people already gathered. When he walks in with his head bandage, splint and sling, the crowd erupts in weeping, wailing and gnashing of teeth. Everyone rushes forward to help the Major lie down. He begins to writhe and moan again. The people crowd in. Some swoon, weeping bitterly in silence. People from the streets pour in through the gates to see the spectacle. Various people are shouting directions, usually the opposite of what someone else has just suggested.

The Mayor keeps repeating the phrase *"kubeng"* in between tossing, turning and moaning. Finally, I get someone who seems reasonable to help me chase out the malingerers. The Mayor then tells me that I must take him back to the hospital to be hospitalized. I insist his injuries are not serious and he can stay here if he can find a way to have a little peace and quiet. At last, some order is restored and I bolt. The air-conditioned car feels good on my sweat-soaked body.

6:48 p.m.: I enter Sarah's empty living room after having grabbed a cold bottle of hibiscus flower tea from Claver's fridge. It's good to just sit. I see some cold pasta left on the table and dig in.

7:03 p.m.: Sarah and Jonathan return from the meeting at the church. Jonathan and I sit out on the porch to escape the heat a little. I grab my guitar. For some reason every song I start to sing seems really meaningful. I enter a time of personal worship as I present my struggles, fears and hopes to God through other people's songs sung straight from my soul. Jonathan doesn't seem to mind that I'm totally absorbed and ignoring him. He goes inside. I finish and feel the sudden overwhelming sense of God's presence. I start to weep. I bow my head and close my eyes to try and not be seen as the sobs wrack my body.

7:51 p.m.: Anatole comes with some questions about some patients.

8:39 p.m.: I hit the sack.

2 a.m.: Anatole wakes me out of the deepest sleep ever. I rip out my earplugs, take off my eyeshade, and head over to the hospital feeling already drained. A woman has come with what looks like a prolapsed uterus. There's something at the end that looks like a necrotic fibroid. Something doesn't seem quite right but the rest of her physical exam is pretty normal and she's not hemorrhaging. I give her some antibiotics, cover the uterus with some gauze and tell Anatole we'll operate in the morning. I wake up Dr. Claver, since he's the gynecologist and inform him of the case. I fall asleep immediately.

8:39 a.m.: Dr. Claver wakes me up. He says he's going to operate on the woman and asks me if I can do the anesthesia since Nassourrou is sick. I figure it'll be nice and cool in the OR so I don't mind. Besides I figure I won't have much to do.

To make a long story short, it turns out that what was sticking out was actually the end of her small intestine which had been swallowed up by her colon in a process we call intussusception until it came out her anus. I have to scrub in but it takes us a long time to figure out exactly what's going on as it is all just one huge, inflamed mass. After 7 1/2 hours of surgery we finally have managed to take out most of the colon and part of the small intestine. We then hook up the small intestine back to what is left of the colon. Amazingly she survives the surgery.

Unfortunately, she dies four hours later. We did what we could, but I have to wonder if we had made the diagnosis a few hours earlier and operated then, would we have been able to save her? But then again, she waited a long time before coming in. I guess I'll never know.

14 APRIL 2004
MANGOES, BULLFROGS, SEWERS AND HEAT...

I sit on top of Jabel's Land Cruiser, my butt resting on one spare tire while the computer rests on the second spare. Every time a car passes the bullfrogs stop croaking briefly before thundering noisily again, drowning out any other sound. It almost makes me think I'm in a swamp in Louisiana instead of a slum in N'Djamena. The sewage that normally runs safely in trenches by the side of the road has somehow been blocked up across the street forming a sort of local swampland. During the rainy season they say that all the roads become like that with just a narrow strip in the center. People hate cars then because they have to jump off into the murky waters when a vehicle passes.

I was sitting outside this same house a few weeks ago, straddling the cement rail across the muck of human and animal waste. Having just eaten some watermelon, I came up to chat with the security guard, *Papa* Ganda, who Jabel and Caleb call Propaganda. As we talked, I watched four little girls amuse themselves. First they lay pebbles in the dirt. Then they threw one into the air while trying to grab as many stones in the dirt as they could before catching the tiny falling rock. Next, the girls took a circle of rope made out of old bicycle inner tubes and played a game that had something to do with jumping into it, on it or over it according to some unspoken rule while it was wrapped around first the ankles, then the knees, then the waists of two other girls.

Propaganda used to be one of the most feared officers in the *Tchadian* army. During the war with Libya and some of the later civil wars, he used to go into towns killing all the men and raping the women. Later he became a Christian and now reads the Bible more than anyone I've ever known. You never see him without it open. He's Jabel's night watchman now and still enjoys his reputation. No one messes with Propaganda.

The other night someone came by who didn't know him. Big mistake. The man was drunk and loud. Since Jabel and the others were resting, Propaganda told him to move on. He laughed at the old man and asked who was going to make him. Propaganda just said if he's looking for trouble he just found it, then calmly walked inside, picked up his machete and walked out purposefully straight toward the man. Still laughing, the drunkard looked around to see who else was joining in the joke of this grandpa trying to bust his chops. No one was else laughing, everyone was just backing away. Suddenly, the man realized this was no laughing matter and took off running while Propaganda went quietly back to his Bible reading.

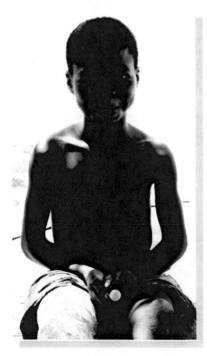

In Béré we are having problems with mangos, or more specifically mango trees. It's mango time and you can buy them for less than two cents apiece. But people still can't get enough. A woman came into the ER having fallen out of a mango tree. She said she wasn't hurt but wanted to know if her baby was okay since she was six months pregnant! Fortunately, they both were fine.

I went on rounds to see the boy who'd fallen out of the mango tree a few weeks ago. We'd wired his jaw shut. Whenever I see him now, he usually has a scowl on his face and looks at me like I had done something horrific to him. I asked the mom how he was eating and she said she was giving him a lot of *bouillie* made of rice, peanut paste and water. Not too many vitamins. So I asked if she could feed him limes or mangos crushed up.

They don't speak French, only Nangjeré but I guess the word *mangue* is universal because suddenly the boys face lit up with a grin so huge I thought it was going to split his head in two, from ear to ear. The next day when I came to see him he looked up at me and gave me another monster smile revealing tufts of fibrous mango stuck in the wires keeping his jaw in place. I couldn't help grinning myself.

Back in N'Djamena, I want to go to the river in the afternoon to go swimming and play soccer with the guys. However, with all the waiting around in offices and "come back later" I end up arriving in Jabel's ghetto about 15 minutes after they've already left.

Not wanting to miss the excitement at the river I borrow Jabel's roommate's bike and take off through the barrios. I soon find out the seat has a certain peculiarity. No matter where I sit on it, it finds its way back to its preferred position of 45-degree angled right up into the crotch. Not to mention the seat is already too low for my long, giraffe-like legs.

So, here I am, a tall, pale *Nasara* riding a rickety bike with the seat pointed almost straight up, in shorts and sandals, riding with legs bent and churning like a broken paddle boat through the slums, sewers, dust and 105 degree heat of a flat, desert African city passing Arabs dressed in long flowing robes and turbans bartering everything imaginable alongside the road. Needless to say, I get more than a few stares.

But, unlike almost every other *Tchadian* on a bike, I'm in a hurry because I really want to swim. So, I'm passing all these guys leisurely pedaling along on their cruisers when suddenly I feel someone coming up on my left. It's a muscular African in shorts and a t-shirt who looks at me and grins as he passes me. There's no way I'm going to let that happen, so I pick up the pace and pass him. He starts pedaling furiously and without saying a word we enter into a neck and neck race. Before we know it, we are approaching the bridge. Trying to make conversation without acting like I'm out of breath and about to die, I ask if he's going to cross the bridge. He says yes and that starts a conversation as we both mutually slow down without giving the other an inch.

Halfway across the bridge I spot the boys down below on a sandbar playing *le football*. I tell my competitor that I'm stopping to greet my friends assuming he'll keep going, but he comes over with me. I wave and tell my friends that I'll be right there. Then I continue on. At the end of the bridge, I again tell the dude that I'm turning off here, so good-bye. He doesn't get it and turns off too.

We continue our silent race off-road now. When we're almost at Jabel's Land Cruiser, my new friend asks me a question.

"What I'm going to do with your bike?"

"Take it over to there," I point to where they're playing soccer.

"We can just chain our bikes together."

"Uh, okay."

We take off for the river, swim across to the sandbar and spend a pleasant hour playing soccer, swimming and watching Jared try to catch some fish. After we're done I throw my bike in the back of the truck and hop in. My new friend does too. We cruise across the bridge. On the other side, my pal gets off, finally says *au revoir* and we part the best of friends.

I just have to ask myself, what made him stop and spend the afternoon with complete strangers? Did he really have nothing better to do or was it just this peculiar African thing about friendships being the most important thing in life? It was all just very bizarre and yet cool and normal at the same time.

21 APRIL 2004
HOWLING

The wind is howling outside the hospital. Dust devils and mini-cyclones tear up the African soil. Inside my head a storm is raging as well. I'm close to being completely burned out. I'm so easily frustrated. My motivation is low. The inevitability of the lack of change is forefront in my mind. I haven't slept through the night since I can remember. I toss and turn in my bed. My thoughts are tortured. *When will it end? What am I doing here? Why am I here? How did I get to this point?*

Maybe it's lack of exercise. I've been to the river swimming three times in the last week. It hasn't helped, however. Maybe I haven't had enough quiet time. Yet, all our visitors are gone and the Dr. Claver is in the capital. In fact, it hasn't been this quiet since I arrived in the Republic of Chad. Maybe I need more time with God. But I've woken up early the past few days for extra prayer and Bible reading. I've even gone through several devotional books without any improvement in my mood.

The feeling that this is the way it is and always will be slowly settles in. I'm here for the long haul. No manner of miraculous, extraordinary cases and no quantity of lives saved can change the fact that things are mostly pretty routine here. The same desert, same sand, same bushes, same trees, same flatness, same colored mud huts, same type of people, same diseases, same filth, same poverty, same landscape, same sun, same heat, same sweat, same work, same food, same...same...Sa.m.E.

I had a dream last night.

I was fast asleep on the porch, outside where it was cooler. A pig woke me up by grunting in my ear. I went inside, fell asleep and entered dreamland. In my vision, I wake up realizing that the electricity is on. I hear the rumble of the generator. Why? I get up and go to the hospital. All the nurses are crammed into the operating room.

"What's going on?" I ask Dr. Claver who's operating.

"Surgery," shaking his head, he turns back to his work. I see a large pig strapped to the operating table.

"What's with the pig?" I inquire incredulously.

"It's pregnant," he replies nonchalantly. "The baby is in distress, got caught in his umbilical cord."

The surgeon is performing a C-section. I now see two pigs on the table. One pig is lying with its abdomen splayed open. The other pig is inside the first pig's belly twisting in a mass of slimy umbilical cords.

"Have they paid for the operation?" I probe.

"I don't know. I didn't ask. It's an emergency. Pigs are very important here you know."

I move to the next room where there's a crowd of locals. Somehow I know who the owner is: a typical woman from the village wrapped in a colorful piece of cloth from Nigeria.

"Have you paid?" I accuse. The woman laughs.

"It's an emergency...we'll pay later," she says with a knowing smirk on her face. Everyone laughs at me. Suddenly, the surgery is over and Dr. Claver is standing before me.

"Get out of here and never come back!" I scream in frustration as I wake up in a cold sweat. Sometimes I wonder why I signed up to be a missionary.

If only I could feel like Africa wasn't the place I'm supposed to be. If only I could shake the strange sensation that this is what I was meant to do. If only I could stop having moments of wonder and joy in the midst of the pain and frustration. If only I could convince myself that I made a mistake in coming here. If only I didn't really feel like I was being refined here in the furnace of the Sahara into the man God wants me to be. If only I could find a good excuse to leave. If only I could think of something else to do with my life. If only I could be content with a normal Western lifestyle. If only I didn't really think it would get better if I stick it out. If only...

25 APRIL 2004
WHY

I am once again reminded of why I'm here. The path meanders through the mud brick huts of Béré. The clouds are splayed across the huge *Tchadian* sky like someone took a huge white paintbrush and made a few bold strokes across the deep blue canvas of the evening. Behind me walks a pretty red-headed Danish nurse with a train of over 20 African children each vying to either hold her hand or hold the hand of one who's holding her hand.

In front of me is the hut of Lazare, the hospital's janitor, which has no roof. He stands up from behind a woven grass matt wall where he has been meditating facing the setting sun. The sun appears to be setting backwards as its top half is covered by a huge cumulus cloud while its bottom half stretches to almost touch the horizon. Above the cloud the filtered sunbeams stream out in hazy rose-colored rays. There is no noise except the chattering of children in *Nangjeré*. I feel a hand in mine. It's a one-armed boy who loves to just hang out at our porch and look in the window to watch us eat or whatever. I've been teaching him a few English phrases, which he loves to repeat.

"What's up, dude?" I say.

"Nothing, bruddah," he replies with a toothy grin.

A three-year old girl with a very dirty worn shirt about ten times too big hanging loosely over a swollen belly comes up munching a green mango, skin and all. She starts loudly repeating *lapia, lapia* over and over as she tries to give me a sideways "five" with her open palm. She laughs when I start repeating *lapia* over and over with her.

There is a group of boys, the sons of some of the nurses, who always love to just hang out around the house. I always speak to them in English but they love it. I grab them and throw them together to the ground as we wrestle and they squeal in joy, covered with dust. One of the sons of our pediatric nurse, Lona, usually runs around naked and always just stares up at me, insisting that I am all his. He gets jealous if I let someone else sit on my lap besides him.

So, Sarah and I are on the path through Béré back toward the hospital. We've just come from the most entertaining event of the month in our village of 20,000 inhabitants, a soccer match with a team from "far away." The field is a lumpy patch of hard packed dirt with a small line carved out around and tattered flags on sticks planted at the corners to mark its boundaries. The goal posts are so twisted that once I was sure there would've been a goal if they'd used straight wood to make the posts. The field is actually well delineated by the crowd pressing just up to the playing field about five to ten people deep without benches, stands or anything.

To make sure the boundaries are respected several gendarmes in varying types of army uniforms patrol the edges. One carries an old automobile fan belt, which he swings in the general direction of anyone close to the line as he yells for the crowd to back up. One actually hits a young boy with a canvas army canteen belt. They are helped by a local in

Arab robes and turban sporting Oakley-type shades, a cigarette hanging loosely in his mouth and bunch of straw that he wields as a weapon. He almost causes a fight with the players when he gets in the way of a throw-in from out of bounds (the player accidentally hit him in the head with the ball, bouncing it out of bounds again).

To heighten the experience, a ghetto blaster belts out Nigerian tunes with classic African rhythms while a dude straight from *Solid Gold* wearing tight bell-bottoms and a brown corduroy shirt jitterbugs in the corner of the field when he's not "helping" the gendarmes keep order. I think he's actually the pastor's son but I'm not sure. An old man with missing and rotten teeth who looks vaguely familiar comes up calling out *"Docteur, lapia."*

"Lona mega?" I reply.

"Lapia, kubeng," he responds while vigorously shaking my hand.

"Lapia!" I repeat as I've just reached the extent of my *Nangjeré*.

Most of the adults have been drinking. I make sure to stay close to Sarah and her *Nangjeré* friend, Julie. As the only white people in the audience, Sarah and I are also part of the entertainment. Sometimes I wish I could just blend in, but like it or not I'll always be a celebrity here. Kids crowd around as an old *Nangjeré* grandma continually makes commentary on the soccer match. Sarah is a child magnet. I'm glad, as it takes some of the attention from me. I may be tall and blond but her very fair skin and wild curly long red hair outdoes me in the "notice me" factor, especially here.

Everyone is sleeping outside these days. It's too hot indoors as the tin roofs and cement block walls just hold the heat in. On Sarah's porch I've rigged a rope to sling my mosquito net from while she has had someone make a framework of rebar that she ties hers to. We've been blessed with a very slow week at the hospital. While hippo bites, cattle gorings, falls from mango trees, getting crushed by ox carts, knifings and such are exciting, it's been nice just to have a few cases of Malaria and some infections to deal with lately. Also, Dr. Claver has been away, which means the TV has been off and there haven't been people around all the time. We also haven't had any foreign visitors here this week, so overall it's been quiet.

One night, as we are sleeping outside something happens that makes me feel like a teenager all over again. Sarah has just shared with me some very personal things. She is at a very vulnerable point. She's shy and afraid. I want to show her that nothing she's said has changed the way I feel about her. I tell her to give me her hand and she slips it under her mosquito net and into mine. Then I pray for her. Afterwards, I just let my hand stay there. She doesn't pull away. I feel the same adolescent thrill I haven't felt in a long time as I slowly caress her fingers.

We lie there in silence enjoying the moment. The stars are out in full force. The moon is a crescent right above the planet, Venus, just like the symbol of Islam. A cool wind blows away the heat of the day. Even the pigs and goats respect the moment by temporarily ceasing their usual background grunting and bleating. I suddenly feel as if a huge load that has been trying to crush me has been lifted. I feel that I could sink through the mattress and slip into a sleep that would last for days while at the same time my heart is racing thanks to Sarah's tender touch.

09 MAY 2004
WAR

Tchad has a long history of war and its impact continues to affect everyday life in this sub-Saharan country. It's routine to hear during morning report at the hospital that a woman came in who'd been beaten by her husband, brother, uncle, sister, or her husband's other wife.

About a month ago, tribal warfare broke out in N'Djamena as a whole quarter was shut down by armed police who shot tear gas and bullets into the crowd while inside the warring members bludgeoned each other with clubs, machetes, bush knives, tools, bicycles and anything else they could get their hands on.

That same week a man was walking near a Jabel's house and was jumped on by thugs from a tree who knifed him and left him for dead. The next morning he was still alive surrounded by curious onlookers. When someone asked why they didn't help him, one shrugged and said, "We don't know him." Another was stoned to death on a nearby side street. I remember well the knife fight that happened inside our own hospital right outside the door of the ER where I was trying to take care of an infant with Tetanus and another child convulsing from severe Malaria.

So, is there any hope for peace in *Tchad*? Not yet. I'm suddenly called from rounds by shouting. Our chauffeur, Bichara, just drove up outside the halfway built hospital wall. He's been out with the district vaccination program at the same time as some of the agricultural community decided to retaliate for what they felt

> THE OTHER GENDARMES WENT CRAZY LEAVING AT LEAST TWO DEAD

was an unfair decision in a land dispute with the Arab nomad cow herders.

A group of rice farmers went to the nearby gendarmerie and when the gendarmes pulled out their guns, one tried to wrest the rifle away only to be shot in the stomach. Then the other gendarmes went crazy leaving at least two dead and multiple wounded. All this happened right in front of

Bichara, who then helped load five wounded into the back of our pickup and bring them to the hospital.

By the time I arrive a huge crowd has gathered as usual to gawk. Dr. Eric Davy and Dr. Cathy Castillo are visiting from the Ventura County Medical Center in California where I did my postgraduate training. I feel like I'm back in residency, except we're unloading Africans with blood soaked clothing piled on top of each other in the back of a beat up truck instead of from a well equipped ambulance with paramedics who've already started IVs and applied dressings. No, this is raw carnage, casualties of war straight from the battlefield.

I quickly question the wounded, who are all conscious, where they are injured. Three have been hit in the legs, one in the belly and the last in the arm. Blood smears the bed of the truck as I commandeer several staff to bring stretchers and take away the one shot in the stomach first. All seem pretty stable on first look and listen. The best thing is that we actually have gloves this time thanks to Eric and Cathy.

We take the man with the abdominal injury straight to the OR while I grab IV catheters, tubing and IV fluids from the Pharmacy. Eric has just taken one of the men shot in the leg to our tiny ER. He's bleeding pretty profusely. It looks like the bullet went through the femur, shattering it. One of our seasoned nurses, Anatole, is with him and since he seems stable I move on.

In the minor procedure room we have two others who've been shot in the leg. On the procedure table is a man who's been shot through the front of the thigh. The bullet burst out the back of his knee with some fat and a shredded nerve or tendon hanging out. He can't move his foot and is writhing in pain as Cathy washes out the wound. Dr. Claver is assessing the other patient who's been shot in the hamstrings but seems to not have hurt anything serious.

I go into the OR. The injured man's abdomen is soft but he has a fast heart rate, a normal blood pressure and a bullet hole entering the right lower quadrant of his abdomen exiting his right posterior flank. I start an IV quickly and run in fluids fast as possible. Sarah administers antibiotics and a sedative. Samedi, the scrub nurse, arranges the instruments while I scrub. About 25 minutes after his arrival, I'm ready with scalpel poised to open his belly.

I slice from his sternum, around the belly button and down close to his pelvis. The small intestine comes pouring out but there is no blood or fecal material. I fish around his lower belly identifying a hematoma where the bullet passed by without entering his abdomen. Then I check carefully the colon, appendix, liver, spleen, and finally the small intestine from beginning to end without finding any injuries. I sew the fascia and skin closed and scrub out.

While he wakes up from his anesthesia, I go to check on the others. The two in the minor procedure room have IVs running, antibiotics in and dressings in place. They are sweating like crazy in the stuffy tin roofed chamber so I move them to hospital beds and go to see the one in the ER. Eric has placed a sandbag on the wounded man's leg to stop the bleeding but the table is still covered with blood.

We lift off the sandbag, remove the dressing, pack the hole with gauze where the blood's pouring out and place a pressure dressing reinforced with the sandbag again. We snag a bed from the medicine ward, roll it outside under the porch and move the patient there while a crowd of about 30 gather around to see what the three *Nasara* doctors will do. Since we don't have a working x-ray machine much less any equipment for traction or orthopedic surgery we have to come up with another solution for the fracture. We place the lower leg in a plaster cast, tie a rope around it, loop it over the end of the bed and lash the sandbag to the tips. The leg is out to length and doesn't look rotated so we assume it is reduced. Meanwhile, the pressure dressing has managed to stop the bleeding.

10 MAY 2004
PEACE

Today, Sarah and I are headed out to the river on a single, well-used bicycle. I'm on the pedals while she relaxes easily behind me on the small platform over the rear tire. I'm out of shape and the bike's tires are flat. Needless to say I'm struggling. It's over 110 degrees outside which doesn't help. Sweat is pouring off my face and body. My thighs are burning. As for my butt, well, let's just say that a bike seat here is really a torture device. Two *Tchadian* boys, also on a single bike, catch up and pass us easily. I glare at them enviously as I am working hard and getting nowhere.

We finally arrive at the river. It feels so good to plunge into that muddy, warm water. I give a brief introductory swimming lesson to one of the boys who passed us and then go off to play in the current. As I rest under the shade of the opposite bank, my feet and legs still in the water, the other boy calls to me asking where Sarah is. I don't see her. I get a little nervous when the boy yells back that he thinks she's headed downstream.

We jump into the water, letting the current take us where it will. The stream gets shallow quickly, so we climb the bank onto a footpath. Up ahead the stream winds around a corner with grassy banks poking out between volcanic rock and scrub trees before disappearing into the African plain. No sign of Sarah.

We round another corner and there she is. She's striding nonchalantly in the ankle deep water. The river here is wide but shallow. Sarah's long curly red hair flows down the bright white skin of her back, reflecting the sun off her baby blue bikini. All along the banks, scores of very dark, curious children stand and stare. Ahead is a ford where groups of Arabs are gathered in long robes and turbans chatting. Meanwhile, similarly attired boys herd cattle across with waving sticks and periodic cries of "Hoah! Hoah!" Sarah seems oblivious to her surroundings.

I run up to join Sarah. As we pass the groups of Arabs I wonder what they think of a bikini or if they've ever even seen one. As we continue around the bend, Sarah asks some of the kids if there is deep water ahead. We have to make a small detour onto the path when a boy running along above the stream warns us of a fishing line. The line is marked with pieces of white plastic waving in the breeze off of sticks stuck in the sand. He also informs us that there are hippos in the deeper waters so we decide to stop.

I face downstream on my back and Sarah faces upstream on her tummy. We just sit and talk as I stare at her thinking how improbable all this is to be in  the middle of a stream in Africa with a beautiful, redheaded Dane, surrounded by Arabs. I turn around on my belly and put my arm around her. She has goose bumps from the cold.

We sit and talk for about half an hour watching huge cargo trucks gun it across the ford while small, banged-up pickups packed with turbaned Arabs splash, spray, spin and twist across. The cattle are sometimes obstinate running from the water just right before entering sending the Arab boys running and shouting after them, waving their sticks. Finally, as the sun starts to go down we have to go back. The return is uneventful except for the excruciating pain of trying to pedal the seven kilometers while being completely out of shape!

01 JUNE 2004
WIND AND RAIN

As I sit sipping my hot sugary milk slightly browned with a sprinkling of coffee, I think back over recent events. It's pouring down rain outside, pounding on the tin roof and lulling me into reverie. The steam from my beverage fogs up my glasses blotting out current happenings in favor of remembering how God recently took me to the brink and brought me back again through wind and rain...

I need a break. When I find out that my friends Jason and Belen are going to be in Nigeria and have planned a short trip to the Koza Adventist Hospital in northern Cameroon, I decide to meet them there. Since I have to be in N'Djamena anyway at that time, I can easily cross the border and meet them at Banki on the Nigerian-Cameroonian border. Sarah decides to accompany me.

We cross the *Tchadian* border into Cameroon at Kousseri and proceed to Banki without incident. On the Cameroonian side of the border in Banki, the customs people are friendly. They offer to send someone with Sarah and me to help us find the border station and my friends. Our guide leads us confidently through the maze of narrow, pot-holed, plastic-filled, dirt streets lined filled with vendors hawking the latest Nigerian goods.

We arrive at the Nigerian emigration office where we find Jason, Belen and their 16-month-old daughter, Mikaela. Then we return to the Cameroonian Immigration where I change money outside on the black market. Upon arrival back at customs our guide tells us we need to pay a 2,000 francs customs fee. We argue back and forth.

"We never actually entered Nigeria so why do we need customs clearance?"

"Yeah, but your friends will have Nigerian exit stamps and Cameroonian entrance visas at Banki. If you don't have a customs clearance stamp from Banki, they may stop you elsewhere and you'll have problems."

"Well, I'll just tell them we just picked these guys up on the side of the road, and the vehicle was never out of the country."

"Okay, fine," he laughs good-naturedly. "Move on."

"*Merci beaucoup,*" I respond as I hold out 2,000 francs. "You've done such a good job guiding us personally through town I'd like to show my appreciation."

The man accepts with a warm smile and a nod of understanding. It's the way things are done here. If I'd paid the custom's fee, the money would've gone into someone else's pocket that hadn't helped us. This way the money goes into the right pocket.

Upon arrival at Koza I'm reminded of how pitiful our hospital in Béré really is. The Koza Adventist Hospital is still a bush hospital, but compared to Béré, it felt like a miracle of modernity: real electricity from wires, air-conditioning in the thick stone-walled doctor's house, refrigeration, a well-equipped operating room, well-functioning lab, thick stone-walled hospital buildings built in 1953 and yet in much better shape than ours which were built in the early '80s.

Maybe I'm imagining it, but the people also seem friendlier and less intrusive. The children don't stand outside the windows or run free at night singing, shouting and dancing till all hours. No one even comes begging for money! I seem to connect on a personal level much better with the staff even after only a few days and a big part of me just wants to ditch Béré and come to Koza where they would welcome me with open arms. Here the local authorities respect the work of the hospital instead of always suspiciously spreading rumors about how we're out to hurt the population and are too expensive.

The next day at church I'm scheduled to speak. The church is a massive stone edifice simply furnished inside with crude wooden benches. The children and choir have just finished singing rousing, rhythm-heavy African tunes accompanied by a variety of percussion instruments. The mood is joyous. They get up to introduce me and suddenly a massive wind of gale force begins to beat so viciously against the church that speaking is out of the question. We go rapidly from sweating hot to chilled, goose-bumpy cold.

The ensuing thunderstorm is so fierce that it blows inside the church through upward facing slats wetting everyone on the platform. People crowd to the sheltered parts but refuse to leave. The kids begin to sing, clap and pound their drums louder and louder until the wind and rain are drowned out. After half an hour the raging storm calms a little and they decide to continue the service. But when someone stands up to introduce me again, the wind also picks up again drowning the speaker out. Everyone begins to laugh.

Finally, I decide to just go for it. I almost go hoarse shouting out my message in French while the interpreter translates into the local Mafa language. Meanwhile, the rain continues its assault on the church. I feel alive, alert, awake, purified and cleansed.

That night as I walk back alone to the house to sleep, visions of how great it would be to come to Koza surface. I stop and stare up at the moon. The wind has knocked out the power lines so the heavenly lights have no competition. The moon is turned so its crescent looks like a big smile. I feel as if God is smiling on me telling me that I am free.

I begin to cry as I realize all the pressure I've put on myself to succeed at Béré. I didn't realize that I'd felt trapped, like I had to stay and succeed or people would be disappointed. All that suppressed frustration pours out of me as my body is racked with sobs that release a lot of built up tension. It's true that it was God's leading that sent me to *Tchad*, but it was my choice. In this instant, I feel that it is God's continued desire for me to be in Béré, but it is still my choice. If I choose to come to Koza or even return to the US, God won't abandon me. The choice then becomes clear to me: I will stay in Béré.

I soon find myself back in Béré. One day, a message comes that I'm to go to a seminar in Lai, 18 kilometers away. I attend the conference, but feel kind of uncomfortable not knowing anyone and being a foreigner. I return home that night. The next morning, the ambulance driver takes me to Lai. Halfway there we begin to see the looming blackness of storm clouds and once again a fierce wind picks up.

We arrive at the river and see that the barge has broken free from its moorings and run aground on the other side. There's no one in sight, not even one of the usually ubiquitous dugout canoes. How can I get across? The rain has turned into a deluge pounding on the roof of the ambulance. The chauffeur echoes my thoughts.

"Why don't you put your clothes in a plastic sack and swim across?"

I think he's probably joking, but I'm serious. So I strip down naked, pack my pants and shirt in several inner tube bags, tie my sandals onto the back with a strip of rubber peeled from an old tube and step into the storm. I slip and slosh through the mud down to the river and plunge into the waves. Lightening flashes, thunder roars, the rain pelts and I swim using a modified breast-stroke pushing my bundle ahead of me across the river about 200 meters. I feel invigorated. I'm in Africa fording a raging river half-naked in a storm to attend a seminar!

I get to the other side and pull on my boxers. I continue shirtless and barefoot up the road past the piles of mud bricks made at the water's edge. I approach a group of *Tchadians* trying to push a cart full of bricks up a muddy slope onto the mud road. They look at me and laugh to see a butt-white, almost nude, barefoot *Nasara* walking toward them. I go up to them and offer to help.

We push, pull, and lunge, fighting the mud and dead weight of the cart the whole time. Then we unload, re-push, re-pull, and finally succeed. I leave, walk up the road, change into my half-dry-soon-to-be-all-wet clothes and forge ahead. On the main road, one of the other seminar attendees picks me up and takes me the rest of the way to the conference center. I'm drenched, cold for the first time in along time, and more than eager to guzzle many cups of hot, sugary milk flavored with a sprinkling of Nescafe.

03 JUNE 2004
WISH LIST

1. One night of not having to sleep in my own sweat or out on the porch

2. One day without having to eat rice, beans or lentils. One day where all I eat is fresh stuff (fruit, salad, yogurt, a sandwich, etc.)

3. One surf session even if there are no waves. I just want to paddle out and sit on my board and feel that anticipation that no matter how flat it is a great wave with my name on it is about to roll in where my fingers get so cold I can't hardly get out of my wetsuit or zip up my pants

4. One meal without flies

5. One day without dust: staring at it, walking on it, and breathing it

6. Air conditioning

7. Flushing toilets all the time

8. Electricity for one full day so I can plug in my computer or turn on the fan or listen to music at some other time besides 6 -10pm.

9. Water I can drink from the tap. One shower when I can just throw my head back and drink up some cold fresh water straight and unfiltered without that partially-refrigerated-with-old-cabbage-smell on the bottle

10. One day of speaking only English with everyone I meet, no French, no Arabic and definitely no *Nangjeré*

11. One day when I can actually have at my disposal all I need to diagnose a patient

12. One ICU stay for one patient so one patient who should live, can live

13. One consultation with a specialist, any specialist I want

14. One day when I can give the patients all they need without worrying about whether they've paid for it or not.

15. One day when the orders I give the nurses will actually be done as ordered

16. One of mom's home cooked meals

17. A game of basketball

18. One day without seeing armed soldiers

19. One day without being stared at

20. One hour without kids standing outside my windows staring in

21. One trip to town without being called *Nasara* once

22. A working vehicle I can take anywhere I want, anytime I want

23. One church service with music that moves me

24. One email session without bugs on the screen

25. One day without administrative duties

26. One guy friend I could just hang out with. Sarah's great, but she is just a GIRL after all.

06 JUNE 2004
HERE WE GO AGAIN

Once again, I can't escape the rhythm of Africa and the endless cycle of life and death. About a month ago I delivered a dead baby by symphysiotomy and vacuum extraction. Unfortunately, I missed the fact that the mom had a uterine rupture until it was too late. When I finally recognized the rupture, before I could even put in an order to transfuse some blood and prep her for surgery, she died in front of me. I watched her just slip into nothing. It haunted me for a long time. I vowed to never miss a uterine rupture.

Eric and Cathy have now been here for a month. They are supposed to leave Béré this morning in order to catch the midnight flight out of N'Djamena. But at 5 a.m., the nurse calls me in to see a woman who is in labor and not doing well. Dawn is just beginning to creep in, giving the early morning the feel of a full-moonlit night. It's completely calm and quiet. I walked through the gate, down the path between the new grass, past the church, under the trees and benches on the right, past the clinic on the left, up the steps, under the porch past the surgery suite, into the darkness of the maternity ward and into the labor room.

This time, I'm ready. Sure enough, the uterus feels funny. I can easily feel the baby's body parts. While the *garde* starts an IV and places a urinary catheter, I rush home to wake up Eric for one last hurrah in *Tchad*. The woman is already in surgery and Samedi has come from home so Eric and I scrub. Eric opens with a midline incision and finds the uterus. He cuts through the thick muscle and pulls the baby out. Unfortunately, he is already long dead.

The mother's abdomen is filled with blood. We suction furiously trying to identify where the rupture is. Finally we locate it on the posterior surface of the uterus extending into the abdominal sidewalls. I call Dr. Claver and he bails us out by performing a life-saving hysterectomy. Eric and Cathy make their flight and the mom recovers without complication.

A week later on a Saturday, another woman comes in to labor and delivery after having tried to deliver all day at the health center across town. Nothing was happening so after trying a vacuum extraction of the baby they sent her over to us. She's been at the health center since 6 a.m. and arrives at our hospital at 7 p.m.. The nurse calls me and I enter the room to examine the patient. The poor woman is very swollen from all the maneuvers done to her at the health center. Once again, the baby's body parts are easily noticeable and there is no fetal heartbeat.

Here we go again. We wheel her off to surgery, open up her abdomen with a midline incision and find the fetus immediately, already dead. We pull the baby out, suck up the blood inside and notice that luckily this time the tear in the uterus is anterior where we usually cut the uterus open anyway. Of course, the laceration is deformed and complicated in the shape of a Mercedes symbol, which makes it a little tougher. This time I'm alone, except for Samedi, but am able to control the bleeding and suture the uterus. We close up and she recovers without incident, but once again the baby is dead.

Wednesday, I pick up my dad, Jim, from the airport in N'Djamena. Thursday, I return to the airport to fetch a piece of lost luggage. Friday, dad and I return to Béré the same day that Dr. Claver moves permanently to work at the Kélo Hospital leaving me the only doctor for a population of 130,000. As soon as I arrive with my dad, they tell me about a woman who just arrived in labor. Here we go again. Fortunately, this time, she came directly to us after trying to deliver at home. We take her to the OR and find that she is just at the point of rupture. The baby is out in less than two minutes and gives a lusty yell almost immediately!

Since we're operating under spinal anesthetic, I lean over the sterile drape and ask the woman how many pregnancies she's had. This is her tenth. I don't bother to ask her opinion, but simply inform her that we'll be tying her tubes so she won't have any more children. I know that would be considered unethical in the US where the woman should consent one month prior to delivery, but that's just not practical here. If she has another pregnancy she has a good chance of another serious complication and even dying.

Sunday we find ourselves short-handed. It's just like the good ol' days. The only nurses on duty are the veterans Lona, Samedi, Anatole, and Rahama. They have over 90 years experience between them at the *Hôpital Adventiste de Béré*. Everyone else is sick, post-call, or a government employee who doesn't work Sundays. Things go fine until about 5 minutes into rounds.

"*Docteur*, there's an emergency in the ER!"

Turns out to be just a migraine. I return and see one more patient.

"*Docteur*, three more emergencies."

I go and see three young men lying on benches in the waiting room. One has been here before with a urinary infection and stones. He has been peeing pure blood for two weeks and I see his bladder swollen up to his belly button. I order an IV, urinary catheter and antibiotics, and prep for surgery in case it's necessary.

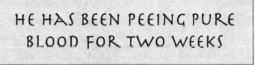

HE HAS BEEN PEEING PURE BLOOD FOR TWO WEEKS

The next patient is a young man who'd been up all night drinking day before yesterday. Yesterday evening he had a sudden onset of severe abdominal pain and bloating. I examine him. He needs emergency surgery. The family leaves to find the money to pay.

The next guy has come in having vomited blood since yesterday evening. He's had ulcer type pain for one year. He also has bright bloody diarrhea. We give him IV fluids, H2 blockers, anti-vomiting medications, a nasogastric tube and call for a blood count, which is normal.

After getting a urinary catheter, the first guy is doing better. The second guy's getting worse, but the family has returned with the money. The third guy starts to vomit up a lot of blood. I write for a blood transfusion and head home to refuel with a quick meal of mushroom sauce over rice that Sarah has prepared. She comes back to help in surgery. In the OR, I notice that the patient's belly has really gotten tense.

I scrub while Sarah does the anesthesia. I open the abdomen quickly with a full midline incision. When I enter the peritoneal cavity out pours greenish yellow stool. The intestines are bloated and raw from inflammation and everything is covered with sticky poop. I pour in liters of irrigation solution, suck it up, and start searching. Sure enough, I find a large hole in the small intestine. I patch up the perforation with several stitches. The appendix doesn't look too healthy either, so I take it out.

Then comes the fun part. I dump in liters of tap water and rinse and slosh and slurp as much contamination out as possible. I finish with a final irrigation of saline solution and leave in three drains. After closing the abdomen, we take the patient out to the wards since we have no recovery room. As the staff cleans the smelly OR, I go to see patient number three.

He looks like he's about to crump and hasn't got any blood yet. With the other case and being short staffed, his transfusion has slipped through the cracks. I go quickly to find Anatole. As I'm talking to him across the fence, the family comes up to say the man is dead. One man saved, another man dead. Such is the cycle of life and death here in Africa.

11 JUNE 2004
ANATOLE

Anatole comes in to see me. He has come into the office with a hand written list of topics he wants to discuss. He starts out by going straight for the jugular.

"Do you know me? Anatole? I know you've worked with me. Maybe someone gave you my file to peruse, but do you know who I am? What my education is? What my training is? How I got here? Why I stay? Where I should be? How much I should be paid based upon all that? Who am I? You have no idea!"

With that introduction, Anatole proceeds to tell me the following tale:

"In 1980, I'd just finished my second year at the *lycée*, I must have been 16 or so. The church board got together and asked me if I would go to the fledgling Béré Adventist Hospital to receive a three-month apprenticeship in laboratory science. They told me it would help the hospital and would be a benefit to me. I wanted to finish my schooling, but the church board had voted so I felt I had to go. I arrived in Béré March 2, 1980. It was the last time I would be away from Béré for more than a month or so at a time.

"The three months went by quickly and I succeeded in everything I touched. At the end, my supervisor, a missionary trained in lab work, asked me to stay on for another six months. Again, I wanted to continue my studies and at least get my *Bac* but the church convinced me to stay.

"Before I knew it, it was 1983. At that time, because of the excellent work I did, I was given a Certificate of Aptitude in Laboratory Science by the Hospital. In 1985, I was sent to Maroua for some seminars and in 1986 to N'Djamena. But still I wanted to finish my schooling and get some official training. The church refused.

"In the mid '80s, a European missionary couple I'd worked with sent me around $5,000 for my further education. The Adventist Mission in N'Djamena took it and told me to wait. My lab partner asked for the same thing and they sent him to Cameroon for two years. He never came back so the Mission didn't want to send anyone else. I never saw a penny of that $5,000.

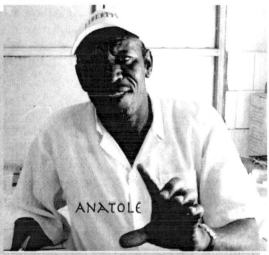

ANATOLE

"Over the years, I did manage to get them to send me to various short training programs on different topics such as tuberculosis (three times), leprosy (two times), HIV/AIDS, onchocerciasis, blood transfusion technology, and a WHO program called "Maternity Without Risk."

"I was there for the cholera epidemic, working night and day. I took night shift as a nurse even though I wasn't one. I came in the morning to give oral medications to the patients, worked in the lab till midday, cleaned up, went home briefly and came back at night to give the rest of the pills to the inpatients. I had to start IVs, draw blood, give shots, do anesthesia for the surgeons and I've been both treasurer and secretary at the church.

"So, doctor, now you know some of the suffering I've gone through and how I came to be here. Now what do you think?"

I don't know what to say. Anatole is one of those people hard to ignore. You can always recognize Anatole, even from a distance, because he is never without his pink baseball cap pulled down low over his weathered, deeply lined face. His brows furrow in intensity almost as quickly as his face lights up with a toothy grin. At work he can always be found with his short-sleeved, long white lab coat over worn slacks and flip-flops.

He works harder than anyone. He can be found six days a week in the lab and with the tuberculosis patients, every third night on lab call, and every fifth to seventh night on overnight duty. He also has been doing anesthesia now that our charge nurse, Nassourrou, has been on vacation for a month.

Anatole keeps detailed anesthesia records on scratch paper since we have no proper forms. No one else even bothers. He will never give up on a pediatric IV unless he's tried at least 12 times and then he'll still try something crazy until he finally gets it. He will stay late every day to make sure the lab results are in. He keeps detailed track of all TB patients in our district.

His thirst for knowledge is insatiable. He has an inquisitive mind and a questioning spirit. He will never take anything for granted without looking at it from all angles and purifying it through the fire of his questioning. He can be counted on to seek me out often when he's on call just so he can learn from a case. Morning worships and church wouldn't be the same without his intense desire to know and experience the truth. But, he has some other questions for me now.

"Is the church ever going to do anything for me after all I've done for this hospital? What will happen to my family if I become sick or die or retire? Will the church care for my family and me or will my 24 years of service be quickly forgotten? I keep going because I see patients improve, lives saved, and diagnoses made because of my sacrifice. I know that one day I'll get my reward, but what about right now, in this life?"

As I sit there staring across at Anatole's earnest face, I am speechless. I have nothing to say in the face of such dedication and self-sacrifice. I only hope I can help him personally in some way, some day.

16 JUNE 2004
DOCTOR NURSE

Someone's banging on the door. Torn out of a deep sleep and dreamland, I try to find my bearings. It's Sarah. It's 2:30 a.m.. A woman just delivered and is bleeding. I give some instructions to Sarah. She leaves. I think for about one minute then drag myself out of bed, throw on scrubs, surgical cap, headlamp and flip flops and pad through the pitch black of the still, moon-less African night.

By the light of two kerosene lamps and my headlamp I see an Arab woman lying in a pool of partially clotted blood. I do a vaginal exam and am greeted with a gush of fresh blood as I pull out some clots. I quickly squeeze the uterus between my inside and outside hands. I massage vigorously expelling more clots until the uterus finally becomes firm. I head back and fall asleep instantly. I awake at 6 a.m..

Diarrhea calls. I've had it for days. It's not bad, just a few times daily, but it just won't seem to go away. As I relieve myself, I read a few Psalms on the throne. Then, I eat a healthy breakfast of mom's granola, powdered Hershey's NIDO milk, and some boiled, guinea hen eggs. Afterwards, I'm off to staff worship at 7:30 a.m.. We sing a song in Nangjeré, read about King Josiah in the Bible, pray, and hear the report from Sarah's *garde* shift.

I gather my bag, throw my stethoscope around my neck and head off to the medicine ward. The nurses are gone today on some continuing nursing education course. So, I've put the cashier, Pierre, in charge of the Medicine Ward and we bring the chaplain, Degaulle, along to translate. The first woman has amebic dysentery and Malaria but feels better and is just on pills so we send her home. Next is a young man with cerebral Malaria who had been in a coma for almost three days, who now is fully awake and eating. We change him over to pills and send him home.

Over in the corner is a woman dying of AIDS with pneumonia and diarrhea that hasn't responded to antibiotics. She is practically a skeleton but still has a fire in her eyes. The last patient is the father of one of the nurses who used to work at the hospital. He's a tough old bird with diverticulitis and is ready to go home too.

Then we're off to the maternity ward. There are four women who delivered yesterday or this morning. All four had girls. One is the chubbiest baby ever and weighs four kilos. All the new moms are doing fine, including the one who bled this morning. I examine every baby from head to toe and find they are all healthy. They all suck vigorously on my finger when I examine their palates. One even grabs my finger with her tiny hand as she sucks away. I'll have to come back and examine two of the newborns later since they are covered with poop when I open up their wrappings. No diapers here!

Pediatrics is filled with ten kids. All but one has Malaria. Most are chubby, well-fed toddlers who should recover fine. One is very malnourished from waiting too long at home before coming in for treatment. He's not showing much improvement today. One is a little thin with some sores at the corner of her mouth. Fortunately, the HIV test comes back negative.

Another ten-year-old had been bitten by a snake a week ago, has a swollen left leg and came to us two days ago nearly dead with severe anemia, a bleeding disorder and Malaria. He's doing fine now after a blood transfusion, Vitamin K and IV Quinine. But he is complaining about his swollen leg.

A baby admitted yesterday morning with Malaria is breathing super fast and is tiring out quick with his eyes starting to roll back. I look at the inside of the eyelids, which are pale signifying severe anemia. We order a type and cross for a blood transfusion. The last little boy has an abscess on his leg and a bone infection that is slowly healing from the inside out with dressing changes using diluted bleach.

I go back to my office. On the way I see Gai, the young man who had the pus around his right lung after a stab wound. I'd had to open up his chest, put in a makeshift chest tube, and treat him in the hospital for several months with a wide variety of antibiotics. I finally sent him home a few weeks ago. He looks great, has gained weight, and it seems his left lung has expanded somewhat into his right cavity to replace the destroyed lung there. There are no signs of infection, which is a miracle!

In the office two of the recent babies' fathers come to get me to prepare their birth certificates. They want to leave with their wives so I have to hold onto the certificates to convince them to stay at least 24 hours to monitor the women and newborns.

Matthieu knocks on the door and informs me that the parents of the kid needing a transfusion refuse to give their blood. The dad was all set up with tourniquet on, needle ready and transfusion apparatus on standby when he tore off the tourniquet and ran out screaming. I go to explain again the importance of giving their child blood. I explain that we have no blood bank. I show them my translator's inner eyelids while saying *rouge* and then show them their child's conjunctiva is *pale*. I tell them that that's why they need to give their blood which is *rouge* in order to make their child's *rouge* again. They finally get it and the dad agrees to give his blood.

I go to do some of the dressing changes since the nurses aren't around.

I GO TO SEE MARTY, THE MAN BITTEN BY THE HIPPO

Sarah's already done some of them before going home to rest, which is a big help. A mom approaches with her one-year-old who'd been burned on her forehead, left upper eyelid and left ear with boiling water. She wants to make sure I don't forget to do her dressing change. I take off the dressing and the wound is healing well. I tell her she needs to buy some ointment and a bandage.

I go to see Marty, the man bitten by the hippo, who's still here but almost completely healed. Of his huge butt wound, all that remains is a tiny area posterior to where the anus should be. Next week we should be able to take down his colostomy. He'll probably be incontinent but considering he's the only person in any local person's recollection to survive a hippo attach he should count himself lucky. He's been walking normally for several weeks now.

I go back to clinic where I see an AIDS patient with diarrhea, a pregnant woman with a kidney infection and Malaria, a baby born with no thumbs or anus who defecates through a hole in her vagina and has Malaria, a kid with a rectal abscess I drained two days ago, two other women with urinary infections and Malaria, a baby two weeks old who has already been treated for sepsis in our hospital and has since had poor muscle tone and twitches and spasms of eyes, lids and limbs. She seems to be doing a little better today.

I go to check up on the baby being transfused. I see the father of one of the other Malaria babies who greets me warmly. I took off his left nipple which had a small cystic breast mass three months ago. He shows me the well-healed scar. There is no tumor or any suspicious lymph nodes. The baby being transfused is already breathing a little better and the eyelids have a little color to them.

The father of the boy bitten by the snake approaches me to ask if I can prescribe some cream to make an abscess come to a head. His son was given an intramuscular injection at a health center before coming to the hospital and he thinks the injection site is infected. I write him a prescription for some Ichthamol Cream, a black tar-like substance, that supposedly should do the job. It certainly can't hurt.

Pierre, the cashier and nurse for a day, consults me for his jock itch.

I get a Malaria smear done on myself. I've had a cold and been blowing huge globs of snot all day. Do you know how hard it is to speak a nasal language like French under those kind of conditions? The smear is weakly positive with lots of white blood cells telling me my body's learned how to fight Malaria by itself. I still buy some Fansidar and Doxycycline just to help out a little. I'm getting Malaria all the time while Sarah hasn't had it once in almost ten months. She brags that it's because her immune system is so strong, unlike my weak American one. I tell her it's because her Danish blood is so bitter the mosquitoes flee for their lives.

I'm about to head home to eat at 1:30 p.m. when a boy comes in referred from a health center for a blood transfusion. He is weak and pale and hot and most certainly has Malaria. His hemoglobin is 11, which is good, but his Malaria smear is grossly positive. I get everything ready with paperwork and orders hoping that Dimanche will show up on time at 2 p.m. like she's supposed to.

It's after 2 p.m. and I'm getting more and more impatient. I just want to eat and get away from the hospital. I send someone at 2:30 p.m. to find her. At 3:15 p.m. I go to where the nurses are having their meetings and meet Dimanche along the way. As I see her coming all kinds of nasty things to say come into my head. I end up trying to blow it off through sarcasm and laughter.

Koumabas calls me from the hospital. There's another pediatric case. The kid looks just as bad as the last one. It must be Malaria. The lab guys have gone home, so I tell Dimanche to just treat the child with Quinine and antibiotics. I finally go home.

I eat some spicy lentil and potato goulash over rice with more of our cook, Salomon's homemade chili sauce and three hard-boiled eggs. I turn on Michael W. Smith's Worship Album and lie down sticky with sweat. I can't take a shower. The water tank is empty. It's 5 p.m.. As I lie there staring at the ceiling and listening to music, I feel peace sweep over me as I sigh and slip into sweet repose.

27 JUNE 2004
RED

A study in contrasts. A paradox. Unpredictable. Challenging. Frustrating and gratifying. If it wasn't for having the fairest of fair skin and flaming, red, wild, long curly hair and freckles, Sarah could be African. Just as Africa is never boring, always adventurous, filled with passion and life, so is this nurse with the unpronounceable Danish name, Gry, that her non-Danish-speaking friends call Sarah.

She grew up a wild child always going contrary to the grain. If you told her to go up, she'd go down. If you told her to turn left, she'd veer right. If you said eat, she'd shut her mouth. If you said don't talk, she'd open as wide as possible and yell at the top of her lungs. Don't meant do; stop meant go; light meant dark; stay meant leave. Her mom was wise enough to provide direction but with a certain amount of freedom to explore and discover for herself the consequences of her choices. The burned hand teaches best.

At the same time she was quiet and reserved, able to spend hours by herself with her horse or a book. She was silently at home in both a stable or a library. She could stare for hours across a pasture, beach or sea. Riding her bike through the rain down narrow Danish streets she'd arrive at home and be content with her chocolate, ice cream and something to read.

In high school she was known for practical jokes and worked at the campus radio station as DJ. She became well known in Adventist circles with friends all over at school, at work as a nurse in the hospital, as part of a church plant.

While content with the simple joys of solitary life she also traveled extensively taking the Trans-Siberian Express from Moscow to Beijing. She hiked the Great Wall, entered the Forbidden City and visited the rocky fortresses of Guangzhou. She lived for a year in Jerusalem working with handicapped kids, frequently taking the road to Jericho through the desert, climbing and jumping off cliffs into rivers along the way, visiting the Dead Sea for mud baths, and braving the dangers of oft-suicide-bombed buses downtown. She lived for six months as a volunteer nurse on the Peruvian Amazon spending weeks at a time in small villages eating only bananas, fish and rice, longing for the luxury of some beans. This goes without mentioning her trips to Ethiopia, Turkey, Belgium, America, and Chad.

Seeing her with children is truly a marvel. She spends hours with them in the hospital drawing faces and designs on their hands, arms, and bellies. She attracts a crowd of barefooted, and often bare-chested, thin African kids wherever she goes and soon has them organized playing some kind of group game that draws an even bigger crowd, including adults who often join in the fun. She passes time with the sick as well: eating their food and having them braid her hair in typical *Tchadian* fashion. Every Saturday, using a picture roll, she teaches a crowd of children and parents three times as big as the rest of the church.

She is fearless. She wandered the streets of Jerusalem and N'Djamena at night by herself. She rides horses alone to go swimming at the local river. She drove a taxi in Odense, Denmark, on the weekends "for fun" in between nursing classes. She spent a month in N'Djamena by herself finding things to do like pulling teeth at the clinic near the main market.

SARAH

She spent three months in Béré before my arrival trying to learn the languages, getting brought before the local authorities and interrogated in French about her involvement in a tragic Pediatric death at the hospital with threat of prison, and getting harassed by the local men about being their wife (or second or third member of their harem). She will jump off cliffs, drive like a maniac down jungle paths, bargain down even the most stingy Arab in the market, work all night caring for all the hospital patients while running the ER and delivering babies by herself.

After telling me that one her favorite places is the library where she can spend hours in solitude, she'll wrestle me to the ground with amazing strength for her wiry frame and, when I counter attack, will refuse to give up even when pinned helplessly while being tickled mercilessly. Eventually I always give up. I've finally met someone more stubborn than me.

She refuses to let the opinions or problems of others affect her. One may call it naivety but it's more like freedom. You really have to be obvious if you want to offend. Otherwise she will think that you can't really mean her. It's a simple other-selfness that is so contrary to our common self-absorption that at first I took it for a defense mechanism. She just simply is so unselfish that, unlike most of us, she doesn't always assume that everyone is talking about her or that the world revolves around her.

If you are ultra-sensitive you'll have a hard time being around her. She is filled with playful sarcasm and one should always be on the guard, ready with a witty comeback if one wants to survive a conversation with her. At the same time she can be a perfect listener and gentle and kind in her responses to personal revelation or the sharing of difficult things. She laughs easily and fully with her face crinkling up, her freckles dancing and eyes sparkling under wisps of stray curly red hair.

She is very unconcerned about personal appearance as far as clothes, yet looks comfortably attractive always. She can have scratches and dirty feet but keeps herself well. She's not a neat freak but likes cleanliness and is decorative and creative, enjoying painting in her spare time.

She may be somewhat of a loner but get her with her close friends like her mom, and she'll become hoarse from too much talking. She emails her mom almost daily and used to speak with her for hours at a time every day in Denmark. She is at ease in a crowd or in total isolation. She will listen attentively with no hidden agenda or impatience to talk herself, while being able to talk almost non-stop if given the right subject.

She loves to read about God. Give her a spiritual book and she will be lost to you. She listens for hours at a time to her favorite pastor's sermons on tape. She gets up early to pray. She always wants to talk about how trust or the lack there of is the key to the spiritual life. Yet she recognizes how hard that is. If she does trust you, she will bare her soul, just don't expect it to be easy to gain her trust as she recognizes that only God himself can be fully trusted.

She is conservative and flamboyant. She will wear long skirts and even Muslim veils at times and the next moment go skinny-dipping at the river. She listens to quiet conservative Christian music and then talks about radical acceptance and change that is needed in the church which is so bound by tradition.

She will diffuse all tension in any situation at the hospital and is loved by everyone. She wins them over with a word or two in their language or a simple reconciliatory statement.

At the same time she won't let me get away with anything and will call me on my selfishness, temper and inconsiderate actions. She just won't put up with my crap. Annoy her enough, like a certain woman who barged in on delivery Sarah was managing, and she'll wipe a glove covered with vaginal secretions all over you. Like I said, more stubborn than me.

Africa is full of contrasts and surprises, joy and sorrow. While I've seen more suffering and death than I would wish upon anyone; while I've lived and experienced so much pain, depression, hopelessness, joy, fulfillment, and wonder than I could imagine; while I've felt more loneliness and isolation and distance from my friends and family, I have found someone more suited to me than I could have possibly dreamed.

Red...I think I have a new favorite color.

02 JULY 2004
HALF-BAKED

I think I'm a bad missionary. For example, shouldn't I love the local people? But I find myself thinking that most of them are sneaky, cheap, dishonest, drunkards, violent, and manipulative.

Once, a woman came in with part of her nasal septum bit off by her husband who's been drinking. Almost every night we see a woman beat up by somebody: husband, brother, father in law, sister, other wife, or son. Walk down the main road on a Saturday and every man you meet will be barely able to walk and greet you with a "*bwwwohhhn swwaaahrrr*" in a drunken slur.

A mother will arrive with a nine-month-old who's been vomiting for two weeks, has Malaria, is lethargic with sunken eyes and seems barely alive, and the father will try and bargain with you to get as low a price as possible for treatment. It's as if he thinks he's at the market bartering for onions. Then he'll promise the world if you just go ahead and treat. He'll pay later. Then after one day of perfusions, the whole crew will pick up and leave in the middle of the night before the baby is well, just so they can avoid paying anything.

I know I'm supposed to love them, and sometimes I do. Most of the time, however, I just yell and try to intimidate them into doing what's best for them or their sick kids.

The other day I was playing American football with some of the kids. That's a good missionary thing to do, right? Then I thought it would be fun to just see if I could peg some of the younger ones. All the other kids got a laugh when one of them would get nailed. Then I threw the ball at a group on the porch and popped Lona's son Fambé on the top of the head toppling him off the railing onto the ground. He landed on his head. I ran over and he was screaming bloody murder while blood poured down the side of his head from a gash in his scalp. I did feel kind of bad; does that make me a little less of a missionary loser?

Sometimes I publicly humiliate the nurses. For example, David consistently doesn't follow specific orders. I'll tell him start an IV and I'll come the next day to find no IV. I'll say over and over you need to write the time you give the medicines and sign it the chart. He never does. I always see him sitting on the bench outside the clinic relaxing or chatting up with some of the other nurses, yet his ward is covered with dirt and vomit.

SOMETIMES I PUBLICLY HUMILIATE THE NURSES

Therefore, sometimes on rounds I use what little sarcasm I've picked up over the years and tear him to shreds in front of the patients and staff. That probably is not the most endearing of my qualities. Aren't I just supposed to realize that we just have cultural differences?

I don't have much patience when the medical team for the local health district comes with a signed requisition for our vehicle so they can go to Kélo and buy *carburant* (which should mean fuel but really means beer or any other alcoholic beverage they can get their hands on). I take the document and in their presence say *"Ça c'est quoi?"* and tear it to shreds. Which of course, in a culture where shame is the worst thing one can do to someone, is not a way to work well with the local authorities.

Also, shouldn't I want to eat local food and integrate myself into local life? But I tend to just hang out in my own house, sometimes with Sarah or the other expats. I will do as much as possible to avoid the millet paste and dried fish sauce, even though in this culture one should never turn down offered food, even if one has just eaten. I always say that I'm full already.

Sometimes I stand up in church and publicly question things. One night Pastor Degaulle said something that was totally against my own interpretation of the freedom of the gospel. So, I stood up and contradicted what he'd just said. I'm pretty much convinced of my own rightness most of the time and don't really care what others think. I'm stubborn and speak often in the heat of the moment—not exactly your passive, peace-loving, culturally sensitive missionary type.

I take perverse pleasure in telling parents what negligent people they are to keep their kids at home for way too long before coming to the hospital. They come only if they're at the point of death. They'll try traditional treatments like cutting the skin over a painful area, eating herbal concoctions or stuffing roots up their butts. Then they'll go to the market and buy whatever pill looks good to them at the time. After that they'll go to the Health Center to be treated several days with a variety of pills and injections.

At last they'll come to the hospital when the kid has severe anemia or is so dehydrated he's as limp as a wet noodle. Of course by then they'll have used up all their money, so they'll promise to pay later or try and bargain. We'll go full steam ahead, transfuse, start IVs, give injections, put in feeding tubes and in the end it's too late and the child dies. Then the parents just leave without so much as saying thanks for trying. They go back to their village and tell everyone to not go to the hospital or your baby will die.

I think I'm a half-baked missionary, but fortunately I'm in a place that's so hot I'm starting to cook until I'm well-done, one minute at a time.

08 JULY 2004
BLOOD

I walk toward the hospital. My *Tchadian* robes swish gently as I stride forward purposefully. It's Saturday. The sun is newly up and I'm on a mission. I want to round quickly on the hospitalized patients and make it to church. But that won't happen today. God has other plans.

I approach the clinic. There is a mother sitting outside on a broken metal chair with a splintered wood seat and no back. An infant is in her arms. Coming out of his scalp is an IV. Attached to the IV is a tube filled with blood. The blood runs from a bag hanging by a coat hanger to the bars on the charge nurse's office window. There is a metal tray on another chair. On the tray is a bloody IV catheter needle. Next to it is a wad of cotton, an empty IV tubing bag and a roll of tape.

I turn the corner and enter the ER. Dimanche fills me in. Malaria. Severe anemia. Took 40 sticks to find the vein. Had to use the scalp. Our third pediatric blood transfusion in 24 hours. Yesterday two died. Same disease. One died in front of Anatole's eyes as he frantically searched for the vein. Would this one's fate be the same?

I grab my stethoscope and make rounds. Before I finish, one of the new nurses, Martin comes to tell me there is another case. I hurry back as fast as I can while wearing a long robe. There in the shadows of the unlit ER is another baby struggling. I quickly examine him. Heartbeat 180.

Conjunctiva white. Palms pale. Respirations labored. Limp. Tired. Eyes shut. This one can't be long for this world. Two of our lab techs, Jacob and Anatole are there already. As they prepare to type and cross the child for a blood transfusion another baby arrives.

I recognize the mother. She is dressed in brightly colored cloth wrapped around her body and head in Arabic fashion. She has henna stains on her hands and the sent of incense and savory oils. She has just had two children hospitalized here. She's pregnant again. In her arms is a three-year-old with coffee-colored skin, huge brown eyes and a white and black bead necklace just at her throat. She is tired and breathing fast. I take her pulse. 160. Her eyelids are colorless as well. Quick decision. I tell them to stop with the other child and type and cross this one first. She is more likely to survive.

The first kid matches blood with both mom and dad. O+. The second child matches with mom, O+, but she's pregnant and dad hasn't arrived yet. Anatole has meanwhile started an IV with Quinine on the Arab girl while Martin has started the treatment on the first. Anatole then draws the blood from the dad for the sickest baby while we wait for the papa of the Arab one to arrive. The transfusion is started. The kid is still alive and soon starts to breathe easier as the life flows back into him.

> I RECOGNIZE HIM IMMEDIATELY. HE WAS THE ONE WHO WAS STABBED...

Meanwhile, the little Arab girl's father arrives. I recognize him immediately. He was the one who was stabbed right near where we were currently sitting outside my office. I had been in the next room with a seizing baby and an infant grimacing with Tetanus. That was three months ago. Hard to believe. We'd operated on him twice and he'd been in the hospital almost two weeks recovering. He looks great now. Jacob draws his blood. It's a match and the girl gets her essential life giving red fluid pumping into her veins.

I go finish rounds. The baby with the scalp IV has finished his transfusion and looks better. As I'm walking back past the ER, Anatole says I need to look at the little girl. She's seizing he says. I go look at her. Her skin is scalding. Temperature 104.9 degrees. She is shivering uncontrollably as we try to cool her down with water and fanning. She just has the chills, not seizures. I speed up the blood transfusion, as her heart rate is still fast.

Martin comes to tell me the other boy isn't doing well. He is lying on the plastic of the exam table with his blood slowly dripping in. Just a few milliliters left. He's exhausted. I notice he's breathing slowly with a few sighs. I listen to his heart and hear it start to slow down. I rub his back and pinch his feet. His heartbeat picks up as he cries in pain and the adrenaline kicks in.

I yell for Jacob to bring the *respirateur* (bag-valve-mask for artificial respiration). I continue to stimulate every time the heart slows down. Jacob arrives with an *aspirateur* for sucking out gunk from newborn's mouths. I yell "*RESSSpirateur, not ASSSpirateur!!*" and he bumbles off to get it. I'm afraid it won't arrive in time. After what seems an eternity, Jacob arrives and I start to try and breathe for the baby.

He fights it. Every time I try to breathe he cries and struggles. He almost loses his IV. I've changed it from blood to a Quinine drip. I listen to his lungs. Filled with fluid. Overload from the transfusion. I call for Martin to inject some Lasix to clear his lungs. He does. I continue to bag and stimulate as the heart beat drops off every time I stop rubbing his feet, yet responds nicely when I start pinching again. Minutes go by. He hasn't peed. I double the dose of medicine. Bag. Rub the back. Keep the IV from being torn out. Try to keep my stethoscope balanced on his chest so I can monitor his heart rate and see if any air is going into his lungs.

He still hasn't urinated. I feel his bladder. Full. I push. Urine squirts out. An hour has gone by. I stop bagging and watch. He seems to be breathing okay. His heart rate is fine; no, it's dropping off again. I restart CPR. Another half hour goes by. Finally, his lungs are clear. The Quinine is starting to kill the Malaria. The blood has refurbished his worn out circulation. He breathes on his own. His heartbeat stays up. It's 3 p.m.. I head home.

Two days ago, Rahama calls me in the early evening to see a woman in labor. She is less than five feet tall and petite. It's her first pregnancy. She is referred from an outside clinic for stalled labor. I grab the aluminum cone with a stethoscope-like earpiece on the pointy end and press it against mom's large belly with my ear firmly pressed on the other end. Slowly but surely I tune in. Yep, the baby's heartbeat is fine. I check the cervix. Completely dilated. The baby's head is very deformed with a lot of molding.

I decide to do a symphysiotomy. I inject local anesthetic over her pubic bone. I prep and shave the area. I get a large scalpel and cut down to the cartilage. Jacob is there and he grabs one leg and pulls it back to her hips. Rahama grabs the other. I've placed a urinary catheter, which I displace sideways with my left hand from inside to protect the urethra while my right hand starts to cut down through the cartilage. Halfway through, I have my assistants push the legs down pulling the hips apart. I hear and feel the pelvis tear open mid-pelvis. They stop at my command. I listen again to the baby's heartbeat. It's fine.

The mom pushes a few times and the baby is born cone-headed, swimming in it's own meconium. I call for an *aspirateur* and this time get what I ask for. I clean the nose, mouth and throat. The baby hasn't cried. I clamp and cut the umbilical cord. The baby is limp with a weak heartbeat. I call for the *respirateur* and start breathing for the newborn while at the same time Rahama cleans and rubs the baby vigorously and Jacob pinches the feet. Harder I say. He pinches harder. Nothing. Baby's limp and blue. I continue to breathe. The heartbeat stops.

I vigorously do chest compressions alternating with bagging using the *respirateur*. The baby's eyes twitch like they want to open. I stop. A weak heartbeat. I continue. Finally, after ten minutes he starts to cry weakly and

LONA

breathe on his own. His heartbeat is nice and fast. His color is starting to pink up. His muscles are starting to have some tone. His reflexes return. We continue to rub and dry and stimulate. Finally, he seems to be doing okay.

This morning I do rounds dressed in scrubs. Lona's wife delivered precipitously at home last night. She and the baby are fine. Lona wants a tubal ligation.

I visit the two babies we transfused at the same time just four days ago. The daughter of our stabbed Arab friend is ready to go home. As cute as can be, she holds out her hand for me to shake before our chaplain, Degaulle, prays in Arabic that Allah will heal her. The other child is sitting up having just eaten. She's ready to go home as soon as Dad finishes paying for the hospitalization. The one transfused through his scalp vein went home yesterday.

I then go to visit the twins born prematurely at about seven months gestational age. I thought they'd be dead by now. They were born early Sunday morning and when I first saw them they were cold and hadn't suckled at all and the mom seemed disinterested. Today, one looks perfect, the other is a little dehydrated still, but both have breastfeed well and seem to be fine. The baby born by symphysiotomy looks great but is still having some trouble latching on to mom's breast. I hope there's no permanent neurological damage from the prolonged resuscitation.

I'm very content as I do the tubal ligation on Lona's wife. There are too many babies, too many sick kids, and too much heartache. But there's some joy as well. It's God's way of reassuring and reminding me that I am, after all, where he wants me to be.

12 JULY 2004
CHAPLAIN

I'll never forget my first impression of him. It is my first church service in Béré. There are about five of us sitting in a circle of wobbly wooden benches without backs. The sunlight filters through the one skylight and slotted holes in the walls that serve as windows. The light reflecting off the dust gives it a hazy, lazy atmosphere.

Degaulle sits across from me in bright blue, high-water pants. His matching button down shirt is very ragged with multiple roughly patched areas. His feet sport sock-less, toe-holed skater-type shoes with *L'Evangile de Paix* printed on the sides in ink. He wears a dirty, well-worn hat with *Salut* printed neatly on the brim. He's tall and thin with piercing, slightly slanted eyes and a huge, quick smile. His eyes bug out from behind enormous plastic square-rimmed glasses held tentatively in place by a string. His joy is contagious as he speaks of sharing his faith with those he works with out in the fields. I am a bit surprised when he gets up to preach. I'm even more surprised by the truth, simplicity and sincerity of his message about why Peter denied Jesus: he straggled behind instead of walking with Jesus, he stayed by the fire instead of being by Jesus' side and he didn't keep his gaze on Jesus even when Jesus looked at him.

I find out later about his past. Apparently, he became a Christian and Adventist in his hometown of Béré as a direct result of the missionaries who eventually built the hospital. He was baptized in 1977 shortly after the hospital was founded. He then went to Cameroon to study theology and returned as a pastor in 1981. He worked all over *Tchad* before finally being relocated to Béré in 1987, a year before being fired for not having the minimum 30 baptisms per year required at the time. Since then he has made a living by cutting straw in the bush and weaving mats. He has remained unofficially the pastor of the hospital church the whole time because the mission office never provided an official pastor.

Degaulle struggled as he watched his wife leave both him and the church so that she can make money during the big market day on Saturday. He has eight children. His oldest daughter is married and lives in N'Djamena. The second oldest son is a teacher at the Béré Adventist School. His 13-year-old daughter is one of the leaders of the children's choir at the church here in Béré. They sing traditional music accompanied only by drums. One of his sons was the jitterbugging clown in bell-bottoms at the soccer match.

He sings with enthusiasm and force in the highest possible key he can choose so that no one can sing along and even he himself can't hit the notes. He dances with arms upraised when the kids get going. Today, he cracks me up all the way to Koumabas' house by singing *She'll Be Comin' Round the Mountain, The Battle Hymn of the Republic* and other old folk songs in almost incomprehensible English.

DEGAULLE

At Koumabas's house we find the elders of the clan sitting on benches in the shade of a large tree. It's a time of mourning for Koumabas's father's second wife who died in our hospital Thursday of a stroke. They carry out the service in traditional Nangjeré fashion. We approach as the sun is sinking low casting beautiful shadows behind the corn encircling the brown mud brick huts.

The oldest son greets us by grasping our hands with his right hand while his left hand grasps his right forearm in a gesture of respect. He motions for us to sit. We all murmur subdued greetings and condolences in French and Nangjeré. Then, after we have shook hands all around we sit down.

The oldest son then comes around again to grasp our hands in the same manner except this time he kneels in front of each of us while humming and moaning softly as we again offer our condolences. He than gets up and we begin chit chatting as if just on any other social visit. Whenever someone new comes or anyone passes by, the superficial conversation is interrupted to repeat the same ritual.

Finally, Degaulle produces a note hand-written on a scrap of paper in very formal French expressing our grief and sorrow and sympathy for Koumabas. Then, one of the women brings hot sweet tea on a platter in small shot glasses. We each take one trying not to burn our fingers on the hot glass while alternately sipping, blowing and setting down the very excellent heat conductors. Sarah sits apart with the women on the other side of the path on mats. She uses the time profitably to entertain and learn by speaking to them in Nangjeré.

Then we walk home in the cool of the evening. Martin finds me on the way and tells me there's an emergency at the hospital. I end the evening with an exploratory abdominal surgery which unfortunately reveals a partial obstruction of the colon caused by a mass, probably cancer.

Degaulle has livened up our hospital life as well. After being hired as chaplain, he has started animating morning worships where he always has the last word. He then joins us on rounds where he interprets loosely, preferring to go off on any little thing if I don't continually beg him to just translate. He also helps with crowd control yelling to help clear out groupies who gather around every patient looking for a little entertainment.

The best part is that Degaulle prays with each patient in their mother tongue whether French, *Nangjeré*, Arabic or *Ngambaye*. Thankfully, we've had no English-speaking patients or I'm sure he'd try to pray in English which would just make me think of "Combing rooond ze mooonton wan shay coomms..." and make me crack up laughing.

18 JULY 2004
WEEKEND

Ah yeah, the weekend. Saturday morning. Get up late and eat a leisurely French toast breakfast with Sarah. This should be a good day. Not too many inpatients. I quickly don my favorite Arab attire. I hear *Nangjeré* chants wafting over from the church letting me know that things are getting underway.

I enter and see a tiny group gathered on the benches. Mud covers the floor from last night's rain. They are singing French hymns pathetically instead of the usual catchy *Nangjeré* songs. I sit. My bony rear isn't happy with the hard wooden bench. David gets up in his new shiny green robes, hat sticking awkwardly out of his front pocket. He gives the report from last week's service. Degaulle pipes up saying we need to set goals for offerings for each class to motivate us and encourage us. He waxes eloquent on the subject. I can't stand it.

Finally, I interrupt and say "*Non, non, non!* We're focusing too much on the wrong things and hindering our freedom that we have as Christians." They look at me condescendingly, wondering what planet I just came from. I walk out.

I go to the hospital. Martin is on duty. The teenage daughter of the old District Medical Officer is here with a headache, fever and muscle aches. I diagnose and treat her for Malaria. We head off to rounds. Sarah's friend, Julie, is with her dad who has been hospitalized with an altered level of consciousness. He has a slow heartbeat from complete heart block. Today, he's recovered somewhat, although his heart still beats without change at 44 beats per minute. His problem is both simple and complex. Simple because all he needs is a pacemaker. Complex because that is impossible here and there is no real medical treatment. I send them home as his blood pressure is now reasonably under control.

The Malaria kids are all doing well, their parents just haven't paid for having their child's life saved. The woman who had a C-section for placenta previa a few days ago is sitting up with her healthy baby boy at her side sucking his fist. Martin changes the dressing on the infected wound of the woman with the strangulated umbilical hernia operated on over a week ago. I stand to the side and supervise. The wound looks clean and is slowly but surely healing from the inside out. It appears the repair of the defect is holding strong. The man with the raw, infected foot and heel that hasn't healed since 1988 hasn't changed much.

Clement, the boy with the tibia infection and fracture, is post-op day number two after one of his many surgeries. We were finally able to get an x-ray, which revealed the bone wasn't healing at all but was actually fractured proximally and distally and was slowly being rejected by the body while some callous was forming in between the tibia and fibula. I went in, reduced the fracture, partially closed the wound, casted it using a stick from a mango tree for extra support, and left a hole in the cast for dressing changes with diluted bleach. Clement is tired but still able to give me a weak "five" as I hold out my hand palm up.

I return to the house. Sarah and I cook spaghetti. I make the sauce and it's killer. Unfortunately, I underestimate the potency of the small Béré chilies. Anatole, his wife and two kids join us for lunch. Anatole can't take the heat of the peppers and eats just plain pasta. We talk a lot and have a great time. Martin comes to find me to tell me about a patient referred from another health center.

I return to the ER to find a young man who's been paralyzed from the waist down for two days. The paralysis started at his feet and moved up. He can't pee, control his stool, or feel anything from the waist down. He has a fever of over 104 degrees. I do a spinal tap. Anatole finds an ovum of a parasite called Schistosoma heamatobium. It can very rarely enter the spinal fluid and cause transverse myelitis. The treatment for the parasite is a single dose of Praziquantal, but unfortunately his paralysis is probably permanent.

Sarah has already left on foot for the river. I grab the keys and drive the truck to meet her there. I dive into the refreshing water and feel it flow over me washing away many things. I stroke powerfully over to the rapids, position myself to avoid the rocks and launch backwards into the current which sweeps me away and washes over my body as I gently paddle to keep aloft. I'm carried past some cliffs with deep roots hanging down exposed. I swim over, find a small ledge of clay under water and shove off with just enough force to grab a root with one hand and pull myself up the cliff using the roots as a rope. I reach the summit and look for Sarah. I plan to hide and jump off the cliff and scare her when she's right below.

However, she stops at a overhanging tree near the start of the rapids. I walk down the path and join her. We grab the branches and swing like monkeys. I jump up and grab her waist pulling us both into the water. She throws mud at me and splashes me with water. We scramble up again whooping and hollering.

I swim some more until I'm exhausted. Then I go to shore where Sarah is reading. There are some kids standing close by staring. I try a new tactic. I stare back. At first they laugh and look away. Then they sneak a look back and quickly turn away when they see I haven't stopped staring. Eventually, it unnerves them and they move off. Victory!

My appetite has returned with a vengeance by the time I get home. I eat two huge plates of leftover spaghetti and garlic bread, sweating and breathing fire as the chili pepper is too much for me, too.

I fall dead asleep until being awakened by a violent thunderstorm accompanied by knocking at the door.

"Retained placenta," the *garde* reports. It's 1:30 a.m.. I pull on scrubs and a raincoat and trudge through the mud puddles, my flip-flops offering little protection.

The placenta is basically almost out by the time I get there. I reattach the clamp on the umbilical cord, massage the uterus, give a little tug and the placenta plops out intact. The woman has a little bit of a floppy uterus but with more massage and a shot of oxytocin she's fine. The nurses have worked for half an hour to revive the baby. He looks great. They told me that after the last C-section when I broke scrub to resuscitate the infant and they watched him come back to life they knew they shouldn't give up easily but should aggressively reanimate the newborns. Have I actually made a difference here?

I return home. As I lie back in bed, I feel the best I have in a long time. Tears come to my eyes as my heart breaks with gratitude to God for bringing me here to Béré.

31 JULY 2004
SCAMMED

I come to work one day and someone has opened the operating room doors. He is currently in the walkway between the clinic and the maternity ward where he has disassembled our x-ray machine and two operating lamps.

"What are you doing?" I ask.

"I'm here to repair your x-ray machine."

Well, that seems reasonable. After all the Ministry of Health had promised to send someone months ago.

"Why have you taken apart our operating lamps?" I continue. "They were working just fine." He doesn't look me in the eyes. He just talks really fast, none of which really makes sense to me.

I go to talk to André. "Don't worry," says André. "I know him." So I let him keep working. Later, the man comes back to see me.

"You owe me money from when I was here before," he says. "Also, I can repair your small sterilizers. And then I'll make you some x-ray viewers for a good price."

"Look, we want our x-ray machine fixed and that's it," I retort. "And put our lamps back together, too. They didn't need fixing anyway."

When he's finished, he gives me his bill. It's ridiculous. He has charged us for repairing the lamps including exorbitant prices for the bulbs. I refuse. He has also put down four x-ray cassettes at $400 a piece. I laugh in his face. Finally, he comes down to $50 a piece. I say we'll take two to tide us over until we can get some donated. I just can't wait to see him leave. He drops a business card in the dust at my feet.

"Call me whenever," he states as he drives off.

The next day I ask Lona where the x-ray cassettes are.

"The man asked me to clean them," Lona replies. "And then he took the cassettes with him. You know, he's the same guy who ruined the generator several years ago claiming he knew how to fix it. I don't know why you let him touch anything."

I ask myself the same thing when it turns out he didn't even fix everything on the x-ray machine. He'd done just enough to show us one good x-ray to "prove" that it worked.

Some time later, a half-drunk man comes up to me with a Barbie doll house.

"Here's the house you ordered," he drawls as I look at him stupidly. "My friend is in prison and needs money. Can you buy this to help him out?"

"Who's your friend?"

"The guy who always repairs your equipment, you know x-ray machine and stuff…"

"Really? What happened to him?"

"Well, he was supposed to make these x-ray view boxes for the Kelo Hospital and then tried to make off with the money without delivering the goods."

"Well, serves him right. I'm sorry I didn't order this house and I'm not giving you money."

"Can't you just give me 500 francs or something? I can't go back to my friend empty handed."

"*Non, c'est pas possible! Au revoir!*"

Later that evening, André completes the story.

"That guy was here a few years ago and took off with all the electric plugs and switches. He also stole the bulbs from the surgery lights and the solar panels that were on the roof of the OR.

"André, just one question: why didn't you say something earlier?"

12 AUGUST 2004
VACATION

Sarah and I decide to take a "vacation" in N'Djamena. The day of our departure from Béré, we stuff four large men into the backseat of our small Toyota Hilux pickup while the front seat is filled with our beefy Arab chauffeur, a petite Danish nurse and an even-leaner-than-he-used-to-be American.

The first leg of our trip begins on the road from Béré to Kélo. Originally built of only the finest of red clays and sands, the route now boasts large ruts delicately carved out by heavy transport trucks and offers the occasional wet-clay, slippery-as-snot experience alongside many detours around impassable mud bogs. In between, there are a smattering of washboard bumps and potholes.

Our first stop is the Kélo market, one hour from Béré. The market is filled with mats piled high with produce amidst the mud puddles and piles of used plastic bags. On the side are small shops selling everything from handmade leather knife cases to paint to wire to axes to canned goods to brightly colored cloth to bread to diesel to rebar to cement to hand creams to soap to whatever else you may need to survive.

Leaving Kélo behind, we discover something that to me has become a luxury: a paved road. At least compared to what we've just experienced, this is a superhighway. Consisting of two lanes without dividers or markings, this freeway offers the ability to make up some time as we can get up to speeds of 120 km/h! That is until we have to slow down for goats, ducks, cattle, sheep, pigs, people carrying things on their heads, potholes, flipped-upside-down minivans, broken down tractor-trailers, villages, stray kids, dogs, bicycles, police and customs checkpoints, and the occasional potty break.

Halfway to N'Djamena, Bongor offers the best chicken in *Tchad*. Along the main thoroughfare, there is a chain of restaurants specializing in the grilled birds. We pull up and choose our meat fresh off the piece of chain-link fence sitting over some coals. We wash our hands out of a bucket using local soap covered in plastic netting, then sit under a veranda on plastic chairs with a plastic covered wooden table. Our culinary adventure starts with a pineapple milkshake while we watch them tear our chicken apart with their bare hands till it's nothing but easily managed pieces.

Finally, it's chow time as the tray of pieces arrives garnished with a few sliced onions and a pile of chili salt soaked in lime or vinegar. After purchasing a couple baguettes to throw in the middle, someone thanks God and we all dig in to the common plate using the fingers of our right hands. Properly, one should only touch the dish and mouth with the right hand. The left hand is reserved for other important personal duties.

The road then gets worse for a few hours until we arrive in N'Djamena. What strikes me instantly is the wealth of N'Djamena. Sure there are uncovered sewers spilling out into the streets, pigs running everywhere with dirty children as companions, mud brick houses, few buildings over two stories high, and trash everywhere, but there's electricity (sometimes), running water (maybe), telephones (if one is rich) and lots of fresh fruits and vegetables!

N'DJAMENA

For our stay we could choose the clean, mosquito-free, safe, well-equipped guesthouses of the International Society of Linguistics or TEa.m.. However, we prefer to save money and stay at the Adventist guest house located conveniently above the Mission office.

The house is in poor shape. The floors are unswept. The kitchen has a grime-covered gas stove with one working burner and mildewed cabinet doors hanging on their hinges. There is no electricity. The bathrooms are equipped with cold bucket showers and un-flushed toilets. The bed rooms boast mosquitoes the size and tenacity of small birds and mattresses that provide a thin barrier between the sleeper and the wooden slats of the bed.

I am lulled to sleep with the sound of mosquitoes buzzing in my ears in spite of the mosquito net. After a miserable night of tossing and turning, I am awakened by numerous roosters and a tape-recorded, rock-concert-loud Muslim call to prayer at 4 a.m.

Our local N'Djamena cuisine consists of rotten pineapple, rice, potatoes, hard avocados, onions, lots of eggs and a surprisingly good watermelon. Our drinking water comes out of a bucket and tastes like plastic hose.

I am here to attend meetings and they are made even longer by the 120 degree weather unrelieved by air conditioning or even a fan. That night, I feel even hotter as I'm hit with a bout of Malaria. Sarah gets it even worse. We've come to recognized only too well the typical symptoms of periodic hot flashes, occasional diarrhea, abdominal pain, muscle and joint aches, splitting headache, and generalized fatigue.

Once the diagnosis is made, I go to the market. Turning right after the taxi stop and office supply stalls, I walk past some vendors of tools and building supplies. Just before the roadside produce stand, I find what I'm looking for. Three booths in a row sport robed Arab men wearing small round hats hawking their pharmaceuticals.

"What do you have for Malaria?" I ask in French.

They show me some Amoxicillin. "*Ça c'est très bon ça.*" The vendors try to con me. Amoxicillin is an antibiotic; useless for Malaria.

I point to a couple of banged up single dose boxes of Fansidar and some Quinine pills from a tin can.

"How much is that?"

Before haggling for a good price, I confirm that the white pills are indeed Quinine by tasting one to make sure it's real. I am gratified with the characteristic bitter taste of true Quinine. After a few minutes of bargaining, I'm satisfied with the deal and buy some for both Sarah and I.

We both feel better by morning as we prepare to head back to Béré.

14 AUGUST 2004
LOVE

Sarah is sitting on the couch, burning up with Malaria yet again. It's a calm Saturday afternoon. Sunlight filters through the window lighting up the dust. Flies buzz lazily around the cool cement floor. Sarah is weakened, her brow wet with sweat. She's wearing a tight t-shirt with "Redhead" splashed across the front. She smiles sweetly as we talk of nothing, nothing at all.

Without much thought—although the issue has consumed every waking moment of my conscious mind—I feel the time is right. I look Sarah in the eyes as she brushes away a strand of red hair.

"Do you think the wedding should be in Denmark or the US?"

She looks at me with a grin splitting her face. "Denmark, of course!"

Yes. Love found in *Tchad*. Unexpected. Marvelous. Scary. Marry a Dane? December 30. Denmark. A small church. International flavor.

Simplicity. Red wearing white. The next adventure. Wonder. Awe. Amazement. Gratitude. What next? I can't wait.

24 AUGUST 2004
BICYCLES, TWINS, AND DANCING ON SAND PILES

I cut through the uterus and grab the left leg of the infant pulling it out. I repeat the maneuver for the right leg. Then, I extract one arm at a time. Just the head remains. I stick my finger in the baby's mouth, bending the chin to the chest and slowly pull. He pops out. I hand him over to Sarah who begins resuscitation. I wait for a cry. There is none. Meanwhile I notice the uterus is still quite large.

I look in and there's another amniotic sac. I break it. There's another head. I place my hand inside the uterus to keep the head flexed while pushing with all my might on the uterus from outside the belly with my other hand. I pass the second twin off to Sarah too. I have to break scrub to help resuscitate. Neither infant is crying and both are blue. Samedi starts to sew up the uterus. As I breathe for one twin with a *respirateur* and give chest compressions, I don't even think that this could be me. It's not until later that I realize that this is how I was born: unexpectedly by C-section, a twin who would've died in the days before surgery. Both boys lived, then and now.

Yesterday, I did another C-section on a woman pregnant with twins. It wasn't as satisfying. The mom delivered the first twin at home and then tried a long time with the second, even going to a traditional healer before coming to the hospital. The second was head first with both hands poking out the sides preventing him from being born. He was already dead but we operated to save the mom. That was 2 a.m. Saturday morning. I would preach at the church later that day hoping to not fall asleep in the midst of my own sermon. Fortunately, the fear of public speaking, especially in a foreign language, gave me enough adrenaline to stay awake.

The next afternoon, Martin, the nurse on *garde,* calls me in. Two infants need blood transfusions. One pregnant woman has a hemoglobin of 4.3 and Malaria. Another pregnant woman presents with a urine infection and Malaria. One woman has a hernia and needs surgery. Anatole is there, working like a madman in the lab trying to get the blood types right and transfuse three people at the same time. Sarah is searching for IV access on one pale kid and David is on the other.

Neither of them can afford to pay. But I've started a new system where they can leave something as collateral until they bring the money. So I add to my collection of bicycles. My office now looks like a bike shop with bikes in various stages of disrepair piled in one corner.

The next evening we operate on the woman with the hernia. I find the sac but it looks strange. It looks like some kind of weird tumor with hair growing out of it. I don't feel comfortable with just cutting it off and maybe leaving some tumor inside. I open her belly. There I find a piece of dark looking small bowel at the point of rupture. I do a small resection and anastamosis of the intestine. Then I dissect out the "tumor" and find it's really just the hernia sac with the "hair" being small, clotted of blood vessels where it had been strangulated. Some may call me an idiot. I say it was God's way of getting me to see that intestine so I'd save her life.

03 SEPTEMBER 2004
AIDS, WIDE-EYED BABIES, AND BEARDED ARABS

I'm staring at a shriveled up mockery of a somehow still beautiful woman ravaged by AIDS. Her stick thin sister lies on a mat by the side of the bed, also suffering from the same malady. They've called me because *"Ca ne va pas,"* something's not right. She has a clenched jaw and her eyes are crossed. She's trembling. Everything else seems normal. No seizures or neurological deficits.

Dimanche is with me. We start to talk to the woman. I tell her I know she's afraid. She's afraid because we've just hospitalized her for tuberculosis. She's afraid because she sees her sister wasting away in front of her. She's afraid of the future. She's afraid of death. I tell her it's normal to be discouraged and depressed but that there is Someone who will be there with her in the valley of the shadow.

Her eyes uncross and comprehension registers. I continue. Slowly the jaw relaxes and she starts to nod in understanding. I tell her we are there for her and that the hospital staff is praying for her. Tears well up in her eyes. We finish and I leave. We are in the process of trying to get antiretrovirals for her, as she is reliable and can afford them. Most people with AIDS can't pay for the life-saving medications. I usually have to just watch as they slowly fade away.

Later that day I find myself staring at an eight-month-old baby with a round face. His eyes are wide open as if in a panic. He's staring straight ahead without seeing. I have a mask over his mouth and nose and am breathing rapidly and shallowly for him. He has severe *Falciparum* Malaria and has just had a blood transfusion. The first Quinine drip is slowly running down into his tiny vein. His heartbeat is almost too fast to count. He is exhausted. I'm giving him a break by breathing for him.

As I stare at him I think how he is only one of many. How many have we seen the last month? Over 30? His parents sit nearby. People stop occasionally to stare at the strange white man doing who knows what interesting thing. I send them away. The parents are dressed in dirty, worn hand-me-downs, probably from the West. Their hands are calloused and their lined faces betray a hard life making them appear to Western eyes as twice their actual age.

I look back at the baby. I somehow feel very strange. This is a mysterious moment. How did I end up at this moment in time in this place? I see the baby and somehow I love him. At the same time I wonder what I am bringing him back to. If he survives will he just die next year of the same thing? Will his life have been filled with joy as a kid's should or will it be filled with hunger and fear? But at this moment I can think of nothing I'd rather do than breathe for him and watch his tracheal tug and sub costal retractions subside and relax. But it's not for me. I want it for him and for his parents. He starts to twitch in a localized seizure. I continue. Somehow, he makes it and a few days later, is discharged. He hasn't fully recovered yet, but is breastfeeding well.

Another day, a bearded Arab walks into my office after I call his name for a consultation. He is angry.

"Why have you seen others before me when I was the first one in line?"

I get angry in return. We exchange arguments, both of us in broken French; mine with an English accent, his with an Arabic accent. Then, we both decide to drop it and turn to his daughter who stuck a ball bearing from a bike in her ear five days ago. They come from Kélo where they tried unsuccessfully to wash it out with ear irrigation.

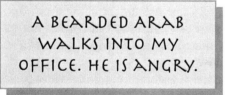

A BEARDED ARAB WALKS INTO MY OFFICE. HE IS ANGRY.

I look in and see pus, inflammation and the tip of a black metal ball. I try various instruments and end up just causing bleeding. She's in pain. We take her to the OR and give her general anesthesia. I spend 3 1/2 hours trying to extract that foreign body. I just can't give up. I feel hopeless and helpless. I just don't have the right instruments or equipment. I'm using an otoscope and some modified skin hooks. I have nothing else.

Finally, we decide to let her wake up. I try one last thing. I grab a hemostat. I'm desperate. I reach in and find it by feel. It slips off. I just can't get around it well enough to grasp it. I try three times. One last one attempt. I try a different angle. I clamp on it and it pops out! I'm about in tears. I know that it was only God. I go outside and show the bearing to the Arab father. He is almost in tears and runs in to see his daughter.

He'd wanted us to persist. He wanted someone who wouldn't give up on his daughter. As I sit down to write the prescription for the much needed antibiotics, I feel lightheaded and a mysterious presence surrounds me. I know I have experienced a direct intervention from above. From frustration and despair, I've been brought to my helplessness and then given what I asked for. I hope I don't cry in front of everyone.

I go home and I'm exhausted. I wake up early the next morning to do an exploratory abdominal surgery. Thankfully I find nothing serious. I do rounds, see patients in clinic and then perform a tubal ligation. When I come out of surgery, they've sent a woman from Lai. The hospital staff there is on strike since they haven't been paid in five months.

The woman is pregnant with massive leg swelling and hypertension: pre-eclampsia. Since she's not yet in labor, Samedi and I perform a C-section delivering a large baby. I don't hear the baby cry. The nurse is sucking out the newborn's nose using a tube attached to her own mouth with a trap box in between. I break scrub and start breathing for the baby with the bag-valve-mask. He starts to pink up, his muscle tone improves and he begins crying. I re-scrub and finish up the surgery.

01 OCTOBER 2004
NOSE PEANUTS

I'm hauling sand. It's what was left after construction of the wall. I decide to landscape a little around the house. It's really ridiculous because now there's this one tiny patch of niceness replete with cactus, volcanic rock and a brick border adorning one corner of a tin roof house that has peeling paint, cracked windows and moth eaten rafters harboring bats and rats.

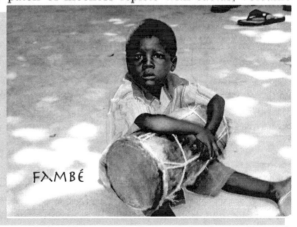

FAMBÉ

The neighborhood boys have gathered as they usually do anytime *Nasara* starts doing anything. Now, they insist on grabbing the shovels and wheelbarrows and hauling sand. One of the boys, Fambé, starts dancing on the sand pile. He's only three. He runs around naked most of the time. And he dances as if he was born to boogie.

Fambé is the second youngest son of Lona, one of our nurses. His favorite pastime is to stare at *Nasara* with a blank look on his face. He won't smile, talk or do anything. One day, he came up to me in church, sat on my lap and promptly ripped my Arabic robes, exposing my buttocks to the rest of the congregation.

Occasionally, I'll be walking to work in the early morning fog and I'll see someone sitting in the dirt waving with a huge grin saying "*Lapia, lapia.*" I'm not sure if Fambé still likes me, however, since I circumcised him. He got an infection because he runs around naked and rolls in the dirt every chance he gets. It also didn't help that he was quite proud of his new look and would show off to anyone.

That night, Sarah calls me to come see a baby with a peanut stuck up his nose. I hurry over and see the child comfortably resting in mom's arms. I walk down the hall to my office and gather my arsenal: otoscope, nasal speculum, forceps, clamps, spray anesthetic. I'm armed to the teeth. I walk back balancing all my goodies in both hands. I turn the corner and see a strange man bending over the kid. It's the father of one of the other patients. I hear loud sucking noises. I'm frozen. He then lifts his lips off the baby's nostrils and spits out a slimy peanut right there in his hand. He nimbly picks it off and tosses it aside. I'm flabbergasted. Feeling a little foolish with my "modern" medicine, I tell Sarah to give them their money back and return home laughing and shaking my head.

09 OCTOBER 2004
MOONLIGHT

The *Tchadian* sky stretches out into what seems like infinity. It's like being in a curved mirror at the circus where everything is distorted and seems larger than life. The light blue sky is brilliantly clear except for one huge bank of puffy white clouds stacked on the horizon. We are escaping from Béré and the hospital. Becky, our second redheaded nurse volunteer, leads the way down the small path away from the back of the compound. Nathan, our blond 6'7" pre-med student, strides casually beside her. Wendi, a volunteer accountant and the third redhead in the group, walks behind me next to Jennie, the second newly arrived volunteer nurse. Sarah, the first redhead, brings up the rear.

The sun beats down fiercely as we enter the rice fields where the path disappears under water for long stretches at a time. The water is hot to our bare feet. The path alternates between fresh sand and sticky mud. We occasionally pass locals on their way to or from the fields carrying flip flops in their hands and bundles on their heads. A friendly *lapia* is exchanged and repeated as befits local custom. Occasionally, a *lapia ei* or *lalé* will be thrown in for variety. Of course, Sarah has to always show off by actually carrying on brief conversations in *Nangjeré*. Although I'm envious of her linguistic skills, a simple *lapia* is the best I can do.

At the river, we are surrounded as usual by half naked children carrying fishing spears who are more than happy to leave what they're doing to watch *Nasara* swim. What could be more entertaining than watching weird looking, white foreigners jump, swim, wrestle and toss mud at each other?

Going back to the hospital, the moon reflects perfectly off the still waters of the rice paddies as the sky is still painted pink from the recently setting sun.

11 OCTOBER 2007
BLEEDING

A baby comes in with a severe infection covering her groin, legs and lower abdomen. There are large, black dead skin patches with yellow pus along the edges. The wounds need to be debrided. I take her to the OR. After putting her to sleep, I cut away all the dead tissue.

That afternoon Sarah comes to me to say the little girl is unconscious. I come and find her recently dead. I desperately refuse to believe it. She's pale. The bandages are red with blood. She's bled out and no one noticed. I do CPR furiously. I am unable to accept that I should have checked back on her several times before going home.

No one else seems to be concerned about her at all. What a waste. We have no post-operative recovery room or any real post-operative care. I see death all the time, but this one gets to me. I should've checked more carefully to make sure all the bleeding had stopped. Sarah is also devastated when I see her later. She feels it's her fault. I hug her and let her know it's not. I feel sick to my stomach.

Dimanche's sister comes in the next morning with abdominal pain. The nurse on *garde* thinks she has a urinary infection. After examining her, I at first think she has appendicitis. I decide I should do a pelvic exam. She has cervical motion tenderness which means she probably has an infection of the uterus or fallopian tubes.

A few hours later, when I go back to see her, the pain is now on the left side. Her story changes too. I wish I had an ultrasound or other tests. I check a complete blood count, which is normal. I put her on antibiotics and continue my work. I don't feel quite comfortable with the diagnosis. After work, Nathan and the other volunteers want to go to the river. Right before leaving I decide to check on the patient again. She's worse.

I look some stuff up in books and ask some more questions. After more reading, I realize I should have checked to see if she was pregnant. She said she has had normal periods, but you never know. Matthieu, one of the lab techs, comes in from home to do the test. The faintest of lines appears on the test strip telling us it's positive. I feel relief. God has helped us find a diagnosis even with our lack of equipment. It's an ectopic pregnancy.

I know I need to operate, but I'm always more nervous when it's a friend or the relative of someone I work with everyday. What if I'm wrong and I operate for nothing and something goes wrong? I'd operated on a woman a few months ago who I'd thought had an ectopic pregnancy and it turned out to be a simple pelvic infection treatable with antibiotics. Was I making the same mistake?

We take Dimanche's sister to the OR. After being prepped and draped, I open up her belly in a low pelvic incision. Dark blood comes out of the abdomen. Sure enough, there's a swollen mass in the left fallopian tube. It has just started to rupture. I clamp off the blood supply on both sides and remove the mass. After irrigating the belly and sucking out all the blood I check for further bleeding. Everything is dry. I close up the fascia and skin and place a sterile dressing.

What if I'd just gone to the river like I really wanted to? I have to have time to myself or I could spend all day, every day at the hospital. It's so easy to get overwhelmed and sucked into work. I could lose myself and who I am in the incredible, never ending needs of a place like Béré. But this time, the sacrifice saved a life. It was worth it.

15 OCTOBER 2004
GUAVAS

I find myself walking swiftly down a path. Through the sunlight flickering off the rustling leaves of the guava trees I see the kids slinking up. I feel the adrenaline surge. The kids always steal our guavas. I know how to stop them. All I have to do is catch one and beat him up like any good *Nangjeré* man would do and the thieving will stop. Unfortunately, beating up on small children has been something I've never been able to do. Now, if it was the pigs that came scrounging for worms every morning, I could beat them up without any qualms. The only problem is the pigs are too fast. You'd never think it to see them, but they're fast.

The kid in the tree sees me. Two things happened simultaneously. I kick off my flip-flops and begin to lope toward the tree while the boy almost falls out of the tree in his hurry to get down. His watchman takes off and quickly veers left. I'm hot on the tail of the second, the one who's actually been in the tree.

This boy I'm running after obviously hasn't been informed of the *Nasara* rules. He just knows someone is chasing him and he needs to get away. He's in too much of a hurry. I pace myself. I keep up with him easily with a measured stride.

He cuts down into a pit where mud bricks have been harvested and falls getting up in almost the same motion. I circle the rim. He ascends the other side with me now hot on his heels. We enter an opening in a mud brick wall and run around a hut into a courtyard. I can smell his fear. I know he's mine.

He realizes he's in a dead end. He finds a narrow break behind a pile of reed mats. I cut him off. He stops behind the mats. Only the mats protect him from what he is sure is a severe beating. He begs for forgiveness and then makes a break for it. I'm only a few feet behind. He might've escaped if it hadn't been for the pigs.

Everywhere a small patch of water gathers, there the pigs will gather as well. They wallow deep in the mud with silly grins plastered on their snouts. When our outside faucet leaked last spring the melodious sounds of contentedly snorting pigs never ceased to freshen the airwaves as they kept it boggy. The pig's snuggling down keeps the wallow wet and slick even when all around has dried out.

In that split second between freedom and catastrophe, our guava thief meets his pig wallow. With a look of surprise and terror, he goes down fast and hard skidding along the slime for a good five feet on his belly. I'm on him in a second. I grab his wrist and pull him up out of the bog.

"Come with me." He  can't do anything but comply because of his fear even though I barely have his wrist with one hand. I have no idea what I'm going to do with him, but it has been good sport by the powers. He finally realizes my weak grip and breaks free only to trip and fall within ten feet. By then a crowd has gathered

NATHAN

and I explain again that while we don't like stealing we don't mind if they eat our guavas if they ask. I release him.

Between chasing kids stealing from our guava trees, playing basketball on our leaning tower of hoop, and playing guitar and drums on the porch, Nathan and I have become quite the neighborhood entertainers. The local children never seem to tire of yelling out our names.

"Jay-mmm-suh, Jay-mmm-suh! Nat-aaahh, Nat-aaahh! Lapia, lapia! Naaaasssssaaaarrrraaaaa!"

They never cease to wave joyously anytime we pass by or take the time to hang out. They are dirty, naked, barefoot, ragged, cheery, playful, mischievous, tireless, incorrigible and about the cutest children to be found anywhere.

Since that infamous day of catching the guava thief, one tiny little boy never fails to come up each day and with a big grin on his face ask in broken French, "*Je mange les goyaves*??" We of course say, "*Oui,* eat all you want!"

11 NOVEMBER 2004
CAMEROON

I'm sitting in the back seat of an old Land Cruiser. I've about finished off the huge bag of Béré peanuts and am munching contentedly on my first apple in months. I swig some earthy tasting water from a *Tangui* bottle and swish it around. The road is winding up and down and all around through incredible greenery and ever more fierce mountains. A waterfall can be spotted here or there. We are up on the side of the mountain and turn a corner where a town starts to appear on the little hills in the valley.

We see our sign and veer quickly right up off the pavement and on to a dirt road, so pitted and trenched it would make a *Tchadian* road seem like hitting deep powder on a snowboard in comparison. We climb steadily and pull into our destination: the Pope John VI memorial conference center. We have arrived in Bamenda in the English-speaking part of Cameroon. Joining us are Adventist health professionals from all over Central Africa.

I spend the rest of the week learning about HIV/AIDS and how to treat those living with it in Africa. In between and after sessions we amuse ourselves by playing ping pong and getting drilled at 6 a.m. every morning by some drill-sergeant-like coach intent on making us soccer machines by the end of the week. Over the weekend, I play soccer barefoot alongside Anatole, Samedi, and Lona against the well-shoed Cameroonians. We barely lose on penalty kicks. The food is good, not withstanding the fact that cabbage makes up a part of every meal.

Wednesday, I find myself again in a bus just outside of Bamenda. The mountains are even more rugged, almost mythical. Waterfalls seem to tumble down in the distance around every corner. A light fog adds to the fairy-tale like quality. We are going to Mbinko Hospital where Dr. Hansen spent most of his time researching leprosy, the disease that now bears his name.

Settled on the edge of a mountain overlooking a lush valley straight ahead and with towering cliffs to the left broken apart by at least three waterfalls, the hospital is in an enchanted location.

The leprosy rehab clinic still runs strong. A school for the deaf is one part of a program to rehabilitate handicapped people and reintroduce them into society. A local wood carver now makes prosthetics for amputees and others at a fraction of the national cost. A carpentry shop apprentices locals and provides all furniture for the hospital. A metalwork shop makes wheelchairs, gurneys and other items for hospitals nationwide. An agricultural project provides food for the lepers and hospital staff. Natural gas is produced and used on site. Ophthalmology provides a reference location for vision problems from the whole region. The staff numbers over 400 employees including a four-member chaplaincy program.

The place has a feel of vibrancy, good will and movement. Change is in the air as I see projects being realized all around me. And behind it all? An almost exuberant confidence and trust in God. Truly inspirational.

The return trip to *Tchad* is mostly remarkable for being even longer and more tiring then the outward bound portion. On the train from Yaoundé to N'Gaounderé we are unable to get sleeping compartments. We spend the night sitting around a table as more and more people, chickens, various food items and boxes begin to pile up around us. A group of passengers in front discusses Cameroonian politics loudly till the wee hours of the morning.

I laugh hysterically as an enterprising Vermox salesman describes in detail the many noxious effects of intestinal worms and how with his product you will be able to crap them all out.

> AFTER ALL, EVEN BILL CLINTON, GEORGE BUSH AND USAMA BIN LADEN ALL NEED TO POOP WORMS!

"And get some for the wife so you can share the experience," he insists. "After all, even Bill Clinton, George Bush and Osama Bin Laden all need to poop worms! So buy Vermox one and all!"

After an eight-hour bus ride to Yagoua, I spend the night on a mat on the floor of the train station in Yagoua. I'm wedged between Samedi, Lona, and Anatole on one side and a stranger on the other.

We wake up at 5:30 a.m. and hop on the back of motorcycles to race through the slowly awakening dirt streets of Yagoua. I feel like I'm almost going to freeze to death as the chill dawn wind rips into my face. We make it through two police checkpoints who look long and hard at my visa yet somehow don't see that it has expired five days ago. We cross the river in hollowed out log canoes. On the other side, Bichara is waiting to take me home to Béré and my waiting fiancé, Sarah.

Home, sweet *Tchad*.

26 NOVEMBER 2004
CHILLS

I close my office door. I feel cold and tired. My muscles and joints ache. I put my Old Navy sweatshirt on over my scrubs. I lie down on the exam table. It's not even my office. I'm in the pre-natal care room temporarily as the main building gets renovated. I'm sure it's just exhaustion. I don't really feel sick. It feels so good to lie down. Since Sarah left three days ago my life has become crazy once again...

I drive her to the N'Djamena airport in our pickup. We walk across the courtyard and into the waiting area past huddled groups of *Tchadian*s, many wearing the traditional robes and round hats or turbans. Sarah packs lightly. I am carrying her backpack and she has a tiny carry-on bag. Acting like we know what we're doing, we walk past the guards, through the cage like entrance and into the check-in room. I hold her hand. We load her bag onto the belt and I hug her good bye.

People around us watch in wonder to see a man actually show affection to a woman in public. When I let Sarah go and she starts to enter the ticketed passengers only section, a woman comes up and tells me I can go with her. She is apparently moved by our display of affection. She says we can go up to the observatory to watch the plane come in.

The woman checks Sarah's passport and then we walk up the steps to a huge glass window with open slats letting the cool N'Djamena night air blow in. We stand there laughing and talking watching the plane come in, the only one of the evening. Finally, I know I have to say goodbye. I feel weird, surreal. It hasn't sunk in that she's leaving and that I won't see her again until a week before we get married.

I have the strange sensation of wondering if I even know this beautiful girl with wild red hair beside me. I wonder if I'll feel even weirder after a month apart. I wave goodbye one last time and walk down the stairs, past the passport checkpoint, out the guarded cage-like entrance and into the eerily lit, yellow N'Djamena night. I cross the pavement and get into the car. I feel like a zombie thinking how normal this all seems and yet within a few hours Sarah will be in Europe in a completely different world...

A knock on the door interrupts my reverie. A nurse opens the door and peers in. "*Docteur, excusez-moi, mais il y a une urgence.*" Three sweaty, out-of-breath men push past the nurse carrying an elderly woman who's moaning, but not responsive. Probably Malaria. I examine her, order some tests, prescribe a few medications and send her to the ward.

I'm really starting to feel the chills. I head to the lab and have Mathieu, the lab tech on duty, poke my finger for a Malaria smear. I go back to my office and lie down, slipping quickly into that nebulous zone of not awake, not asleep, not thinking, not dreaming, kind of aware but out of it.

In my subconscious world, I'm on the way back to Béré after seeing Sarah off at the airport. Nathan and two other volunteers are with me. We race through the pothole filled roads to Guelengdeng.

As we prepare to leave Guelengdeng, the truck suddenly stalls when I brake and put in the clutch. It's the same problem we'd supposedly fixed in N'Djamena. Now, leaving Guelengdeng we also start to lose power. I'm not sure we'll make it to the next main village, Bongor. However, I find that by pumping the gas pedal I'm able to keep a little power and the pickup limps into town.

We stop right where we normally eat chicken, drink pineapple milkshakes and buy soap. As soon as I open the hood, a group crowds around quickly hoping to benefit from *Nasara*. Everyone's a mechanic, several are drunk and I don't trust any of them. All I need is to change the fuel filter. We have an extra one with us. I ask for a 12 mm wrench. A bystander hands me one that is well-worn.

After trying several times in vain to loosen the screws holding the filter in place, I inform the crowd that this wrench doesn't work. Instantly, several pairs of hands reach over try to show me that I'm just a stupid *Nasara* who needs their expert help. First, they grab the wrench out of my hand and then almost strip the nut before I can wrestle it away from them. I spot a public transport van just ahead. I ask the driver if he has a good 12 mm wrench. He lends me one and I soon have the filter off. Then someone comes with a tire chain welded to a pipe, which I use to unscrew the head of the filter.

I hear someone call my name, a welcome change from the ubiquitous, *Nasara*. I turn and recognize the chauffeur from the health district of Béré. He just happens to have stopped in Bongor on his way to N'Djamena. He knows a little mechanics as well and makes a few adjustments to the idle and the truck fires right up. I thank him and prepare to continue on my way.

First, though, I have to settle accounts. The man who brought the pipe and chain apparatus demands to be paid. I extend a 500-franc note. He refuses saying he prefers nothing rather than accepting that small amount. I say fine, see you later. One of our other passengers, the chaplain's daughter, adds 500 francs making it 1,000. He still refuses.

All the bystanders say I should give him more. I tell him I just spent time with the second best mechanic in N'Djamena who charges 4,000 francs an hour and since he wants more than 1,000 francs for 15 minutes he must think he's a better mechanic. He continues to refuse. I get in the car. His friend takes the 1,000 francs.

The "mechanic" tries to make me feel guilty by coming up to me and informing me that even though I'm robbing him blind he wants to wish me a *bon voyage* because he's a good person. I tell him thanks and start up the engine. Finally, he realizes he isn't going to get any more and his attitude changes. He takes the 1,000 francs, smiles, shakes my hand and wishes me a real *bon voyage*. This *Nasara* has learned a thing or two about local bargaining techniques.

We arrive without further incident in Béré that evening.

Back to reality. I'm really starting to feel the chills. I have goose bumps all over and my hair is standing on end. My teeth are chattering and my legs shivering. I go to the house and climb in my zero degree down sleeping bag still trembling. The muscle aches are severe now and my head is pounding. I drift into a troubled sleep while thinking back to yesterday evening after arriving back from N'Djamena…

At 8:30 p.m. I'm sitting on the porch ready for our evening prayer time with the missionaries. Just as we begin, Anatole comes running up. There is a patient who just came in with suspected intestinal obstruction.

I go up to the hospital. After finally succeeding in placing a nasogastric tube, I try to place a urinary catheter in the man before surgery. It won't pass. The tip comes out bloody. I try again. Finally, after four different types of catheters and no success, we decide to just start the surgery. It's about 10 p.m..

I scrub while Samedi preps the abdomen with Betadine. Samedi scrubs, we put on our gowns and drape the patient. After a prayer by Anatole, I grab the scalpel and slice quickly from sternum to pubis. Going through skin and subcutaneous fat, I hit the fascia and slice through. The pressure inside the belly bulges out as I dissect carefully into the peritoneal cavity. With my fingers protecting the intestines, I cut rapidly through the rest of the fascia till his belly is laid open from top to bottom.

Black, foul-smelling small intestine pours out along with thick, dark red fluid. The sigmoid colon is hugely dilated with a necrotic loop of small intestine wrapped around its base. I try to reduce the colon through the trap unsuccessfully. I poke a hole in the bowel wall letting out the gas and some nasty fluid then pull tight a purse string suture to close the hole. I reduce the sigmoid, freeing it up from its trap. It is fortunately still viable.

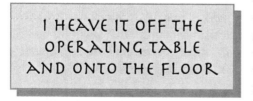

I HEAVE IT OFF THE OPERATING TABLE AND ONTO THE FLOOR

The small intestine is dead from about eight cm proximal to the large bowel halfway back to the stomach. I clamp the bowel on both sides of the dead section. Then I poke through the mesentery and clamp, cut, and tie across the blood supply freeing up the dead part. Once the necrotic bowel is removed, I heave it off the operating table and onto the floor.

I suture the two cut ends of good intestine back together in two layers. I release the clamps and there is no leakage. I irrigate the abdominal cavity and suck out all the contaminated liquid. I leave in two drains and stuff the intestines back into their rightful place. I then close him up.

By the end of the operation, I can barely stand. I feel drained. It's 1 a.m.. Walking back I feel the chills for the first time and have to warm up under a hot shower for half an hour before being able to fall asleep.

Now, it's the next day and I'm in my office drifting in and out of consciousness. Matthieu comes to tell me my Malaria smear is positive for Falciparum, the worst kind of Malaria. I take five Mefloquine tablets and go home to the warmth of my sleeping bag.

11 DECEMBER 2004
THURSDAY

It's hard to get out of my warm bed. The nights have been actually cool here lately and getting out on the cool cement floor is all the more difficult. I finally make a break for the bathroom and am thankful for one of the few luxuries we have here: hot showers. I dress in scrubs and head to the kitchen on the other side of the duplex for breakfast.

Nathan starts me off with a pile of eggs, well cooked to kill anything, as they look pretty sketchy when cracked open. I take some of the now-stale bread baked by Salomon, and dip it in a few eggs mixed with cinnamon to make some French toast. The final element of our *Tchadian-*American breakfast is the big bowl of milk bought fresh from the Arabs in the market yesterday that has turned solid overnight. The yogurt mixed with fresh limes, bananas and sugar is excellent.

I walk over in the early morning haze to our temporary waiting room under the mango tree. Behind me is the skeleton of our clinic with its roof and ceiling completely removed and all furniture and equipment moved to the main hospital ward. Our cashier, Pierre, reads from the Psalms and we pray before hearing morning report. Samedi, the *garde* gives a brief summary of all that's happened overnight and we pray again. It's 8 a.m. and the day is about to begin.

I enter my temporary bureau, the midwife's office, and am bombarded by a foul smell that has been getting worse every day. We put out rodent poison a few nights ago and everyone tells me all the mice have died in my office. I tell one of the janitors, Ferdinand, to pull off the two boards covering a pile of wires in the corner. It appears to be the mouse nest. I grab my army shoulder bag that serves as my doctor bag and prepare for rounds.

Before I can start, the pharmacist, Koumabas, needs some more supplies from the main pharmacy. After giving him the syringes, needles and meds he asks for, I check in on Ferdinand. He's discovered one dried, splayed out mouse high up in the wires and a fresh kill down below along with tons of plastic, papers and a surgical cap that the mice have used for their nest.

I head out to the wards. I see Anatole's child first. Apparently, the mom prefers to be hospitalized on the porch, instead of in the wards. The whole family is spread out on a variety of mats and Arabic rugs. The kid has Malaria and still has a very rapid heartbeat but otherwise appears to be doing somewhat better despite vomiting a couple times. I go inside.

The unlighted wards are perpetually dim and filled with shadows. I visit Pediatrics first. One adolescent with cerebral Malaria and possibly syphilis is ready to go home. A nomadic Fulani child with Malaria is also ready to be discharged. The little six-year-old with meningitis and resultant

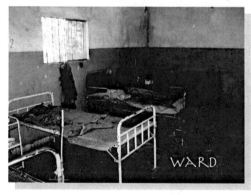

right-sided paralysis has awakened from his coma today and started to eat a little soup.

The young boy with the osteomyelitis of his femur gets his dressing changed with a diluted blend of Clorox. Next is little Angeline who has been with us for over four months for treatment of her infected tibia. We had to remove part of the bone, but the wound has finally closed. Today, I plan to replace her leg cast that has supported her damaged bone for months. It's made of plaster wrapped around two small tree branches for strength.

I move on to the adults. The first patient is a sad case of teenage pregnancy. She labored for four days at home before going to the health center where they let her labor one day more before referring her to the hospital. Instead of coming to the hospital she continued to labor another four days at home until she delivered a dead baby while shredding her cervix and bladder.

When the girl finally came to the hospital two weeks after being referred, she had a raging infection with dead tissue hanging out of her vagina and a ten cm tear in her bladder. Her infection has now been treated and we've tried two repairs on her bladder with restoration of almost completely normal anatomy. Unfortunately, there is still a small fistula. The District Medical Officer, Dr. Ongram, has been trained to repair these types of fistulas. I'll refer her to him the next time I see him.

The second patient is an adult with Malaria ready to go home. Next up is a woman with a huge jaw abscess from neglected dental caries. She's doing better after three extractions and antibiotics. I move onto an elderly gentleman with a huge inoperable bladder tumor who is on palliative care. Another woman with Malaria and some strange shoulder pain is fine except for the hypersensitive painful, non-swollen shoulder that just won't get better no matter what treatment we try. Following is a man admitted last night with ascites and lower extremity edema. Questioning reveals a heavy drinking past. I assume he has liver cirrhosis and plan a paracentesis later to draw off some of the fluid in his belly.

As I head back to the office, I stop to change a dressing on a man who'd passed under my knife for a finger amputation a couple weeks ago. Then I see Angeline and her mom who've paid for the new cast. I pull out the newly donated cast saw, hook up to the lab's small generator and tear through the old fiberglass. Jennie and Nathan then help me rub off the thickened old skin over her leg and wash her down. The leg is kind of floppy since the new bone hasn't completely reformed yet. I wrap her leg in cotton and apply the fiberglass cast from thigh to foot. Angeline only cries a few times and then, still sniffling, she gives me one of our traditional high fives.

Back to my clean-smelling, mice-free office for clinic. It's 10 a.m.. Five of my nine patients are HIV positive. Two of the girls are relatives of one of my patients who just died on Monday. All three have AIDS. The one who died was the one who had the resources to buy anti-retroviral (ARV) medication. She took it for three months without any improvement. For her it was too late. One of the girls I see today, Honorine, on the other hand, started ARVs at the same time and has now gained over 14 pounds.

It's good to see all of my HIV patients. I see them often enough to actually have formed strong relationships with several of them. Honorine just finished her last ARV pill and doesn't have money to buy more. She is an orphan and has some property in the nearby town of Kélo. It will be sold in a few weeks. Unfortunately, that is too late to buy the ARVs as even a day or two of missed treatment can allow the HIV to become resistant. I lend her the money and she takes off immediately for Kélo. Her life depends on it.

I finish clinic at about 1:30 p.m. and head to do the paracentesis on the man with the ascites. I stick a large needle and catheter in the left lower quadrant of his belly and the anticipated straw colored fluid flows out. I send some to the lab and let four liters drain off.

As the swelling goes down, I examine his belly and am surprised to find his liver quite enlarged rather than the shrunken one that one usually finds in cirrhosis. Also, the consistency of his abdominal wall is thickened and doughy. Instantly, another possible diagnosis enters my head: abdominal tuberculosis. If this is the case, it's good news for him because TB is treatable. On the other hand, cirrhosis has no cure and is universally fatal without a transplant. I put him on a two-week trial of anti-tuberculosis medications.

Just then, Dimanche, this evening's *garde*, comes up to tell me there are two patients who've just arrived. They've been referred from the hospital in Kélo because their generator is broken.

I go to see the first at about 2:30 p.m.. A young man who shows the wear and tear of a hard life is lying temporarily on one of the delivery beds. His hair is wild and sticking straight up like Buckwheat's. He has a deep old scar on his left forearm and various smaller scars scattered across his torso. According to the story, at 5 p.m. yesterday, a bull gored him. His intestines popped out and he went to the hospital in Kélo. The nurses there covered the intestines with Betadine-soaked gauze and gave him antibiotics and pain meds. He was then told to come to Béré.

I look at his belly. It is soft with good bowel sounds. He has bowel function intact as he claims to be passing gas normally. I take off the dressing and see a 10cm portion of irritated small bowl already starting to adhere to the skin. I give him a sedative and try to replace the intestines at bedside. He doesn't tolerate it.

JENNIE & DIMANCHE

We rush him to the OR where I give him a dose of Ketamine, prep and scrub the abdomen and push the intestines back inside. Clear fluid comes out of the belly. By the angle of the wound it appears that he was gored almost parallel with the abdominal wall and it is unlikely that the intestines have been punctured. I leave a drain inside, close the fascia and leave the skin open. I pack the wound with diluted bleach-soaked gauze.

I go to see the next patient. It is 4 p.m.. She is a young girl, seven months into her first pregnancy. She has been bleeding for a day and has abdominal pain. I check for the fetal heartbeat; it is absent. There is minimal amount of bleeding and she is stable. I order IV fluids and plan surgery for 6:30 p.m. when our generator comes on. I go home. I haven't eaten since breakfast.

I eat heartily of Salomon's excellent vegetable sauce over rice and then sit back to relax until the generator comes on. I insert *Step Into Liquid* into my computer and get lost for an hour and a half in the surfing world.

At 6:30 p.m. on the dot the generator comes on and I rush over to the hospital. Samedi has already brought the patient to the OR and is getting her set up. We put in a urinary catheter and I give her a spinal anesthetic. We prep the abdomen, scrub, drape and then pause for prayer. I then cut through the lower abdominal skin straight down to fascia. In less than five minutes the baby is out, premature and long dead. We find she has had a placental abruption where the placenta separates from the uterus before the baby is born. We close quickly and by 7:30 p.m. I am back home and ready for some more of Salomon's sauce.

At 8 p.m. the lights go off. I gather with Nathan, Jennie, and Becky out on the porch under another fantastic, pitch black, star filled *Tchadian* sky. We pray and I feel a peace pour over me that cannot be described. Strangely enough, I am completely content. I walk slowly back to my room and go to sleep almost immediately.

20 DECEMBER 2004
ROAD TO A WEDDING

I'm biting back the tears in the cold pre-dawn air as I race along on behind André as his motorcycle bounces along the bumpy road from Béré to Kélo. All I have is my small backpack and a secret dread that I won't make my flight. I'm scheduled to leave Tchad tonight. I get married in ten days. Taking public transport from Kélo to N'Djamena isn't the most secure way to travel. Maybe I'm destined to never marry after all. I'm very close, but until those words are said I can't be sure.

We arrive in Kélo after one and a half hours. My eyes will remain bloodshot and teary for three days from the cold, wind, and dust. We pull into an open courtyard filled with milling, robed Arabs. An array of Toyota mini-buses in varying stages of being overloaded awaits our arrival. One appears about to leave for N'Djamena. André leads me over to a thatch-roofed shelter with no walls supported by four twisting logs.

A turbaned, bearded Arab speaks to me in French tinged with a guttural, Arabic accent. I buy a hand written ticket. I sit on the front seat after tossing my backpack on top of the other luggage already in the rack. I happen to sit next to one of André's wife's classmates from nursing school.

Then I notice my backpack being loaded onto another bus. I go out to protest and find they want to switch me to another bus because they've overbooked. I protest but to no avail. Then, André returns and with the help of his wife's friend they convince them to let me squeeze in, since I'm trying to make my flight.

I spend the next seven hours with one butt cheek on a hard bench and the other free floating in the air by the sliding door. Wedging me in is the young Arab doorman who opens and closes the door barely packing himself in against me. My legs have to be forced left and cannot move at all. I find solace in conversation with the nursing student and in reading all of the biography of Paul Farmer called *Mountains Beyond Mountains*, which proves to be quite inspiring.

After many stops, I nourish myself with a green papaya carved up with a borrowed knife at an Arab tea and hot milk stand. I also eat two bananas I've brought with me and a couple of doughnuts cooked in a deep frying pan over coals by the side of the road. We have a blowout that causes no harm to the vehicle. We put on the spare and then stop at the next town to replace the inner tube.

Finally, we arrive in N'Djamena. The bus station is part of the eastern market. Fortunately, I see we're near the house of Job, one of my friends. It's only about five blocks from the bus stop. I grab my pack and try to ignore the constant stares and cries of "*Nasara, Nasara.*" Job is not at home. A family member tries to get me a taxi but finds it too expensive when they see he's traveling with a *Nasara*. I go sit out of sight until he finds another taxi at a fair price. We travel to the big central market where the taxis normally stop. We pay the taxi-man a little extra to take us to the airport. I've arrived in time.

It feels very weird getting on the plane. I realize this is the first time I'm boarding a plane in a third world country in order to take a vacation. Usually, it would mean I'm heading home, but now I realize I'm actually leaving my new home. I will be back. The Air France ticket attendant wants me to check my backpack. As I desperately try to make it fit in the sizing apparatus he finally just smiles, shrugs and motions me on.

The flight to Paris lasts only five hours. I'm kind of in a dream world as I view the modern world for the first time in a year. But, it's not as strange as I thought it would be. I get on the flight to Denmark, ready to see Sarah and my family. Maybe the wedding will happen after all!

01 FEBRUARY 2005
I'M BACK!

I'm back from my wedding in Denmark. I'm nervous. What can I expect? I've been in the cold, northern, developed world for one month now. What will it be like in the hot, dry desert of underdeveloped *Tchad*? Will it be hard to readapt?

I descend from the Air France plane onto the runway in N'Djamena. I'm excited. The air is cool and dry with that same distinctive *Tchadian* scent that first caused me to feel that *Tchad* was where I was supposed when I first came here in November of 2002. It seems so long ago now. I'm thrilled to hear *Tchadian* Arabic again as I wait for my passport to be signed and retrieve my baggage. Of course, this time I'm not alone. I've come back to *Tchad* no longer a bachelor. Sarah is by my side.

I don't know if there really is a change or just my own perspective has changed, but it seems N'Djamena is less dirty and there is more of a hopeful atmosphere in the air. There are more foreigners on the streets now. Things seem more available in general. On the way down to Béré all the police checkpoints have disappeared.

The road from Kélo to Béré has started to be graded to make up for the damage caused by the transport trucks during the rainy season. The hippos are still there. The barge across the Tandjilé River has become a bridge again as the water level has dropped. The sign saying *Bienvenue à Béré* hasn't changed. There's the hospital's white water tower and before we know it we are back.

I find that everything is familiar. I have truly come home. Good, bad, ugly, warts, quirks, frustrations, joys, beauty, simplicity, filth, all the contradictions that comprise Béré, it is still home.

The peace lasts only a short time. At first, everyone is just thrilled and excited to have me and Sarah back. There are congratulations all around on the wedding. Life is good.

Then, slowly but surely everyone starts to realize they don't have to be responsible any more. The Director of the hospital is back. I swore that this time I wouldn't let them stress me out. But, little by little people subtly place their problems, grievances and other things before me. I wouldn't mind if it wasn't a constant barrage of things that people could handle and have been handling fine in my absence.

The place didn't fall apart when I was gone. It functioned fine and there were even a lot of improvements. The fence around the housing has been started, the rehab of the clinic building continues to advance, the TB ward has been repainted, and latrines were built. So why does everyone now seem helpless and overjoyed at the prospect of dumping any and every little problem in my lap?

André, who I've been counting on and has come through in my absence as acting administrator suddenly can't do anything without coming and asking my permission first. The lab guys tell me they have to wash and reuse the slides since they ran out of new ones yesterday. Of course, they didn't bother to mention they were getting low. The government has been out of HIV tests for two months. Apparently they are selling them on the side to make a profit, leaving us helpless in the face of the epidemic.

And of course, there are the medical challenges. A boy comes in with a swollen face, legs and belly from losing protein through his kidneys. It's probably a side effect of poorly treated Malaria. We treat the Malaria and start him on something that might help his kidneys. I go to see him several days later. As he goes to pull off his shirt so I can listen to his

ANDRÉ

heart and lungs, he starts having problems. At first, we laugh because he has intertwined his two shirts so his arms are trapped. Then, we realize he's having a generalized seizure.

He's finished treatment for Malaria, so it's probably not cerebral Malaria. No fever rules out infection. It could be low sodium or calcium or some other metabolic disturbance, but our lab can't perform any of the tests that we normally could in a modern hospital. Of course, we have neither CT Scan nor MRI. So I just give him some medicine to stop the seizure. Looking at the chart, I notice a nurse gave him a diuretic during my absence, so he might have low sodium and potassium. I give him an oral replacement to be given when he wakes up. I bow my head and silently pray. It's a helpless feeling. I don't know if I'll see him the next morning.

The next patient in our newly painted pediatric ward is a 12-year-old with a wound on his leg for four years. The x-ray shows massive deformation of the femur from infection in the bone down into the knee. Chances of saving the leg are poor.

One of the nurses, Rahama, mentions that the boy who I thought we'd miraculously saved last year is draining from a similar wound in his leg. He'd fallen from a mango tree shattering his jaw and giving him an open femur fracture. We'd wired his jaw, cleaned out and immobilized his femur. His jaw had healed normally and it appeared the leg had too. Now apparently the open wound had let in an infection that is now presenting itself. I'm discouraged. I'd wanted to refer them to a larger hospital but they'd refused, just as they refuse to come in again to see me now.

Then, there's the girl who'd been burned two weeks ago and just came in covered with a traditional treatment made of a rabbit hair paste. Surprisingly the stuff has worked pretty well and most of the burns are healed. Only a small section behind and in front of her left thigh is infected and needs more standard wound care. She's doing well.

Next is a girl who had a longstanding parotid gland abscess that now has developed into a fistula leaking salivary fluids. They refuse to be referred anywhere else. What do I do?

Not to mention the three women who came in Saturday. One with the placenta covering the opening of her uterus so the baby can't come out. Of course, the baby's already dead and her hemoglobin is a quarter of normal. We operate and save the mom's life, but another dead baby is always discouraging. I come out of surgery just to find another woman with the umbilical cord hanging out and the baby also already dead. She delivers the corpse vaginally a few hours later. Only one woman, a tiny teenage nomad, delivers a live baby. We have to cut an episiotomy and bring the baby into the world with a vacuum attached to its head to suck it out. The baby enters the world screaming and is completely alive in every way as if to spite the death that has been so ominously hanging around.

KOUMABAS

Sarah and I invite the hospital staff over to see pictures of the wedding. There's a picture of me swinging off a playground rope in Madrid.

"This this is a picture of a monkey we saw in Spain," I joke.

"*Ah bon?*" says Koumabas seriously. Everyone laughs.

"Koumabas," explains Samedi. "*C'est Dr. James.*" Later on, we show pictures of Sarah and me in the Paris airport stuffing grapes in our cheeks and lips just to be silly.

"This is another monkey we found in the Paris airport," I say again laughing.

"*Ah bon?*" Amazingly, Koumabas again is serious. Everyone is incredulous.

"Koumabas," laughs Anataole. "*C'est le médecin...James*"

"*Ah bon?*" repeats Koumabas, a silly grin frozen on his face.

08 FEBRUARY 2005
DEATH

Pediatrics is always first on the list for rounds. Before, the ward was a small dark room with dirty walls and floors littered with mats, wire charcoal cooking baskets, pots, pans and various brightly colored cloths covering patients lying on metal beds without mattresses. Now we walk into a brightly painted ward with fish, hippos, huts and horses painted on the walls along with colorful sketches done by some of the kids.

The first child I see is a nine-month-old with Malaria. He's doing fine. He's starting to breastfeed again and his heart has slowed down. The next girl has malaria and anemia. Already transfused once, she's doing better but still has a really fast heartbeat and is somewhat pale. I'd ordered a repeat blood count on her yesterday, but the parents have refused.

I next visit the boy with the infected femur. We'd unroofed bone, left drains in and casted the leg to support it. He seems to be doing better. His appetite has increased and there's hardly any liquid in the drains. The whole thing doesn't smell as nasty as it did at first.

One bed over is a four-year-old with Malaria and four different parasites in his intestines. He's fine and I send him home. I also send home a six-year-old with severe scoliosis who'd broken his ribs playing soccer. I guess he doesn't know he's supposed to be handicapped.

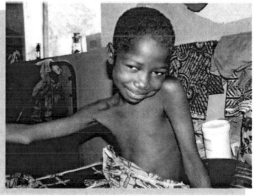

The final patient is a little girl with burns on her abdomen and both thighs. She had been treated at home for two weeks with a traditional rabbit hair paste and then came to us mostly healed but with a few infected places around the edges. Those wounds are now almost completely closed after dressing changes and antibiotics. She's also our resident artist and has the cutest shy smile ever. She helps us as usual by carefully taking off her bandages to let us see the wounds.

I'm head over to the adult ward. There are a variety of patients who are postpartum, recovering from Malaria, and post amputation of diabetic toes. Then there's a man named Koko.

Koko has been sick for two months. He came to the hospital when I was in Denmark for my wedding. He was treated for Malaria. At the time, he'd already been losing weight for one month. After being discharged from our hospital, Koko went to Kélo. At the hospital there he was treated once for Malaria as an outpatient and then hospitalized a few days later and treated for Malaria and amoebas. Last week, he came back to Béré and was treated at our hospital for Malaria again and finally typhoid fever.

I saw him for the first time two days ago. He's thin and somewhat wasted. It's his stomach that bothers him. Yesterday he was eating a little but his stomach was swollen and very tender. He had bowel function. Overnight his bowel function stopped and he started vomiting a lot. He looks bad. His stomach is bloated and doughy and filled with air but soft and tender all over. I suspect perforation from typhoid, abdominal tuberculosis or some strange complication of AIDS. I'd thought about operating on him yesterday and I think the same today. I'm uncomfortable with it though, he might die during surgery in his weakened state, but it may give him his only chance of survival.

I ask everyone to leave and ask him if he's ever tested positive for HIV. He says he's never been tested. We don't have any HIV tests right now, but he says he does want to be tested if they become available.

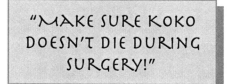
"MAKE SURE KOKO DOESN'T DIE DURING SURGERY!"

I decide whatever he has needs to be operated on. Even if he doesn't survive the surgery I'm pretty sure he won't survive if I don't operate. I don't feel comfortable with the decision but then decisions here are rarely simple. We don't have much to work with except clinical signs, instinct and intuition.

I move on to the outpatient clinic where I see a plethora of pathology ranging from constipation to hypertension to loss of appetite to testicular mass to incomplete spontaneous abortions to lipomas to hemorrhoids to Malaria to infertility to too much fertility. I also spend some time supervising the nurse doing consultations and teaching the nursing student. My desk is piled with books that I have to consult frequently.

André passes me in the hallway and says, "Make sure Koko doesn't die during surgery." *Thanks, André, I'll be sure to remember that. Why would he say that anyway?*

I finally make it home at 3 p.m. for a lunch of fresh cinnamon bread and rice with one of Salomon's sauces. Sarah, Nathan and I play a few rounds of Rummy to while away the time.

At 6 p.m. we bring Koko to the operating room, prep him, give him Ketamine, open his skin and find a seriously thickened peritoneum and a balled up mass of small intestine stuck together. A thick greenish fluid comes out. Everything is covered with white dots. Tuberculosis. I free up some of the adhesions, irrigate well, leave in two drains and close up. He's doing fine.

We wait for him to wake up. Pulse is fine. Blood pressure is good. Oxygen saturation is normal. We have no cardiac monitor. He doesn't want to wake up. His kidneys have stopped putting urine into his catheter bag. His heart rate slows. His O2 sat drops. We start bagging him and doing CPR. His O2 sat comes back. We give him the couple of medicines we have: Atropine and Bicarbonate. No pulse. Nothing. We do CPR for 20 minutes. He's dead. André's a prophet.

We pull out his drains, IVs and catheter. I call in the *garde* who gets the head of the family. About 50 people are waiting outside. They go to get a car to take the body away. Nathan, Sarah and I wait with the body. Nathan offers me some Oreos. I accept. I'm drained and sickened. The family enters the compound with the truck.

As soon as they pull up, the wailing and howling starts. Women flailing their arms and crying "Whoooo Whoooo whooo" and "Baaahooooh, baaaahhhhooooo!" I'm suddenly scared. I slink off in the moonless night to the small side gate as the truck piles high with many live bodies and one dead one. I watch from a distance in the dark. It's creepy. Drums pound loudly and the primal howls and wails move off into the distance with the truck. I go back and eat some sauce and rice. I talk to André. Apparently everyone but me knew Koko was HIV positive. I fall asleep but sleep fitfully, my dreams nothing but nightmares.

23 FEBRUARY 2005
SWEAT

The sweat doesn't even bother me anymore. I don't even notice unless I think about it. Like the beads forming on my forehead right now and the small rivulets hanging out in the folds of my belly. I take multiple showers a day just to feel a few seconds of coolness. I have an unquenchable thirst. The other day I found myself dripping into a wound I was trying to suture. I figured that wasn't too good for the patient ,so I was forced to turn on the generator and crank up the air conditioning to cool down the OR.

We go often to the river. I drive up in the truck never knowing what I'll find. Often it's just Arab cattle drivers shouting *"hhhoeh! hhhoehh!"* to get their herds across the river. Often we only find the traces of their passing: piles of manure and that unmistakable cow smell. The water is surprisingly cool and swift as it skims over the shallow sand bottom of the ford.

Many times we watch people coming back from market. The men usually have slung over their shoulders the curved bush knives with a spine sticking straight out from the inner center of the curve. The women often carry huge loads in massive basins balanced easily on their heads as they sway back and forth in a gracefully smooth walk. Some carry bright umbrellas to ward off the merciless sun.

One drunk man is the happiest *Nangjeré* I've seen in a while. He insists on holding a conversation with us for as long as possible. When he finds I want to take his picture he insists on calling back all his women to be in it. Another grizzled fisherman just shakes his head as he goes back to his nets and dugout canoe. We are careful as we swim to dodge the nets and lines strung with multiple hooks across the width of the river.

Coming back to Béré and the hospital, I see the group from the church at Kalmé is about to leave. They have walked from 12 kilometers away to be with us. I join the group. We slowly walk the dusty streets leaving a cloud kicked up behind us. The kids keep up a constant stream of rhythmic songs in *Nangjeré* accompanied by gourd rattles and a long lead bell-shaped instrument hit with a stick which calls forth deep, earthy bass notes.

Small children surround me. Most have no shoes. Almost all have holes in their shorts and shirts, if they're wearing clothes at all. None are clean. Yet I've never seen bigger smiles every time they catch my eye. I walk with a silly grin on my face humming along or singing a word or two whenever I can.

On the way back I carry Fambé on my shoulders. He's scared yet thrilled by the ride. He almost chokes me to death, yet seems disappointed when I finally set him down.

A prostitute comes into the hospital the next day. She's from N'Djamena and is decked out in a rich, wrapped robe. She is still beautiful. But she is pregnant, in pain, and has symptoms of immunosuppression. She's never been tested for HIV. We are out of tests. Her legs are thin with swollen ankles and feet covered with nodules of various sizes. Looks like Molluscum contagiosum. She is at term by the size of her uterus and feeling contractions. The nurse has brought her to see me because on exam she thinks a foot or leg is in the birth canal.

Unfortunately, it's not the baby. The cervix is normal and still closed. But she has a large mass near her bladder blocking off half the baby's exit route.

She also has Malaria, dysentery and dehydration. She's very pleasant but also in discomfort. She has come to Béré from N'Djamena because she has relatives here and has heard good things about the hospital. When I tell her there's probably nothing we can do about the mass she says that's fine, she came to take care of the baby and make sure he gets out okay.

We treat her Malaria and diarrhea and plan her cesarean section for three days later. The night before, she starts to have regular contractions and goes into labor. As she appears to have recovered mostly from her infections, I call Samedi and Nathan, and we take her to the OR.

The spinal anesthetic goes fine. She is scared. We reassure her and pray with her before starting. She seems to calm down. I cut down quickly and open the uterus. Tons of fluid stained with thick meconium shoots out. The baby has a huge head but comes out rather uneventfully. I pass the newborn off to Dimanche and Nathan for resuscitation. Soon the latest addition to the world is screaming reassuringly.

I pull out the placenta and then take the uterus out onto the belly. I squeeze it to help it contract down to stop the bleeding. I grab a ring clamp and fish in the puddle of blood welling up for the edges of the uterine incision. Samedi suctions, retracts and mops up the blood expertly. There's still a ton of bleeding. I look at the left edge and a cold shiver goes up my spine. I remember hearing about a doctor friend doing a C-section in Africa who got into the uterine artery and the woman bled to death. It appears I'm in the same situation.

Samedi presses on it with some gauze. I quickly grab a suture. My hands are shaking. I tie a quick figure of eight. A little less bleeding. I go for another one. Finally, after two more sutures and what seems like hours later, the bleeding has stopped. I suture up the rest of the uterus. She begins to feel pain and move her legs, our spinal anesthesia has worn off early. We give her Ketamine and she's soon out again.

At the suggestion of Samedi and Dimanche, I do something completely unethical according to my US training. I tie her tubes without prior consent. *Did I do the right thing?* Only God knows.

As I'm cleaning up the blood that had spilled all over the floor I think about something else: all that blood is almost assuredly filled with billions of HIV viruses. For some reason, I'm not afraid of it. I have respect for HIV, but not fear. However, as I see all that blood over my boots, on my scrubs and covering the floor, I can't help but feel a little strange. It looks the same as all the other blood I've seen, yet in a very real way it is different, dangerous, deadly.

It's dark outside, yet still a furnace inside. My energy is spent. My throat is parched. My head is throbbing. My lips are dry. My heels are cracked. My body is sticky with old sweat. *Where can I find relief?*

01 MARCH 2005
SUPERSTITION

It starts out innocently enough. I go to see a patient who's come in overnight. She's lying in bed on her back with labored breathing. She's semi-conscious and drool is coming out her mouth. A pool of urine wets the mattress under her. She moans and barely moves her extremities but otherwise is completely unresponsive. Both pupils are normal and reactive. There is no evidence of trauma.

She was walking in the dark and fell in a hole. On further questioning the family says she apparently fell beside the hole not in it. It wasn't the hole that caused her to fall. Her vital signs are normal as are her heart, lung and abdomen on physical exam.

I order a Malaria smear and some other tests before continuing rounds. A few hours later, I get the results back for the Malaria smear, which is positive. All the other tests are unremarkable. I order a quinine drip and go back to work.

At 1 p.m. I go into the OR to repair a hernia on an elderly gentleman. As I am gowned up and about to start, one of the nurses walks in to tell me that the woman has died. None of the family is surprised. They expected her to die. Now, I hear the rest of the story.

The man I am currently operating on is the woman's brother. When he sold a cow to pay for the operation, she protested. She told him she wouldn't go and see him in the hospital if he used the money for the surgery. He left his village to come to Béré yesterday in order to be at the hospital early for his procedure. She later had regrets and left home to join him at the hospital. That's when she fell down, and shortly afterwards, died. In this culture, if you do something that you later regret, something bad will happen to you.

So, of course, the solution is to never regret anything. That's why I never hear apologies because it doesn't really matter what you do as long as you're not sorry for it! It's better to just have an excuse, no matter how lame. That way, you won't be struck down by whoever or whatever it is that does the striking!

I'm slowly learning little by little why I feel frustrated. I'm in a serious culture clash. If I do something for someone, I'd like to be thanked for it. I will stay up all night, become totally wasted, work while sick with Malaria, and do whatever it takes, if someone will only appreciate it.

The *Nangjeré* language doesn't even have the word *thanks.* They've borrowed *merci* from the French but still rarely say it.

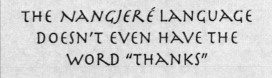

THE *NANGJERÉ* LANGUAGE DOESN'T EVEN HAVE THE WORD "THANKS"

While I easily forgive and forget, and will often apologize, here, it is culturally inappropriate. In fact, asking for forgiveness is considered dangerous. One could die if he has regrets, apologizes, tries to make things up or attempts reconciliation!

I somberly return to the dead woman's brother lying on the operating table, covered with a green drape, and continue the surgery. I find the hernia sac, tie it off, close up the defect, suture the layers closed and clean up. As I go get a drink of water in my office, I see the family silently carrying off the woman's shrouded body.

05 MARCH 2005
AGAINST ALL ODDS

It starts out with a single haunting voice chanting out a rhythmic song in Nangjeré. A gourd filled with seeds quickly picks up the beat and fills in with a soft swooshing sound, like gravel on a beach tossed by the waves. After a few lines, a drum made from a hollowed-out log covered with still hairy goatskin picks up in an off beat as all the voices begin to echo the words of the leader. Then a low thumping fills it all out, hitting you right in the chest with an alternating deep boom boom boom, and a higher pitched hollow knocking. The deep bass comes from a small boy beating a long, hollow square pyramid made of lead that he raises up and down off the floor to change tones.

It's hypnotic and I'm exhausted. My body slouches forward. My elbows on my knees, my eyes close. My feet can't help tapping and my hands softly tap involuntarily even though they don't have the strength for a real clap. My head bobs slightly up and down as my thoughts drift back to this morning...

"Lona wants to see you about some woman in labor and delivery," Sarah shakes me awake.

It's been a long night. My Malaria smear was positive again yesterday. After my second dose of quinine, I fell fast asleep. Then, some people came on motorcycles and began talking and eating loudly right outside our window. I was so groggy, however, I couldn't make sense of anything. I thought they were patients coming to complain that we'd stolen the pumps off their bikes they'd left as collateral for their hospital debts. I drifted in and out of my fogginess all night without really feeling rested. Lying in a pool of sweat doesn't help.

I get up, shower, and put on a pair of pants and a shirt and go to the hospital. I see Lona as I enter the compound. He tells me about a pregnant woman with Malaria who wants to go home after two days in the hospital. I agree. The man whose hydrocele we operated on has a fever. I check on him and he has a small wound abscess. I open it up and pack it with diluted bleach-soaked gauze. I head over to Pediatrics to check on the children suffering from Malaria.

Little James looks at me with a mixture of curiosity and fear. He's one of the first babies I delivered here and probably the first of several now to bear the strange name of James. He's doing fine and I send him home.

...I'm nudged back to the reality of a Nangjeré worship service, as a small girl in tattered rags climbs onto our crude wooden bench. She worms herself between Sarah and me and gives me the biggest, whitest grin ever. I'm soon back into my swaying trance as I can hear the sound of the motorcycle pulling up in my semi-conscious state...

Lona and I go over to the gate. We find that one of the health centers has referred a pregnant woman with a breech presentation. I check the fetal heartbeat and it's slow. I verify the mother's pulse to make sure I haven't accidentally measured hers. As I do, the fetal heart rate slowly picks up till it's back to a normal 150-160 beats per minute. The baby is obviously in distress. The abdomen looks a little weirdly shaped but I think it's probably just a really full bladder. I know we don't have much time to get the baby out if we want to save him.

I send Koumabas to find Samedi. Jacob, one of the lab techs who likes assisting in surgery, is already there to help. Dimanche has just arrived to relieve Lona of *garde* duty. Lona is free to help me get the woman on a stretcher and carry her quickly into the OR. Sarah comes up just then. Koumabas is back and says Samedi is on his way.

I grab one of the green cloth-wrapped C-section bundles, throw it on the instrument tray table and unwrap it in sterile fashion. I open onto the table two pairs of sterile gloves, a scalpel blade and three sutures. Sarah has started the IV and is letting fluids run in quickly.

Samedi arrives. Lona turns the woman over on her side while I open a syringe and spinal needle onto a sterile field made with a glove package. I wipe down the woman's back with Betadine. She can't really double over and has tensed her back muscles. This will be difficult. I put on the gloves, draw up the lidocaine, find the intervertebral space and push in the needle. Fortunately, clear fluid comes out on the first try. I inject the anesthetic and pull the needle out as Samedi turns the woman on her back and lowers the head of the bed.

I put in a urinary catheter and find pure blood. She probably has a ruptured uterus. We really don't have much time now if the baby is to live. I quickly scrub, gown and glove, and drape the abdomen. I nod to Samedi. He prays in *Nangjeré* and I grab the scalpel and in two strokes am through the fascia down to muscle. I quickly cut the fascia with scissors than poke through the muscles with my fingers and pull them apart to the sides. I keep digging and pulling with my fingers until I enter the abdominal cavity. I find a baby's back. The uterus is torn in the lower anterior segment. There are a lot of clots but not much active bleeding.

I reach my hand down the baby's back to its butt and raise it out. Then I swing out the legs one at a time and pull out the body. Each arm is then delivered, a finger put in the mouth to keep the baby's chin on his chest and the head comes out easily. He's huge and broad shouldered. I clamp and cut the cord. He's limp. I hand him to Sarah. There is no cry.

I return my gaze to the woman and pull the uterus out of the belly onto the abdominal wall. I keep listening in the background, waiting for a baby's cry. It doesn't come.

"Bag the baby," I cry. "Oxygen, oxygen, oxygen!" Of course, we don't have any but at least by breathing for the baby, some oxygen will hopefully get into his circulation.

The uterus is torn down through the cervix and partially into the bladder. Fortunately, there's almost no bleeding as all the edges are covered with clots.

"Is there a heartbeat?" I yell to Sarah. "No, nothing," she replies.

"Keep bagging. *Jacob, il faut stimuler l'enfant!* Slap its feet or *quelque chose comme ça!*"

I suture the bladder together and then the cervix over it up to the muscular wall of the uterus.

"There's a faint heartbeat," Sarah calmly mentions. Dimanche has come in. She grabs the baby by his feet and swings him back and forth upside down while supporting his head and neck with the other hand. Still no cry.

"Keep doing what you're doing. *C'est bon!*"

I cut off the clot till the uterine muscle starts bleeding again. I clamp the arteries and suture the uterus to close the tear.

"He wants to cry, he's trying to suck and he's opened his eyes," Sarah reports, but there is still no cry.

I suture the peritoneum over the uterine wound and tie her fallopian tubes. I sew up the fascia and skin and turn to the baby.

He's still floppy but he's staring, has a great heartbeat and is breathing on his own. We smack his feet, rub his back, grind his sternum and rub his jawbone a few more times. We finally give him to his mom. He actually latches on and starts to breast feed a little.

...The music in the church continues to surge through me down all way down my nerves causing many involuntary motions. Sarah pokes me and says to look at Joseph. The 60-year-old grounds keeper with the wizened, white-scruffy-bearded face wearing a pink shirt and maroon pants is up dancing with arms raised right in the face of the percussionists working them into an even more profound musical experience. The chills go down my spine and arms to my legs. People may say it's just Malaria but I sense a connection to Something unseen.

Sarah nudges me again. André is on stage with a massive smile on his face and one arm raised up pumping the air. Tears well in my eyes as I sense that in this small place somehow we have touched something beyond our comprehension. It seems that on the other side they too must be rejoicing as somewhere close by a small heart continues to beat against all odds.

18 MARCH 2005
TWINS

A million thoughts tumble and whirl through my head like the rocks and pieces of smashed bricks tossed by the kids outside. Just like the mango tree outside assaulted by the kids with their missiles, I feel under constant attack. If enough things are thrown at a mango, some are sure to hit, damage, and maybe cause it to fall and crash through the leaves and branches to the ground. It's the incessant battering of small things that keeps my mind in a jumble and my thoughts from differentiating between what's important and what's simply annoying and pointless.

A deep anger has surfaced inside me over the last couple days. I don't know why. It can't be explained by one, single thing. Maybe it's the million and one small demands every day.

Maybe it's the feeling of being used by the friend who is helping to renovate the hospital. Maybe it's the insults hurled at me by the women when I ask why they're stealing huge bags full of mangos off my trees so they can go sell them back to me in the market. Maybe it's the kids who steal my barbed wire and poop in my tool shed. Maybe it's the sheep spending the night outside my door, bleating and screeching their heads off. Or maybe it's the goat peeing like a racehorse right under my window.

Maybe it's the feeling of never being able to get away or have a moment to myself when I'm not being stared at. Maybe it's the patients' lack of gratitude. Maybe it's the feeling of being in over my head and doing things to people that I'm not qualified to do simply because there is no one else around. Maybe it's the lack of directness. Maybe it's the gossip. Maybe it's the forced friendliness. Maybe.

Maybe it's the unexpected, which has come to be expected. There's always that one case that makes my anger disappear and reminds me why I'm here.

The woman is severely pregnant. I say that because I've never seen a bigger pregnant belly on anyone. She's not even that big a woman. Of course, she doesn't really know how long

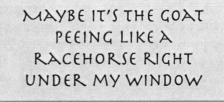

MAYBE IT'S THE GOAT PEEING LIKE A RACEHORSE RIGHT UNDER MY WINDOW

she's been pregnant. The uterine height measures 43 cm. That means she either has too much fluid, too much baby or too many babies. Without an ultrasound I'm just guessing, but I think I did hear two different fetal heartbeats so I think she has twins.

By the way, she's HIV positive and her name is Yvonne. We had identified her on normal screening a few months ago. We explained to her what that means for her pregnancy and how we can try to prevent her child from getting infected with HIV. She had been pretty regular in coming to prenatal visits, but has missed the last few appointments. Now she's huge.

Her cervix seems favorable so we decide to try and induce her labor. It doesn't work. We then schedule her for a C-section. She says she needs to go home and will come back later. She doesn't.

A week later, two nights ago, Yvonne comes back. I'm so dead asleep, I don't even hear the night watchman, Keining, knocking. It's Sarah who wakes me up. I step groggily to the door after fumbling for my headlamp in the dark. I ask Keining what's going on. He replies with the usual, "*Il y a un cas.*" I tell him I'll be right there.

As I walk over to the hospital, I enjoy a rare moment of silence and tranquility. The air is cool and still. There is no moon and hardly any stars. It's pitch black and eerily quiet.

I arrive to find that Yvonne is now in labor. But it's the baby's face that wants to come out first instead of the back of the head. It's almost impossible for a baby to come out in that position. Besides, a C-section will help prevent transmission of the HIV to the baby. I ask why she hasn't come back sooner for the surgery. She said she couldn't find the $40 to pay for it. Dimanche, the *garde*, pulls me aside and tells me the rest of Yvonne's story.

Yvonne was the third wife of a man who died a year and a half ago of AIDS. As the third wife of a husband who died of AIDS, she was abandoned to care for her kids without help. As a result she's been selling herself to men for 50 cents a trick. With six to seven customers a day, even while pregnant, she is able to put food on the table. Suddenly, in the early morning of a dark *Tchadian* night all my confusion, anger and frustration disappears as a dose of cold reality slaps me right in the face.

We prepare immediately for surgery. As I enter the dark OR, lit only by the weak light of my headlamp, I feel a little strange. The story unfolding before me resembles my own beginnings in many ways.

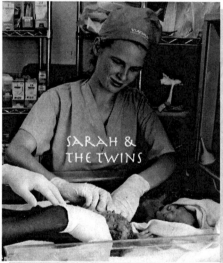

SARAH &
THE TWINS

March 29, 1973. A beautiful, tall 22-year-old blond is in the hospital to deliver for the first time. The pregnancy has been uneventful. Now her labor has stalled. The doctor orders an x-ray, which was standard in the days before ultrasound. When the doc gets the results, he asks the young, nervous husband to step outside. As the door closes behind the dad, he catches a phrase that causes his heart to skip. "Well, the x-ray doesn't show everything, but there's at least two in there."

I grab a green cloth bundle. I open it carefully revealing two folded green surgery gowns and a drape showing years of use and reuse. The instruments are peaking out from underneath. I open two sets of 8 1/2 gloves, a scalpel and four sutures and open them onto the instrument table. I set another pair of gloves, a spinal needle, a syringe with needle and a vial of lidocaine on another table, ready for the spinal anesthetic.

The doctor decides to do a C-section on the young woman with "at least two." Her labor has stalled and the x-ray reveals that the one twin is upside down and the chins have intertwined like pieces of a puzzle. The young woman is my mother. What was going through her mind that day almost 32 years ago as the doctors prepared her for surgery? Suddenly, instead of her first child, she's faced with "at least two" children at once.

She doesn't know exactly how many she'll have when she wakes up, but she'll have twins for sure.

We bring Yvonne in, give her the spinal, and pray. I cut down quickly into the uterus, pulling out two screaming, vigorous, twin boys in one of the few uncomplicated C-sections that we do here. I wipe the first one down quickly to remove the HIV infected blood as quickly as possible. I feel strange and kind of detached as I think how such a simple thing might be the difference between life and a slow death from AIDS. That normal-looking red blood all over the operating field and dripping onto the floor is filled with HIV. This microscopic germ is strange. It can't live without its human hosts and if fact dies quickly outside of the human body. Yet, it can quickly take over a living body until that body wastes. This makes HIV one of the most dreaded diseases of our day.

After surgery, I walk back to the house thinking of many things: my own birth, the tragic death of my twin brother over three years ago, and the uncertain future of the two most recent twin arrivals on our planet resting in the care of their HIV infected prostitute mom. I realize that maybe one reason I was brought here was for them: the untouchables, the outcasts of our day, the HIV infected people living in poverty in the third world.

Already, they are among my most cherished patients. This, despite the fact that there isn't much I do for them clinically. We have no anti-retroviral drugs for treating AIDS. About all I can do is be sure that they feel the presence of a person who isn't afraid to touch them and has no fear of their disease. I'm honest with them. I don't try to ignore their disease and I give them hope when everyone else has given up on them.

31 MARCH 2005
WATER

Water makes up 60% of the human body. Drink five liters a day and you can resist Malaria. Dig down 15 feet by the side of your mud hut in Béré and you have a contaminated water source. Dig down 90 feet at your hospital and you have pure water. A mango tree stays green in a dry, *Tchadian* wasteland by sending deep roots into an underground reservoir. The tree then uses that water to produce the world's best fruit in the middle of the dry season in sub-Saharan African. Those water-filled mangos nourish kids left to hunt and gather for their daily bread. They won't starve as long as long as they can throw stones, climb precariously weak branches or wield a bamboo rod with a wooden hook on the end. Of course, it helps if they don't fall and break their jaw or leg. But even a wired jaw won't keep a kid from somehow eating mangos and grinning at the doctor with mango fibers stuck all through his wires.

Plip, plop. Plip, plop. Can it be? Yes, rain. It never rains in March in Béré except right before 16 foreigners arrive to camp out for ten days having been assured that they won't get rained on. In the end, the rain doesn't come. The 16 volunteers from California survive the heat, dirt, packs of kids and limited food supplies.

A hose carries water half way to their building site. They use the hose to fill buckets. Half the water spills out of the buckets on its bumpy pushcart ride to the job site. The water is mixed with cement and sand to make mortar. The watery mortar is placed between home-fired mud bricks and a new building emerges from the mud. At the end of their stay, water falls from the sky for ten minutes, temporarily cooling their Malaria-induced feverish brows.

VOLUNTEERS FROM CALI

Three major operations are performed during the group's visit. Sterile water mixed with salt flows through a tube and into a vein in the patient's arm. This intravenous access allows an anesthetic medication to flow into his blood letting him survive the surgery without feeling pain. The water then flows through his blood, is filtered in his kidneys and comes back out mixed with waste products in his urine. That same sterile salt water is poured into the wounds before closing, diluting the bacteria and preventing infections. The bloody, vomit covered OR floor is then doused with water and pushed down the drain. The instruments are washed with water and then sterilized with heated water under pressure in an autoclave.

I approach the river between Béré and Lai. I have five people inside the truck with me and there are 15 hanging on in the back. They are covered from head to foot in red dust and diesel exhaust. We've just come from the bush church in Kalmé. All of us are looking forward to refreshing ourselves with a swim in the water. As white bodies emerge in swimming suits to descend down the small cliffs to the tiny beaches along the river, we draw quite a crowd of gawkers, mostly children. Cries of *"Nasara! Nasara!"* welcome us in the usual *Tchadian* way.

I'm one of the first to crash down the sandy bank, rip off my shirt and plunge into the cool, flowing Logone River. I feel it envelop me, cleanse me, cool me, free me, energize me. I pop to the surface and swim against the strong current the short distance to the shallow sandbar, which dominates the middle of the river. I lay on the bottom with just my head sticking up, fighting the swiftness of the water streaming past.

The others soon join me with a football and two Frisbees. This attracts a swarm of naked boys like flies in a hospital ward. They are naked and unashamed, except when standing when they feel obliged to cover up with a single, cupped hand. The end of the sandbar drops sharply from one foot to about ten feet deep. This allows for spectacular diving catches of appropriately thrown footballs. Soon kids are swarming, splashing, diving, thrashing, clambering, jumping, yelling, catching, tossing awkwardly, smiling, and laughing.

Still wet from the swim, I jump back in to drive back to dry, dusty Béré. Just beneath the surface rests enough water to irrigate the entire area and keep it green and productive year round. Instead, we appear to be in a desert, by definition an area without much water.

02 APRIL 2005
HEAT

I have never known what heat was until now. I thought that maybe living in Florida qualified me as an expert. Maybe visiting the deserts of southern California or living on the Amazon would give me some credibility. I imagined that maybe after a year in sub-Saharan Africa I'd have idea about being hot. But now, I know that I knew nothing. There is a reason why Béré is in the part of Africa called the Sa-HELL.

The temperature is over 130 degrees. A cool evening is 96 degrees inside. Sweat is my constant companion. In surgery, with the air conditioner running full blast I soak my scrubs and drip sweat onto my patients despite my best efforts to keep a sterile field. Drinking water becomes my obsession. I feel a strong desire to fall to all fours and join the goats at the salt lick. Sleeping is impossible, as I must flip my pillow every half hour to let the soaked side dry out. The stillness of the night with its hanging heat and dust weighs me down.

The newly remodeled clinic building is a little cooler with its aluminum roof instead of galvanized steel. Running the generator during the day instead of at night lets us use the ceiling fans bringing a little relief. Amazingly, a hand crafted clay jar makes our drinking water comparatively cool. Not having a fridge means food doesn't last. But we don't feel like eating anyway.

Sarah manages to find some ice in the vaccine fridge today. I have a brief epiphany of joy as the ice-cold water flows into me. The only other relief is the ecstasy of placing my sweat soaked face and hair in front of the air conditioner after surgery. I rest my head about five inches from the vents and let the cool air pour over me until the generator is shut off. Then, it's back, suffocating, unrelieved by wind or night, the searing heat that is life in Béré.

08 APRIL 2005
SCROTUM

"I just don't get it, why would anyone want to keep something like that at home?" Lona echoes all our thoughts as we stare at the man's crotch.

I have been called in as usual in the middle of the night for an *urgence*. The man complains of pain in his groin starting yesterday. I ask him a few questions.

"You never had any problems before?"

"No, it just came on suddenly."

"No vomiting?"

"No. It just hurts, bad."

The man is lying on an exam table wearing nothing but a wrap-around skirt with a large bulge between his legs. As he gingerly lifts up his skirt, I see a two-football sized scrotum emerge into view.

Hydroceles are collections of fluid around the testicles usually caused

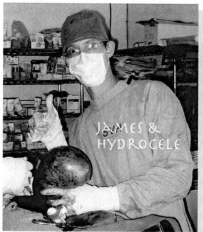
JAMES & HYDROCELE

by filarial worms clogging up the lymphatic drainage. I just stare in awe. I mean, we often make jokes about the size of the hydroceles that we see here, but this one is by far the biggest! Obviously, this didn't happen over the last few days!

I hospitalize him and schedule surgery for the next day. During the operation I remove three liters of straw colored fluid. I'm forced to hack off a ten-inch chunk of scrotal skin with hydrocele membranes attached. I then have to suture the remaining membrane behind the testicle and somehow manage to get the rest of the skin back together. Afterwards, it is far from aesthetically pleasing. However, at least he can wear his skirt easily and walk without waddling bowlegged.

The next guy I see doesn't have a hydrocele. It would be less complicated if he did. His scrotum is only about the size of a large grapefruit. The mass appeared suddenly and he started vomiting. Now, he's writhing in pain. He had a hernia operated on years ago on the same side. It started coming back over the last two years. He's always been able to push it back in until now.

His inguinal area is bulging out all the way down into the scrotum. I can hear bowel sounds with my stethoscope and even see the peristalsis of the intestines through the scrotal skin. I knock him out with Ketamine and Valium, but can't reduce the hernia.

I rush him to the OR, prep, scrub, drape, and start the operation. I slash in a diagonal across the mass and dissect down into the hernia sac. I find the small intestine, the cecum, and the appendix inside. All of them are looking a little dusky from being strangulated. Even after opening the sac, the bowel won't go back in. Finally, I use scissors to cut through the muscle making the hernia bigger. I see the intestine get pink again as blood flows back in. Finally, I can reduce the abdominal contents and close the hernia.

The third sac of the week belongs to a young man with a small orange-sized hernia that has been irreducible for the last five hours. He comes in at 11 p.m.. I'm exhausted and don't want to have to operate that night. Samedi injects the Ketamine and Valium. I push. I manipulate. I massage. I wring. I force. I drip great, big piles of sweat all over him.

I twist and pry and prod until my hands, arms and fingers are cramping. I don't see any progress after an hour. I pray. I implore. I beg. I continue in desperation. I don't feel I have the strength. Slowly, I feel wiggling and hear gurgling. The hernia starts to go in. Samedi takes over for a while. We persist for 20 more minutes and the hernia is finally reduced.

That's the beauty of the scrotum!

09 APRIL 2005
DARKNESS

Suddenly, it's pitch black. It happens every night around 8 p.m.. Shortly thereafter there is also quiet as the generator shuts down. For some reason, tonight is darker than usual. It's like being in a cave, turning off your flashlight and trying to see your hand in front of your face. Sarah and I sit patiently waiting with the other volunteers. Someone lights a match.

But what about the darkness inside me? What about the blackness squeezing out any light from my soul?

Death has struck again. If you've wondered where that dark hooded guy with the sickle over his shoulder hangs out in his spare time, it's Béré.

I'm standing on the porch talking to two teenagers. André walks up.

"Our president is dead." At first, I think he means *Tchad's* President. André soon clarifies. "The president of our Mission."

I met Pastor Herimanana at an HIV conference last October in Cameroon. A down-to-earth guy, he had a real heart for the sick and hurting, especially those suffering from HIV/AIDS.

Thursday, he finished his visa paperwork in Yaoundé. He was on his way to Douala to catch his flight to *Tchad,* when the driver lost control of the bus. He was killed instantly.

André keeps hitting one hand with his other hand crying out *"C'est pas possible, c'est pas possible!"*

The darkness descends.

I hear in morning report today that the little Arab boy with the burn on his chest isn't doing well. His mom bugged the night nurse three times to go get the *Nasara,* meaning me. We all had a good laugh.

On rounds, Sarah comes up and says the boy is yellow all over and his belly is hard. I'll be to see him in a few minutes when I finish with the other patients.

Five minutes later, I hear a small child scream and wail. I look outside. The cute little sister of our young patient is running around, throwing herself on the ground with the most heart-rending cries. A nurse comes to say the boy has died.

The boy's been with us for weeks. He'd come in dehydrated after a month of home treatment for burns on his chest, arms, hands and feet. But he was getting better. A few days ago, he was a chubby, happy baby. His two little sisters love to play with Sarah and hang all over their doting, Muslim dad. He always has crackers in his pockets where even the littlest child can find them.

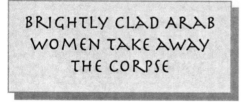

BRIGHTLY CLAD ARAB WOMEN TAKE AWAY THE CORPSE

A large group of brightly clad Arab women in head scarves comes in crying to take away the corpse. The mourning sounds like laughter until I look at their stricken faces. The oldest little sister bangs her head on the ground, tears streaming down her cheeks. A nurse tries to keep her from hurting herself by placing her head in the absorbent lap of an aunt.

The once happy baby is now a rapidly cooling body lying on his back, eyes staring into the darkness.

I return to rounds and stare blankly at the floor for a while. None of the patients or staff says a word. They must wonder what the problem is. People die all the time. It's a part of life, a part I just can't get used to.

A few minutes later, the business manager of our health district comes in. He pulls me aside to inform me that our newly appointed *chef* of the child vaccination program died yesterday of AIDS. The nurse in charge of supervision of the health centers, Dagal, also just died of AIDS. Dagal was a scoundrel, but at the same time I'd hear him occasionally mention God. It was as if his life was a struggle between two warring factions fighting for his soul. Who knows who won in the end? Right now it seems like the darkness is getting the upper hand.

I stumble on, groping, in the darkness of my thoughts. I find a little inner strength and somehow finish rounds. I head to my office where André hands me a letter from one of our nurses' aides, Rahama.

She wants to take her husband to see one of the more powerful witch doctors in the area. I call in Rahama and we decide to go to her house. Samedi joins us. We soon find ourselves walking through the dusty streets, past Samedi and Anatole's mud brick houses, around the corner near the big mango tree, through the hole in the mud wall and onto the mat under the large shade tree in Rahama's courtyard.

Rahama's husband, Kemkoye, invites us to sit. We do. Samedi and I are wearing matching light blue scrubs. Kemkoye has a brightly colored shirt on. His face is an expressionless puzzle. I start the conversation.

"I must warn you about going to the witch doctor. Not only are you unlikely to find a lasting solution for your eye, but you're messing with dangerous, and real, forces of darkness. Is it worth it, even to find a little relief? Or as Jesus said years ago, to gain the world and lose your soul?"

The mask stares past me. The red, cloudy eye pierces the darkness of a corner of the courtyard. He hedges and bets, never changing the expressionless tone of his voice.

"I can't afford to go to the ophthalmologist."

"In two days we're going to N'Djamena. We can take you free of charge to Kousseri. There's some ophthalmologists from *Médecins Sans Frontières* there, just across the Cameroonian border. I'll take you there personally."

Kemkoye doesn't want to be convinced. Samedi says a few words. Half an hour later we leave with him at least willing to consider our offer.

At 2 p.m., I see Rahama again. She enters my office. Her face is a storm cloud of darkness. Abruptly, she spurts it all out.

"Kemkoye insists on going to the witch doctor. I have to go with him." Rahama rises to go. "I'm at the breaking point. I'm so discouraged."

Her face confirms it. She is hopeless.

"Pray for us *beaucoup*." As the door is about to close behind her, she turns and says, "It's in your hands now, *docteur*." Without a look behind her, she heads off into the increasing darkness of a sunny day.

I find myself that afternoon curled up in a ball on my mattress in the corner of my room. Music coming from the computer across the room tries to soothe my mind in vain. The pillow is wet. It's neither sweat nor Malaria this time. My tears are flowing. The sobs almost strangle me. They are the cries of an uncomprehending soul desperately seeking answers. I close my eyes. I've got a few answers from here before. Let me try again in desperation. Tossing and turning, I cry out in the midst of my own present darkness.

15 APRIL 2005
LIVING QUARTERS

My living room in Béré is simple. There are holes in the ceiling over the table in the corner. In the rainy season we put pots on the table to collect the drips. The table is covered with fake plants, a kerosene lantern, a laptop computer, a satellite phone, a calendar, a box with corks, a clay pot with notes inside from people who've borrowed money and a straw basket woven locally and filled with pens, rubber bands, paper clips and various other odds and ends.

A woven wicker waste basket sits to the side. A metal file cabinet with no door and a few shelves has been converted into a bookshelf containing Christian books in French, a *Tchadian Arabic Dictionary* and grammar book, CDs, DVDs, surfing magazines and a few odds and ends like *Don Quixote* in the original Spanish, *A Tale of Two Cities, Perspectives on the World Christian Movement, The Gospel According to Biff—Christ's Childhood Pal*, and Spanish playing cards.

In the corner are three African drums of various sizes, a guitar case, a car battery, a rusty machete, a broom, sandals and a few odd clay pots. A wicker couch covered with a curtain, a small table in the other corner, four chairs and a coffee table complete the furnishings. Two *Nangjeré* throwing knifes, a safari hat and various postcards adorn the otherwise bare, white walls.

From outside the front door comes the sound of an old typewriter painstakingly tapped by André on his porch across the courtyard. A metal, rebar frame on the verandah houses a sagging, limp mosquito net. The cement railing has chipped paint and many missing blocks leaving some suspended virtually in mid air.

Out the side window one hears the twittering of birds, scratching of chickens and the mumbling of kids at play. A bare, dirt yard has piles of raked weeds and leaves ready for burning and smoldering piles and ashes from this morning's fire. Several guava trees have cracked leftover bricks arranged in something resembling circles around their trunks so they can be watered. An old clothesline is currently bare of its usually brightly-colored African clothes or drab hospital scrubs. A rooster and a hen with her chicks scratch at the base of the newly watered trees.

The recently built wall is made of locally fashioned and fired mud bricks with sand-heavy mortar up to about three feet high where a thick, chain-link fence takes over. The heads of children are barely visible on the other side where they have gathered to drink from the hose draped over the bricks and through the chain-link to the outside. Some sort of game with a small, deformed ball is being played to the side. An older boy rides by on a rickety bike with a hundred pound sack of rice tied to the back.

Behind the kids is our neighbor's stack of newly fired bricks. The mud bricks were assembled in a rough pyramid with holes on the outside layer and underneath where sticks were shoved and lit. All night long the family and neighbors gathered around the warm glow until morning brought a blackened outside crust housing bright red, fired bricks within. The neighbors' mud brick, thatched houses weathered by years of rain rest just behind the fence. They almost seem like a part of the natural landscape, unlike our cement and tin roofed behemoths and rude metal fencing.

OUR HOUSE

The elementary school is a few hundred yards off the corner of our fence, abandoned now in the hot, 120-degree *Tchadian* afternoon. Everything seems oppressed by the heat. Even the air seems afraid to move lest it start to sweat or expend too much energy in providing its wind. The only thing unrestrained by the heat is the universally boundless energy of the kids, one of whom hangs casually off the chain-link while the rest have changed games slightly, now tossing the ball in the air in a circle with who knows what objective.

Leading three cattle, a man walks out of the hole in the neighbor's wall that serves as a door. The cattle have huge, floppy humps between their shoulders and three-foot-long curved horns. A chain or rope through the nose allows these otherwise unpredictable steers to be guided even by a child. The man leads them off for some undetermined task: perhaps hauling wood, carrying bricks, pulling a cart, or just to be watered and grazed.

In the kitchen, Sarah sits at her desk with white lace curtains behind her. She is intently flipping through pages scratching her neck with a pen. Her hair has been pulled up tightly and she wears a tank top in a vain attempt to escape some of the heat. A rooster crows. Ephraim calls for his papa. A boy runs past the fence with a stick pushing a rolling metal lid. The briefest of winds evaporates the sweat running down my back providing temporary refreshment.

The hospital is quiet but at any moment that dreaded clap-clap could appear on the porch in the form of a scrub-wearing, white-coated nurse calling me forth from my Malaria-induced musings back into the world of the Béré Adventist Hospital.

26 APRIL 2005
GETTING CLOSE

It's kind of strange. I only really get close to patients if they have problems severe enough to keep them hospitalized for a long time.

There's Marty, the fisherman bit by the hippo. We still keep in touch. It seems every time I go to swim at a certain spot I see him. Last Saturday, he stopped by to give Sarah and me some fish he'd caught. Apparently, he's back fishing the lake with the hippos. But that friendship was at the cost of excruciating daily dressing changes on a two-foot long, six-inch deep wound on his buttocks.

Gai, the tall, lanky young man with one lung also sees us often at another swimming hole we frequent. He's usually off hunting with his bush knife but stops to say hello. He stops by the hospital from time to time as well and we're always glad to see him. He became our friend because of living with a chest tube for weeks, having his chest cracked in the OR with placement of a second chest tube and being hooked up to a crude suction machine every night when the power came on.

Clement and Angeline, the unlikely couple of kids with twin infected left tibias are too little and too cute. They've spent months off and on at the hospital as we desperately fight their sneaky, malicious infections. They are still being casted and we've tried so many different surgeries with very little gain we sometimes wonder if they'll ever walk normally again. But we've seen them grow up from shy little babies to mischievous children. Clement loves to sing and follow Sarah around the hospital on his little crutch. Angeline loves to help Sarah keep the patients' visitors in line by squirting everyone with a syringe full of water.

The list could go on and on: people brought into our lives through painful circumstances and suffering who somehow change us and become part of us through the process.

Currently, there's Suzanne and Yvonne. After a year of virtually no wound infections we were faced with two consecutive C-sections that turned into catastrophic post-op nightmares. Suzanne came first. Hers was a simple routine C-section except that the child was difficult to resuscitate and died two days later. She had a normal post-op course but then came back a week later with a pus coming out of her wound, diarrhea, and a distended abdomen.

The receiving nurse started her on antibiotics and treated her for Malaria. She started to improve. I saw her a day later and opened the wound up more, as there appeared to be an abscess inside. Overall, she was doing well, walking and eating.

Fifteen minutes after I opened the wound, her husband came running to find me.

"My wife just had a ton of diarrhea. Come and look, doctor."

I went and found her standing in a puddle of foul smelling fluid.

"What happened?" I asked.

"I don't know," she replied. "It came from my wound."

We took her to the OR and ended up having to open up her abdomen, which was filled with pus and inflammatory debris. She was left with a huge inverted T-shaped wound open in the midline down to the base of the uterus.

CLEMENT

She's been here over six weeks and has recuperated nicely with only a small portion of her wound still to close. Unfortunately, she has developed a nasty bed sore on her sacrum. Sarah and I have become close friends with Suzanne and her mom. They don't speak French and I don't speak *Nangjeré*, but our non-verbal communication is enough. They joke that Sarah needs to give me more back rubs since I work too hard.

Just a few days after Suzanne came in with her wound infection, Yvonne came in with almost exactly the same thing. You'll remember that she is the woman infected with HIV who gave birth to twins by C-section. We took her to the OR, washed out the wound, put in drains and are doing dressing changes daily.

We helped Yvonne get formula from the Catholics so the twins wouldn't get HIV from the mom's breast milk. They did fine for about a month and we grew quite fond of them. They named them James and David after me and my twin brother. David was always the stronger one.

Unfortunately, David and James developed diarrhea and Malaria at the same time. In a strange parallel to my own life, David died after two days while the weaker James pulled through and is doing fine. I guess now I have two twin boys named David to look forward to seeing again some day.

05 MAY 2005
A TALE

I feel lost in a story that seems to be flying by. It's moving, intense, captivating, and exhausting. Each page is turned so fast I can only catch enough glimpses to get the general idea of what's going on. Yet, each page once turned is permanently turned; I can't go back.

A woman has been in labor for two days. She was seen last night by a retired health care worker and sent to us this morning. Her baby's too big. The head is all molded and almost sticking out. But it's just skin on his head that has been squeezed out. The skull won't fit through.

I have been called from my breakfast. I run to the OR. I grab a syringe, anesthetic, an instrument box, a scalpel, a urinary catheter and some gauze and gloves. I rush back. I shave, prep, and slice down to her pubic bone. I start to cut through the cartilage. The scalpel breaks inside. I can't find it. I yell for a flashlight and another scalpel. I mop up the blood with the gauze. I call for some nursing help. Lona and Rahama each grab a leg. I cut deeper, going by feel. I tell the nurses to pull her legs apart. I hear a crack and feel her pelvis widen at the front.

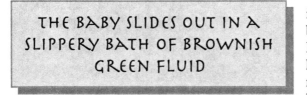

THE BABY SLIDES OUT IN A SLIPPERY BATH OF BROWNISH GREEN FLUID

The baby slides out in a slippery bath of brownish green fluid. He's huge, has a slow heartbeat and poor muscle tone. He never breathes. Despite CPR and resuscitation for ten minutes he never cries. He's dead.

Meanwhile Lona has delivered the placenta and casually says she's bleeding. I'm compressing the baby's chest between my fingers and thumbs, desperately trying to circulate some blood. I look and see that Lona has draped gauze over the perineum. Strings of coagulated blood drip down into the green basin as the entire area turns bright red. I leave the baby. I pull off the gauze. The entire birth canal is filled with blood and a piece of tissue hanging out. I yell for more compresses. Rahama runs to get them. I cram gauze sponges inside and pull them out so I can see what's going on. Nathan has arrived and holds a flashlight over my shoulder.

It appears the cervix has completely torn itself off circumferentially and is literally hanging by a thread. I clamp the base. Then, I soak up the blood in the wound and with the flashlight try to find the piece of broken scalpel. I can't see a thing. I fish around with a needle driver and bang against something. I dab up blood and look again. I see the broken scalpel blade and pull it out. Then I irrigate the wound and suture it up. I then sew up a tear around her urethra and a small posterior laceration as well. I cut off the dangling strip of cervix, take off the clamps and am relieved to see there's no bleeding. It's taken an hour and a half.

What role do I have to play? Why am I even in this story called Hôpital Adventiste de Béré? My being in this tale is as likely as Little Orphan Annie showing up in Jaws. I get this feeling as if the other actors are whispering behind their backs, when they think I'm not looking, asking how did he get a part? And, doesn't he realize that his lines are poorly said and his acting totally out of place?

I'm called over to the TB ward. Someone's not doing well. I see one of our long-timers is in bad shape. He came from Kélo and had started to improve and put on weight. He has a congenitally deformed left arm where the hand faces the wrong way and the whole thing is too short. Yesterday, his cousin told me he had a fever, which I assumed was Malaria. Sure enough, the smear is positive. I write for Quinine and Fandsidar and forget about it.

Now, he's death warmed over. He's unconscious, gray, has a slow heart beat, his cheeks are sunken and his breathing is more like an occasional deep sigh out of reflex rather than a serious effort at obtaining oxygen. I expect him to die in front of me. I sit there and stare at him for ten minutes. If I'd only gone to see him yesterday maybe I'd have seen he was bad and been more aggressive with treatment. It's so easy to ignore the TB patients. They're hospitalized only so we can observe them taking their pills. I'm so busy. I usually see them once a week at best.

A little girl, also hospitalized with TB, is sitting at the foot of the bed weeping. She is the cutest, cheeriest, most helpful girl ever. She always yells, *"James-uh"* and waves as she passes by carrying laundry or water on her head. This week she helped us trim the mango trees wanting to saw as much as she can, even if it doesn't really do much. Now, she cries for someone she wouldn't know, except for their common disease. I feel useless. I want to cry too. I want to run home and hide. I want to be a little kid again. But I just stand there doing nothing and then walk off lamely, a blank stare on my face.

Yet, somehow, it works. Beyond all rational thought, the play goes on. The plot thickens. The suspense builds. The rivals grow to respect each other. Love is found in the most unexpected of places. Laughter pops up randomly. Joy is discovered.

A well-groomed, stocky man walks into my office with jeans, a tucked-in flannel shirt and alligator skin boots. He hands me his resume. He is the referring doctor for a patient I've just seen. I was surprised to get an official looking letter with a reference from a traditional healer that morning. He'd tried to treat her pelvic pain for three days without success. Now he's brought her to the hospital. How cool, I'd thought.

Now he's presenting me papers telling how he's met with other traditional healers from Benin and other African countries for an exchange of ideas and how they're researching traditional pharmaceuticals. I'm impressed. I ask him how he was trained. That's when things suddenly turn bizarre.

I notice he's holding a carved horn as if it was a newborn baby, tenderly and pressed against his chest. He calmly tells me that he was drowned as a child. As he was floating on the bottom, five spirits entered him and revived him. Now, they tell him which plants to use for which problems. I don't know what to say. We continue otherwise to chat as colleagues. I tell him we've found flukes in his patient's urine and have prescribed treatment. He is gracious, polite and refined. It's not at all the way I'd expected my first encounter with a witch doctor to be.

RAHAMA

We are in the midst of real spiritual forces here. A few weeks ago, after morning report, we somehow got on the topic and all the staff started recounting tales of the supernatural.

Rahama told of taking her husband into the bush to see a healer. He boiled water, made him stand in the vapor and then threw something at his eyes. Animal bones immediately flew out of her husband's eyes and fell to the ground. She was shocked but had the presence of mind to gather them up. She showed them to me the next day.

Samedi once saw two men who came by to show off their powers. One took a sharp bush knife, suddenly turned, and whacked off his companion's head. Everyone present saw it fall to the ground. Then the man picked it up and set it back on his friend's shoulders and he started talking and moving normally.

André has seen people put curses on things. If you then try to walk off with that object, you become frozen in place until the person comes back and sees who it was who was going to steal from them. The others all confirmed that this is common.

Then, there are the simple things like when my friend Job was here from N'Djamena. As he prepared to return home, he said he's never heard goats and animals make so much noise or be so bothersome. He said they must be possessed. I'd thought the same thing but was afraid of sounding silly or paranoid if I mentioned it. Why else would they poop on our porch exclusively, pee right outside our windows, bleat uncontrollably for no reason just as we fall asleep and basically do as much as possible to assure we get no rest.

Spiritual forces are palpable here. I believe that God will protect me. But can I fight to defend the others at the hospital who fear these forces? I've seen many patients die who should've lived. There is always some witchcraft or *sorcelerie* going on. As the patients say, "He's been poisoned," meaning a spell has been cast on him. Almost everyone has some charm or fetish hidden somewhere on his body to protect him. What can I do? I feel helpless and inadequate.

I wonder if, like Sam Gamgee as he wanders the wilds near Mordor, if they will write about me in the stories. Do I have an important part to play in this cosmic tale? Will I have made a difference when the curtain falls and the credits roll?

Somehow, I know that in the end, as I sit around the campfires of heaven, I will have stories to tell. People will say, tell me more about Samedi, and Lona, and Anatole and especially, about Sarah. Did you really...? Are you serious? No way!

That's what keeps me going. Especially since a place like this is beyond my most fantastic nightmares. Life begins to take on the character of a myth, a legend. I feel detached at times, looking at myself, wondering if this is reality or just another movie, a story, a tale, something someone made up. Maybe Someone did, and the ending will be beyond my wildest dreams.

30 MAY 2005
PROMENADE

Gueltir, the principal of the school, sets a brisk pace. We're walking side by side down the dusty streets of Béré. There are no street signs, no pavement, no sidewalks, no traffic lights, and no evidence that we are in the 21st century. We walk past mud brick huts. The inhabitants are lying under mango trees on woven reed mats, pounding millet in crude wooden mortar and pestles, carrying big bundles of firewood on their heads, cooking over open fires, and a host of other activities—the same things they've been doing unchanged for centuries. In essence, Béré has managed to capture timelessness. At least until a motorcycle drives by or a man crosses the path with his world-band radio blaring.

We are headed to visit one of the junior high schools in Béré. There are three in town. The first is a Catholic girls school, no boys allowed. The second is a public high school bursting at the seams with 1,500 students. Classes meet in crude mud buildings or in *hangars* built of woven reed walls and roof supported by crooked sticks stuck in the ground.

The school we are going to visit is a private junior high built in 2001. Gueltir informs me it has been all but abandoned because the owner is occupied with other things in N'Djamena. Besides, for the moment, all the teachers are on strike everywhere except at Gueltir's elementary school. None of the state salaried teachers have been paid for three months. Fortunately, with some help from the US, our teachers are paid every month on schedule which is rare in *Tchad*.

GUELTIR

We arrive at our destination. The school is pathetic. The three mud brick buildings surround a courtyard with an open, empty well in the center. To the left and to the right, the buildings have three rooms each, side by side. Straight ahead is the two-room administration building. The doors are made from thin wood frames with green painted corrugated roofing nailed on. They hang haphazardly, locked precariously with tiny padlocks that come apart when opened.

Inside, the uneven dirt floors support some rickety benches and tables leaning crazily at all different angles because of the floor. Termites have been snacking on most of the benches leaving pockmarked fragile structures waiting to collapse. Two of the walls have windows. The side facing the courtyard has windows made of the same material as the doors and they can be opened. The opposite side is made of mud bricks crisscrossed to leave openings in between for air circulation. The roofs are corrugated tin balanced on twisted sticks tied to the bricks with metal bands. One wall is painted black to serve as a chalkboard.

The ad building has one desk, a small bookshelf with a couple of empty chalk boxes on it, a sealed trunk and a locked cabinet. A small chair leans precariously against the wall. I tell Gueltir I'm amazed at the conditions. He wonders what I mean. This is luxurious compared to how he went to school under a mango tree. In fact, on the way here, we passed a school and a church that were made entirely of mats. It's not easy for a *Tchadian* to get a proper education.

We head across town passing through the market as it closes. We arrive at the house of a local *docteur choukou*. He welcomes us into his courtyard, brings out chairs, and invites us to sit. One by one the members of the household come to greet us. The women bow to the ground and extend their hand to shake with the other hand supporting it at the elbow in a sign of deep respect. Our friend's wife brings us a metal bowl of water and a table is called for.

We begin by discussing the local gossip. It appears everything is known about everyone. He wonders why I didn't leave to go to Koumra this morning with André. He thought I'd left. I just found out about it last night and decided it was too late to go. Apparently, he knew I was supposed to go before I did. We move on to the raising of ducks, how to plant fruit trees with bull horns buried beside, when the rain will come and a variety of other topics.

The pastor of the 2nd Evangelical Church joins us. He is Dimanche's father. We extend him another round of greetings and acknowledgements.

Finally, I get around to the purpose of our visit. I tactfully mention that we are all here for the health of the community and that one thing I've noticed is that kids often get referred late for treatment of Malaria. In fact, we just finished rescuing a small, one-year-old girl that had been treated by him for several days before coming to the hospital. I say that it's something in general we see that kids just don't do well with Malaria unless they're hospitalized.

He seems to understand. In fact, he seems happy at the exchange. I don't bother to mention that I think he has no right to be treating patients at all since he is not trained except in basic CPR and first aid. He's still going to continue to treat patients at his home. In fact, in the middle of the conversation, someone comes up and greets him as *docteur*. All we can do is try and help him to not hurt people.

It's getting dark. We bid goodbye. Our *docteur choukou* accompanies Gueltir and me out to the main road. Without a guide, I'd be lost in the maze of paths and huts. He promises to come see me soon at the hospital. Gueltir and I head home. We pass an outdoor cabaret. The warm rumble of muffled conversation floats over the air along with the smell of local rice and millet wine.

Surrounding the cabaret are the small-time vendors. Each has a small table with a kerosene lamp. The table is covered with small plastic sacs of tea, sugar, detergent, or peanut oil along with cigarettes, small crackers and various other items. Overhead is a mat supported on four sticks poking into the ground. Business is booming. We continue on through the dark streets bereft of any artificial light until we see the fluorescent glow of the hospital through the trees and we know we are home.

13 AUGUST 2005
ALL THINGS NEW

We're on our way back. I feel a strange mix of fear, excitement, anxiety, courage, hope, wonder, tentativeness and anticipation. After two months in the USA, Sarah and I are back in *Tchad.*

Arriving in N'Djamena, I am struck by a profound sense of change in the air. Not just because of the time change, the culture change, or the first world to third world change. No, things really are happening in the *Tchadian* capital. We enter the airport and find everything under construction. The days are cool and rainy. Everything has turned green, transformed by the wet season. We'd left a desert. We find an oasis. Even the trash and smells seem content to be temporarily hidden behind the new life bursting all around us.

Sarah and I arrive with a colleague of mine from medical school, Troy Dickson, and his wife, Kim. We meet Pastor Job at the airport. Feeling like the returning prodigal son, I'm thrilled with his warm embrace. We register Troy and Kim with the national security counsel. Then, Job, Bichara and I take the truck to the Grand Central Mosque to change money.

Looking for our usual black market contact, we circle the one-way street counterclockwise around the center of Islamic culture in N'Djamena. Sure enough, our man emerges from the crowd of white-robed, white-capped African Arabs reclining on mats in front of an empty storefront.

"As-salaam aleikum, " I greet him in Arabic.

"Wa aleikum as-salaam. " he replies. "How are you, my friend? Come, let's have some Cokes together."

Bichara closes and locks the truck, while Job and I march off following our regular black market moneychanger. We remove our shoes, cross the mats between the reclining Muslims and into the empty cement room at the back. We relax on our mats as another dignified Arab brings us our sodas. I carefully sip mine as we make small talk. I tell about my trip. They discuss what is happening in N'Djamena and around the country. Apparently the roads are getting paved, the President was sick in France but has recovered and is back in town, and business is improving slowly.

After 15 minutes or so, I remark that I have some money to change. I ask what the going price is. I say I'd heard we were up to 530 francs per dollar. Job quickly pipes up with, "560 per dollar". Our friend immediately agrees to 530. Thus begins the bargaining. Finally, we seem at an impasse at 540. We aren't satisfied. I pull out the calculator and do some quick figures.

"*Mon ami,* you will make 400,000 francs on this deal at 540 per dollar. You will admit that is a lot. If you give it to us at 550 you will still make 200,000 francs. Not bad for a few minutes work, huh?"

He smiles broadly and nods while motioning with his hand to give him the dollars. We count it all out. I put the francs in a brown paper bag and stuff it to the bottom of my backpack. We rise to leave.

"*Au revoir!*" our friend wishes us well, waving as we get in the truck.

"*Agodt afé!*" I reply in *Tchadian* Arabic. We head directly to the bank to deposit the money. The black market has saved us approximately $2,000 that would've been lost to the bank and we've established a valuable relationship.

At the airport that night, we pick up the two medical students, Carol and Sara, who've arrived for a summer internship. We leave for Béré the next morning. In those brief days in N'Djamena, I have heard some disquieting rumors making me anxious to get back to Béré and the hospital.

We enter Kélo by the southern roundabout instead of by the back way through the market. The landscape has been incredible: luscious green plains, full rivers, millet, rice, corn and other crops pushing

> THE TWO CLOSEST HOSPITALS ARE SHUT DOWN AND OUR STAFF IS AT HALF STRENGTH

up toward the deep blue sky dotted with puffy, white clouds. The only thing missing is herds of antelope, zebras, giraffes and elephants. We leave the pavement in Kélo plunging into the red mud of the road. The numerous puddles spray the truck with a slimy red film. This route takes us by the public hospital. The rumors are true. It is closed. Not a single person can be seen in or around its dark buildings.

The government health care workers are on strike. They haven't been paid in five months. Kélo and Lai, the two hospitals closest to Béré, are completely shut down. Our staff is at half strength with only three nurses and one lab tech. We have gone back to *Tchadian* civil war era times with the three veterans, Anatole, Samedi, and Lona, holding down the fort as they have for so many years.

Even with this grim news, I feel a sense of excitement continue to build as we approach Béré. I recognize everything, yet it's all changed. I missed the rain's usual slow transformation of the landscape. When I left, the temperature was 130 degrees and the countryside was a brown, lifeless desert. Now, two months later, I enter green tropical paradise with 70-80 degree weather. I find myself excitedly talking non-stop to Troy, Kim, Sara and Carol about all the things I've experienced over the last year and a half. I am coming home.

We stop eight kilometers from Béré to see the hippos. We climb out and down to the edge of the river. Not 100 yards away are eight large hippos showing off with grunts, gap-toothed yawns and impressive lunges out of the water. Slowly, some local passers-by stop to see the strangers. We chat easily about the rains, the crops, and meanness of the hippo in general. Someone mentions Marty, the fisherman bit by one of these same hippos over a year ago. Apparently, they all know him and are eager to report on his continued good health.

We hit the road, cross the river on the barge, and slosh through the muddy roads till we see the *Bienvenue à Béré* sign. Just ahead, the hospital's water tower is visible over the mango trees in the distance. I feel an indescribable combination of chills, warmth and the overwhelming desire to cry, run, and laugh all at the same time.

As we pull in we see some of the staff in front of the church on benches. Friday evening worship is in full swing. They wave furiously and get up hurriedly to meet us in front of the house. André's grin stretches from ear to ear as he emerges from behind a large, 40-foot blue container sitting on our front lawn. He is shaking his head in joy as he embraces me with the biggest bear hug ever. In fact he can't stop laughing and hugging me. The others crowd around shaking hands, smiling, asking a million questions a minute. Bichara tries to stoically take charge of unloading our bags through the general pandemonium. I glance over at the hospital and see two beautiful outdoor bathrooms for the patients and staff and a new walkway linking Pediatrics and the rest of the hospital.

André manages to get in a few words. "We weren't sure if we'd be able to finish the roofs or not...the container...what a challenge...God held back the rains as we struggled to unload all day...just after reloading it poured down...the strike...Lona, Anatole, Samedi, David...working hard...we've been blessed with the new government nurse, Josué...you can't believe what a leader he is..." And he rambles on and on.

I verify later, the roofs on the hospital ward, labor and delivery and operating room have all been repaired. My heart is filled with joy. Everyone has pulled through in my absence. Without a doctor and at half-strength they have managed to not only keep the status quo, but have made a huge steps forward. André sits me down two days later and explains all the important decisions, resolution of staff conflicts and other administrative things he's done since I've been gone. My heart swells with gratitude.

19 AUGUST 2005
NUMB

I stare blankly at the small hand and arm. I sit on a stool in front of a delivery bed. My hands hang at my side. My whole body feels heavy. My eyes would close if they could to banish the sight forever from my consciousness.

Before me, on the floor sits a large, blue plastic basin. In the basin are some bloody pieces of gauze, a few blood clots and a disembodied arm and hand. The arm is perfect. The nails, the tiny fingers, the palm creases, the forearm and elbow are all perfect. The only deformity is deep purple color of the skin and the fact that there is no accompanying body. I sit here numb in front of the arm's mother waiting for the rest of "it" to come out. As the minutes drag by, my mind drifts.

I am pulled to the door by a rattling banging of fist on metal. My wife, Sarah, has left for N'Djamena. The monsoon rains pound the tin roof mercilessly. Keining, the night watchman, stands outside all but swallowed up in a bright yellow rain slicker.

"*Bon soir*, Keining."

He doesn't reply, just reaches solemnly into his jacket and pulls out the worn half of a paper notebook we call a *carnet* or portable medical record.

I take if from Keining's outstretched hand and read inside. Young woman. First pregnancy. Dates unknown. Bleeding since 4 p.m., two hours ago. Cervix dilated at 3-4 cm. IV started with normal saline. Refer to the doctor.

I give the carnet back to Keining. "*J'arrive.*"

I pull on my scrubs. So much for a quiet, rainy evening reading in my favorite chair. I go next door and quickly down some cold spaghetti and eggplant sauce. I tell the medical students, Carol and Sara, I'm going to the hospital and they can join me if they want.

I slip on my sandals, pull my hooded sweatshirt low and step into the downpour. The ground has disappeared. I slosh through water up to my ankles following the moonlight splayed across a million tiny circles splashing on the surface. It is a lovely dream about to become a nightmare.

I reach the shelter of the overhang beside the operating room. I enter the hospital ward turning right into the tiny labor and delivery room. The first surprise is that I see Rahama there. I think how nice of her to come help at night. She never does that. Samedi is with a small, frightened girl. She is completely naked. Her legs sprawl at weird angles on the table. Pools of blood stretch along each side of the bed. Blood clots and a few pieces of gauze are lying between her legs. She writhes but doesn't really speak.

I ask how far along she is. Rahama replies that she's about four months. I then realize that this is Rahama's daughter. Samedi is just finishing putting in the IV. The IV fluids drip in. I ask for gloves. Normally there are always gloves in Labor and Delivery. There are none tonight. I inexplicably start to become very nasty. I start to talk coldly to Rahama and Samedi asking how come there can be no gloves. When I left on vacation there was a ton. I tell them cruelly how they always just use stuff up. I feel very out of control and realize it, but somehow don't care. I am bothered, frustrated, and in over my head.

Samedi rushes off to the *garde* room and brings me some gloves. I try to examine inside the girl. She won't move into the right position. She doesn't understand French. Then, she doesn't seem to understand the translation. She fights and squirms. I can't even begin to examine her. I start to yell at her.

"Don't you understand we're trying to help you! A little cooperation would be nice!"

Rahama starts to yell at her, too. Nothing. We struggle. Rahama starts to slap her. Finally, I can examine her. There are clots but no real active bleeding. Must be an incomplete abortion.

I run out to get the instruments to do a curettage. The rain intensifies. I give Samedi a urinary catheter to put in her. He can't get it in. I try to help without gloves getting blood all over my hand. I call for gloves. There are none. There is no gauze. I wash my hands off.

Samedi continues to struggle with the catheter. I start to rain down deprecations on the entire lack of adequate staff and materials and how can we work under these conditions. Samedi has no luck. Carol brings me some gloves. I finally get the catheter in. The girl has continued to struggle and get hit in the face by Rahama.

We turn the girl on her side to prepare for a spinal anesthetic. The spinal needle won't go in. The puncture starts to bleed. We have no gauze. Medical student Sara runs to surgery. I wait, seething. I wipe off the blood and am able to get the anesthesia at last. The girl quickly relaxes and actually falls asleep during the rest of the procedure. She's exhausted.

I am able to examine her easily now and after dilating the cervix discover that the fetus is more like 7 months than 4. I can't do a D&C. We listen for fetal heart tones. There are none. On exam it feels like a breech presentation. I try to deliver the first leg and after pulling it out, find it's really the arm. Now I'm stuck.

This position will never allow the dead fetus to come out. I don't want to do a C-section since the baby's already dead. I try to push the arm back in. The humerus cracks, but it goes in. I try to turn the infant inside. No luck. I feel sick at the thought that enters my head. I might have to pull it out piece by piece. I reach inside.

The arm is out again. It is a deep bluish purple and perfect. I grab some scissors and cut through the skin. Three cuts and I'm through. I drop the arm and it spins in slow motion through the air before bouncing in the bottom of the basin splashing up a few drops of dark blood.

> I DROP THE ARM AND IT SPINS IN SLOW MOTION THROUGH THE AIR

I reach inside and am able to pull the head down. It has been doubled almost completely backwards over the baby's little back. What now? The cervix is still only 5 cm dilated. I place my hand on her uterus through the abdominal wall and feel only rare uterine contractions. I stop, dejected, and stare blankly at the small, detached arm and hand in the blue basin on the floor in the pool of blood, clots and gauze sponges.

We send Keining, the night watchman, to find Anatole. We need to get Oxytocin from the lab fridge. The girl still sleeps. Rahama sits quietly.

"I don't know what I'm going to do," Rahama says, looking at me. "The expense for all this falls on me and I don't know what I'll do."

Rahama always lives in debt, barely scraping by, getting advances on her salary to try and feed her husband, kids and relatives who depend on her. With the famine, the increased prices and her own crops from last year being burned up, she lives in constant anxiety about how to make ends meet. This is the straw that may break the proverbial camel's back. I sense her desperation.

The Oxytocin arrives. The girl awakes. She is shivering only covered by a thin sheet. I grab my sweatshirt and lay it on her. Rahama tries to protest saying it'll get all bloody. I say not to worry about it. The girl snuggles under and goes back to sleep. I stay for 45 minutes with my hand on the uterus monitoring the contractions. I adjust the oxytocin drip until she has regular, intermittent contractions with normal relaxation.

Rahama has washed the instruments. The blood still lies pooled on the floor and table but has started to dry. Rahama says she'll monitor her closely now to make sure the contractions don't get out of hand.

I head back home. The rain has stopped. My feet have become pickled in my soggy shoes. The puddles are still there. My forearm and hands are cramping from reaching trying to pull and tug and turn a dead baby. My mind has effectively walled it off so that I'm still in dreamland. I continue to slosh home, wash up and crash into an empty bed. I have a feeling of emptiness so complete that I can't even think of anything to worry about. I fall into a deep, troubled sleep.

04 SEPTEMBER 2005
SPEAKING IN TONGUES

Speaking in tongues would come in real handy right now. Soon after Jesus left them, his disciples were given the instantaneous ability to speak fluently languages they'd never known before. That was a long time ago. Here and now I just struggle along hoping to understand a few words of what's said around me.

Chad has 130 languages and dialects and two official languages: French and *Tchadian* Arabic. Before coming to *Tchad*, I thought if I could just learn French I'd have no further linguistic difficulties. Who wants to learn some obscure language anyway? Well, after almost two years in *Tchad*, that would be me.

Many of our hospital staff speak at least five languages including French, Arabic and a smattering of local languages. The dialects heard commonly, if not daily, at the hospital are Nangjeré, Moundang, Fulani and Ngambai.

Without Rahama I'm lost. I call a patient in. It's a Fulani woman. She is dressed in brightly colored frilly blouse and wide skirt. She has dreads, a nose ring, and multiple leather pouch fetishes hanging around her neck. She carries a baby strapped on her back with another bright cloth that completely clashes but somehow seems right. Her husband is wearing a tattered light blue *jallabiya* with a white turban wrapped amply around his head and neck. I begin.

"*As-salaam aleikum.*"

"*Wa aleikum as-salaam.*"

"*Inti afé?*"

The woman then spouts off in Foufouldé, the language of the Fulani. Her husband translates into *Tchadian* Arabic. Rahama translates into French, which I usually understand. Rahama has the gift of interpretation. She's done it long enough that she knows the answer I'm looking for. So, if the person doesn't answer the question correctly or doesn't understand she'll clarify until the right answer comes. Many people will just directly translate the words instead of interpreting the meaning. Eventually, I am able to diagnose and treat the woman.

I go on rounds. I've heard certain things translated enough that I have picked up some key *Nangjeré* phrases. I approach a one and a half year old with Malaria and start my questioning.

"*Ba ma balou ga?*" (Has he vomited, upchucked, heaved, honked, ralphed, lost his lunch, tossed his cookies, puked, blown chunks, or spewed?)

"*Balou ddi.*" (None of the above.)

"*Ba ma sua kouba?*" (Does he breastfeed?)

The child's mother responds with a nod and a click in the throat.

"*Ká ka kang ga?*" (Any more IV fluids left?)

"*Kang ddi.*" (Nothing.)

"*Xalas, ma ere 'ya bba.*" (Treatment's done, go home.)

Then, grandma comes in and starts to greet me in *Nangjeré* in the long drawn out African style. All I can do is smile and say, "*lapia*" over and over without understanding a thing.

FULANI CHILDREN

Gueltir knocks on the door. He's arrived to give me my first official *Nangjeré* lesson. We start with the *Cantique Nangjeré*. I can sing a ton of songs, but not understand a word. I think it's time to change that. We start with the blessing at the front. It's only four short lines. One hour later, we are both exhausted trying to help me understand it.

The problem is that *Nangjeré* is very simple and grammatically different from English or French. Also, it's not taught in schools and so no one knows the grammar or the rules of the language. So, when teaching, a native speaker interprets the meaning which is the best way to interpret, but doesn't help someone trying to understand and learn the language.

It was hard for me to get Gueltir to translate word for word as he complained that when he did it that way, it wasn't good French. The other difficulty I have is that *Nangjeré* is a tonal language. In other words, *kà, ka, ka'* and *'ka* all have different pronunciations and meanings. At least that's what Gueltir says. It's all one and the same to me.

Sarah and I learn languages differently. She learns by ear. She listens, hears, talks and learns. That's the way we all learn our first language when we are kids. However, just like many native speakers, she may not be able to tell you why a certain thing is said a certain way. She has an amazing gift and already speaks Danish, English, German, Spanish, and French fluently as well as a little Croatian, Hebrew, *Tchadian* Arabic and *Nangjeré,*

I, on the other hand, need books. I need to understand the structure and grammar, the why. That's why *Nangjeré* is so difficult. There are no books and no dictionary.

With *Tchadian* Arabic, I'm having more success. I've bought a book of grammar, a dialogue book and a dictionary. So, I'm starting to feel a little better. Maybe this speaking in tongues thing will come eventually; even if it is by learning it the hard way.

Today, I'm back at work rounding on pediatrics again. I'm feeling pretty cocky after my night with the *Tchadian* Arabic dictionary and my first *Nangjeré* lesson with Gueltir. I approach the first patient.

"*Ba ma balou ga?*" Blank stare. Okay, not *Nangjeré*.

"*Hu gai giddif?*" Arabic maybe? No signs of comprehension.

"*Docteur,*" a nursing student offers. "She only speaks *Ngambai*."

Xalas, I give up!

11 SEPTEMBER 2005
NAVIGATING THE MIND

I lie on the couch. My arms stick to my bare chest. My eyelids are so heavy I can't keep them open. Hens cluck outside, their chicks tweeting alongside. André shouts something in Moundang, which sounds like Chinese badly spoken. In the distance, thunder threatens to disrupt the heavy heat that hangs in the air like a cobweb stretching desperately to ensnare its next victim. The taste of M&Ms rests in my mouth like the sticky, sweet film of scum on top of a stagnant pool where mosquitoes breed ready to spread their deadly curse of Malaria across our small village.

Thoughts flit through my head hoping not to be caught. I glide through the wards in my mind as in a misty cave, dimly lit by torchlight. There to the left is a smiling face of a well-looking woman with a cast on her right leg. She smiles, holds out her hand and says, "*lapia.*" Three small children play some game with a plastic bag at her bedside.

To the right, Lona leads me to the new arrival. An elderly woman betrays her age by her silver hair rather than by her unwrinkled skin and body. She lies stretched out on her back. I examine her abdomen and write prescriptions in her little *carnet*.

I enter the next room, barely noticing the cracked, dingy blue paint. The ceiling panels hanging like moss from an ancient cave. Under a white mosquito net sits the business manager from the Mayor's office. His knee wound has become infected leaking out pasty remnants of his gout deposits like toothpaste gone really, really bad. I unwrap and change the dressing.

I proceed to the next mosquito net cocoon hiding not a butterfly but a man lucky to be alive. He is lying in puddle of his own stool, which is leaking out of a poorly done colostomy on his left abdominal wall. Five days ago I was intimately acquainted with his abdominal contents from midnight until 6 a.m.. Inside his belly, I first untwisted and then removed his dead sigmoid colon, which had turned on itself in a bizarre act of suicide called a volvulus. Today, he is eating, has no pain, and his wound is clean. The colostomy is functioning despite being done wrong, as I learned by reading up on it after the operation.

I move to the outside door passing our tall, thin friend who still has his left leg. When he first came in, I was sure he would need an amputation. His thigh wound is still rather large, but is now beefy red with no swelling or signs of infection. Of course, after two months at home and no real physical therapy department, he is a long ways from bending his knee normally. But, he has his leg.

I walk under the porch. I am surprised at not having to dodge the normal assortment of mats and brightly colored Arabic rugs. I enter the dungeon of pediatrics.

Darkness and the smell of urine and old pus assault my senses. The smells soon disappear as my brain learns to ignore them. I disperse the

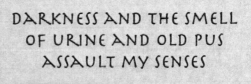

DARKNESS AND THE SMELL OF URINE AND OLD PUS ASSAULT MY SENSES

darkness by simply opening the sheet metal shutters. A row of red beds stretches in what seems like infinity interrupted by a smattering of mosquito nets and tubing hanging haphazardly from a varied assortment of poles, sticks and protuberances. I feel I should have a treasure map in my hand, a hat on my head, a whip by my side and a wry smile playing about my lips if I intend to navigate well this ancient tomb.

I notice that the second bed to the left has a new child. The one who'd occupied that bed the previous five days is unforgettable. A tiny eight-month-old with the typical fever, diarrhea, vomiting and anemia was admitted and treated with IV Quinine and a blood transfusion. But despite our best efforts, this tiny life continued to totter on the edge of eternity. Each day brought no improvement. Her Arab father was a constant presence, ready to do whatever was necessary to save his daughter's life. His obvious love was inspiring.

But the diarrhea continued. The refusal to breastfeed was discouraging. The fast heart rate and breathing was ominous. Finally, two days ago I noticed a change, but not the one I was expecting or hoping for. I noticed a small piece of paper folded many times and tied to her wrist. Then, I took note of the heavy bundle of leather pouches tied around her neck. I spoke to the father.

"Are you a Muslim?"

"Yes."

"Do you believe in the one true God?"

"Yes."

"Do you believe He is all powerful?"

"*Mashallah!*"

"Then why do you put your confidence in these fetishes to save your child's life? If it is Allah's will she will die; if it is Allah's will she will live. But if she lives, you may give credit to the fetishes rather than Allah. Why not take them off and put your trust in the all-powerful God?"

"*Docteur*, you are right."

I pray with them. I walk away. I come back the next day and the child is well. The child has no pouches or things tied around her. They go home that same day.

I continue on pediatrics and remember what happened two weeks ago. A mother lying on the floor begins to writhe and twist and moan. I feel instantly this is something supernatural. Through a nursing student as translator we pray for her. She calms down. We speak with her.

She used to know God. Then, a catastrophe struck. She lost her husband and faith at the same time. She visited a witch doctor. The seizures started. We pray for her again, assuring her that our God is all-powerful and she can be free. She is calm. Her child is still sick, though.

The next day, she is gone along with her child.

21 OCTOBER 2005
BORDER CROSSINGS

Sarah and I jump into our pickup, a Toyota Hilux. The truck is typically *Tchadian* in that it looks much older than it actually is. Inside it may only be a little over two years old but you'd never guess it by the dents, scratches, cracked windshield, broken mirror, twisted bumper, bent tailgate, and grill literally hanging on by a few wires.

My dad, visiting for two weeks from the States, climbs in the back with two other *Nasara*. We pull out of the guesthouse with a rattle, squeak and roll. As we enter the street there is a grinding at the level of the right front tire and a stuttering with each turn of the steering wheel.

We bump along the dirt road until we find the roundabout where we hit pavement. The asphalt is filled with potholes and turns out to be about as bad, or worse, as the unpaved section. Turning left at the French Embassy, we pass a typical N'Djamena midday scene.

Turbaned men struggle with overloaded pushcarts carrying plastic jugs of water or fuel, ten-meter long metal poles, or dirty, Arabic rugs going to the river to be cleaned. A horde of bicycles weaves in and out of traffic. Most two-wheeled vehicles have a passenger: a human being and a wrapped up bundle or a live animal tied up and waiting its fate at the market. Pedestrians are anywhere and everywhere. Uniformed students and fatigue-wearing soldiers with guns share the road with robed and turbaned Arabs, ragged children and common laborers. Muslim philosophers sit under trees and outside shops trying to conserve energy during the Ramadan fast. Women sell anything from pineapples, watermelons, and bananas to cell phones and cigarettes.

I weave in and out of the myriad bicycles, motorcycles, pedestrians, yellow Peugeot taxis and large SUVs. At the same time, I try to avoid as many potholes as possible. Keeping a sharp eye and a heavy hand on the horn, I find myself on both sides of the road and sometimes off road. I pass the US embassy and then one of the few real gas stations  in town. Most fuel in *Tchad* is sold on the side of the road. Each fuel stand is covered with an assortment of old bottles corked with bunched up plastic bags and containing a variety of petroleum products.

I arrive at the Chagoua roundabout, a major entry point to the capital. The old bridge across the Chari is now mostly used for motorcycle and pedestrian traffic. Vendors selling bread, bananas, oranges, dates, coffee, tea, donuts and boiled eggs line one side of the circle. On the other side are a small mini-bus stop and the firewood merchants. The bundles of sticks have been brought down-river in wooden log canoes. We continue along the Chari to the main bridge and cross the rain-engorged river.

Descending the bridge on the other side, I see the police. My first reaction is to keep going. Unfortunately one catches my eye and waves me over. I shouldn't stop. But I do.

The policeman sidles up with a mocking look on his face. I know what's going to happen. I rebel. I'm tired of being seen as a source of easy bribe money just because I'm a *Nasara*.

"Why are you bothering us?" I ask him in French. "I know what's going on..."

He asks for the car's papers and of course finds out that we haven't paid some tax and haven't had our annual vehicle inspection. Maybe he's right. The chauffeur normally is supposed to take care of all that. But I see all kinds of vehicles passing us in obvious street-unworthiness that aren't pulled over. The police prefer to get money from *Nasara*.

I argue, using all the tricks I think I've learned only to realize that it's hopeless. He threatens to impound the vehicle. I know that even if he doesn't have the right to do that, he can do it.

I try to get the car's registration back. I know that if he has the papers he will use that as more leverage to get more bribes. Finally, I ask how much of a fine I should pay. He says 6,000 francs. Not nearly as much as I feared, maybe my bargaining did some good. I pay it and we continue on our way as I boil inside at the corruption in *Tchad*. The worst is, I'm helpless to do anything about it.

I turn left and instead of going straight down the road to Béré, I hang a quick right toward the Cameroon border. Here the road traffic is the same as in N'Djamena with the addition of many handicapped *Tchadians* in their motorized or hand-pedaled three-wheelers. They carry sacks of sugar across the border from Kousseri to N'Djamena. Each day they are allowed to bring in one sack duty-free. This allows them to make a profit and gives them a livelihood. Of course, a little "soap money" placed in the appropriate hands allows them to bring in more than one sack.

I approach the red and white striped metal pole that serves as a customs gate. It is slowly raised in front of me and we pass underneath. I pull to the side of the road right before the single lane bridge across the Chari River leading to Kousseri. As I step out of the air-conditioned interior, the dry heat that defines life in N'Djamena blasts me in the face. The sweat forms almost instantly on my forehead and I can feel it starting to drip down my back and legs.

I walk down the dusty slope to the small cluster of dirty, yellow brick buildings. The red, yellow and blue striped *Tchadian* flag hangs in front. *Emigration-Immigration* is printed in black over the door. Huddled inside is the usual crowd of merchants coming to and from Cameroon and Nigeria. There is also one other *Nasara*.

The room is dark and consists of a high counter on the right behind which stand three officials and on the left a single wooden bench. The back of the room has a partly open door leading into an even darker room where a desk is piled high with papers and documents. The counter is covered with stains and littered with a few pens, some scattered forms and a circular metal rubber stamp stand and its variety of well-worn wooden *cachets.*

I have all the passports from our truck with me. I start to fill out the forms. Job comes in a few minutes later with the passports for the rest of the group who've just arrived. We are 17 in all. Job and I furiously fill out the forms. One of the officials, a woman, tries to help but, since she doesn't read English, requires frequent translation. Slowly, another official starts to hand copy all the information into a thick bloc-note book. The sweat has now drenched me. The air is suffocating. I see my dad outside talking with some other *Nasara.*

Finally, the copying is done. The official calls in an Arab courier, puts all the passports in a paper folder and the courier walks out the door with our documents. I sit down to wait. Sarah walks in and we chitchat. Time passes. Finally, the man comes back with the stamped passports. Now they need to be signed at yet another office. Job hands the officials 3,000 francs "for their trouble." We exit and enter the office just to the right.

JIM

A Muslim man is lying down on a bench. He gets up when we walk in and sits down behind a desk. As he signs all the passports, I fill out a tiny slip of paper with the truck's licensing information. I am to hand this paper to someone right before crossing the bridge. I take the signed passports and am about to leave when the official looks at Job and says *"Kikef?"* The official translation of *kikef* is "What's up?" In this case it means "What, no bribe?" Job hands him 1,000 francs. The man is not happy, but Job walks out the door laughing and shaking his head. I follow.

I think we're done. Wrong again. Job leads us across a small ditch and into yet another office. Fortunately, this officer is one of Job's many friends. He signs and stamps all the documents one more time, but this time no bribes are needed. Finally, we finish. Sarah and I jump into the truck and crank on the air.

We line up with the group of motorcycles, bicycles and pedestrians waiting to cross the bridge. Finally, when the green signal comes, we approach a little straw shack providing shade to some other officials. They are in the process of interrogating the driver of another car. Sarah calls him over, gives him our little slip of paper and we move forward another 20 feet. There we stop to pay the 1,500 francs toll to cross the bridge. Another officer asks for our passports, leafs through them rapidly, and wants to know if we are with the mini-van that just passed with Pastor Job inside. We reply, *"oui"*, which is apparently the right thing to say as he waves us on.

We cross the narrow bridge and now have to approach the Cameroonian immigration officials. This time there's only one office and we don't have to wait for the officer to copy it all into his book. He just takes the information slips, stamps and signs our passports and waves us on. The whole process of emigration and immigration has taken two and a half hours.

We're now in Cameroon for a few days before returning to *Tchad* to repeat the process all over again.

24 OCTOBER 2005
SATURDAY

I step outside. The buzzing hits my ears. A million insects like microscopic cockroaches fall as if they were small kamikaze pilots trying to demolish the big toads hopping gingerly away from my feet. Unfortunately, they mostly hit my back and neck. I walk out into a foggy, full-moonlit night. The drums pound in the background. A chant wafts on the air softly numbing the senses, like the unceasing pounding of the ocean on the shore.

My chest burns as my lungs suck in the hot, searing air. It is Saturday and everyone has left church to go to the river for a baptism. The young guys follow me home. They ask me if I'm taking the car. I say of course not. I haven't exercised in weeks. I change from my Arab robes into some long shorts and a plain white t-shirt with sandals.

I pass the mud puddle in front of the hospital's main gate. The ducks waddle off quacking and swaying as if drunk. We round the corner at a fast pace. A group of young guys surrounds me. The youngest is six, the oldest is in his late teens. We pass through the remnants of a millet field. Like a ghost town, it has just a few reminders of its past prosperity still standing. Marching past the night watchmen's hut and through a few more mud puddles, we hit the main road.

Red clay stretches off into the African plain surrounded by yellowing rice in paddies as far as the eye can see. A few boys fish with homemade sticks and twine in the standing water that houses the rice. The red road is pocked with massive mud holes and deep grooves from the large transport trucks. We are still keeping up a brisk pace and already I'm wishing I'd brought water. The sun bakes my head making even sweating to keep cool seem like an exercise in futility.

A small Peugot truck is stuck between a rice paddy and the road where it tried to skirt a mud puddle. The mud is over the tires and into the chassis. I call the boys over, take off my sandals and step into the muck as I begin to discuss a plan of action with the turbaned driver. The back of the truck is piled with four barrels of diesel and a ton of miscellaneous sacks and plastic containers. I call all the boys over as they pass by.

We attach a rope to the back and some pull while others lift and push on the side facing the rice paddy. I look over and see a well-dressed man hit some slick clay and fall off the back of his bike like a *Three Stooges* movie. He's okay, but getting the truck out has been put on hold as everyone stops to have a laugh at the poor man's expense. Pride goes before a fall as the rope breaks and we all also end up on our butts in the mud.

We change strategies and unload all the bags, plastic containers, and one barrel. Then with coordinated heaves and hos, many manly grunts, and much soiling of clothes, the truck finally escapes out of the hole and gets back on the road. With the blessings and thanks of the driver ringing in our ears and mud between our toes, we take off again for the river.

I suddenly feel very energized and take off running at a determined pace. The boys gladly fall in line bragging of how they'll run me off the road. They claim they could run all the way to Kélo without stopping. Unfortunately, I can't keep up the pace for long. I have to slow to a fast walk.

The boys begin to talk. Most of them are to be baptized today, and they have questions about sorcery, ogres and other supernatural stuff that is a part of their everyday lives. They want to know how that relates to their new belief in one supreme God. They are smart and have a lot to say. With such stimulating and intelligent conversation we arrive quickly at the river. Desperate to cool off, I dive in, barely missing an underwater fishing line.

The drums pound, the long metal cylinder booms, the rattles are in full roll, and the chanting brings each person into and out of the water. Waist deep in the current, I wait. Laughs and swaying and dancing abounds. People drink water straight from the river using the one plastic water bottle that someone has thought to bring. Pierre fetches the water, wading out with his shirt off, revealing his ample gut rolling over his trousers.

In this setting, I baptize someone for the first time. I couldn't imagine a better place to do it. In a muddy river, after pulling a truck out of a bog, wearing shorts and a plain t-shirt, I get to perform this ritual with guys I've just been running and having deep spiritual conversations with. It's my first time and I wouldn't trade it for anything.

02 NOVEMBER 2005
BAT

The baby has what sounds like asthma as I listen with my stethoscope. However, the baby's only one month old so it might be bronchiolitis. In either case the only thing to do is treat with nebulized Albuterol and oxygen. We have Albuterol, but no oxygen. Then, I remember we might have something in the new shipment of old medical equipment. We search in our storehouse and find the oxygen concentrator. We've never actually used it, so we don't know if it works.

Lona is running the nebulizer machine. The lights are on because the sun has just gone down. We have two hours of scheduled electricity. We find a transformer and plug in the oxygen extractor. It works and the baby seems to be doing well on it. We watch his oxygen saturation rise on the monitor. It started at 85% and is now up to 95%.

The *garde* calls me to see a 12-year-old boy with a swollen stomach and no stool or gas for a day. He needs an exploratory operation. We go to

A BAT LANDED ON THE BABY'S FACE

the OR. His thin body is in contrast to his firm, bloated belly. Sarah finds an IV fast and gives him his Ketamine. I scrub, prep and drape. With the scalpel I quickly cut him open from sternum to pelvis. His intestines pop out and spill across the abdomen. I don't see anything obvious at first but there are red patches all over the intestines surrounded by little darker areas. Something is weird. I think it might be Typhoid fever.

Then, as I run the intestines, I discover that part of it has twisted on itself. I untwist it and quickly most of the dark areas pink up. There are a few sections that stay dusky. That part is dead. I know I can't leave it.

I place on bowel clamps around the necrotic section. I clamp and cut through the mesentery. Once all the blood vessels are tied off, I cut the dead intestine out. I suture the two cut ends back together in two layers of running sutures. I release the bowel clamps. There is no leakage. I leave in a drain and close the fascia with sutures and the skin with staples.

I go back to check on the one month old. I see a dead bat in the trashcan by the door. The nurses look up mischievously. The baby is stable but still wheezing. Apparently, a bat entered the room, hit the fan, and landed directly on the baby's face, dead as a doornail! The baby lives through the night and and goes home three days later.

The boy recovers normally and by the fifth day post-op is eating, walking, pooping, and passing gas so I send him home.

The bat is burned in the incinerator.

27 NOVEMBER 2005
THANKSGIVING IN BÉRÉ

I'm preparing Thanksgiving dinner for the staff. I'm alone. Sarah has gone out to an Arab village for a few days. I boil water and dump in half a can of mashed potato flakes. *Voila*, an essential Thanksgiving dish! Since we only have locally pressed peanut oil, the homemade gravy tastes like peanut butter. Salomon boils chicken in tomato sauce for our *Tchadian* "turkey". To top of our holiday dinner I open up a can of green beans, a can of cranberry sauce and two cans of baked beans.

Out in the courtyard, I set out the plastic chairs and our two locally made couches. The sun is going down, turning everything a glowing orange. Samedi is the first to arrive and the only one on time. Soon after Pierre and David show up. Then a cry arises from the street. I look up.

"Nasara! Nasara! Nasara!" The kids are screaming.

SARAH & PEPPER

Next thing I know around the corner of the hospital comes a wild haired red head. She is bouncing along easily on a fine Arab stallion. Her face is covered in dust and pierced with a wild smile. Behind her comes a robed and turbaned Arab on a donkey with a sheep tied behind his saddle. My joy is complete. I didn't expect her till tomorrow. As she swings down from the saddle, I stride over to meet her and sweep her up in my arms. I can tell the trip has been good for her. She looks dirty but refreshed.

As the sun goes down most of the staff have arrived. Samedi and Anatole have been regaling us with myths and legends from the hospital's past. Our chaplain, Degaulle, insists on singing one of the only two songs he knows in English: "Sheeell be comeeeng 'roun zee moun-ten ven zhe comes..." At least it sounds similar to English. I join in.

Everyone chows down and the food disappears fast. Even the team on *garde* duty breaks away for a few minutes to partake. Ahmat and his father, the two Muslims accompanying Sarah also join in.

At the end, everyone goes around saying what they're thankful for. As usual, Degaulle flies off on a random, unrelated tangent. We all try gently, and then forcefully, to bring him back to the point. Anatole surprises me by being so thankful that God brought him to Béré. He's normally so negative.

But now he actually says that coming to work at the hospital saved his life and has made it so much better.

Even Ahmat is thankful that his sickness brought him to Béré. He came with tuberculosis and AIDS. He responded miraculously to the medication and has been our unofficial ambassador since. He thanks God that he came here where his eyes were opened and his body cured. I, of course, am thankful that in the last year God found me a hot, Danish nurse for a wife. It's surprising what you can find in *Tchad*.

Lazare says something bizarre, as usual. But he says it with such enthusiasm and obvious joy that everyone bursts out in applause at the end. Finally, they all leave except Lona's two sons, Fambé and Henri. They spontaneously help bring in the two couches, even though they are only three and five years old respectively.

While the generator is still on, I show Sarah half of the best Thanksgiving movie ever: *Planes, Trains and Automobiles.* Then the generator cuts off and we go back to our room in complete darkness.

All day I've been trying to call my family to wish them a happy Thanksgiving but the satellite phone wasn't connecting. Finally, late at night I get through just as they are finishing eating. They're waiting for the apple pie to come out of the oven. Grandpa, Grandma, Aunt Jeannette, Mom, Dad, and Chelsey are all there. While I'm jealous of the apple pie and the family being together, I have to admit my Thanksgiving has been hard to beat!

30 DECEMBER 2005
PUBLIC TRANSPORT

We are ten kilometers from Yaoundé, the capital of Cameroon. We left Béré Friday morning. It is Tuesday noon. I'm exhausted, which may explain what happens next. We pull up to yet another military check point.

Sarah and I are in the back seat of a Toyota minibus modified to hold 20 passengers. That means we are crammed five across on barely padded benches with not nearly enough space for my long legs to fit. I have therefore spent the last eight hours with my knees and legs twisted into positions I had previously thought impossible for me. Despite closing the windows, everyone is lightly covered in fine a red dust sticking to the hair and eyebrows. The contrast is stunning against the backdrop of the dark, *Tchadian* skin.

Since entering southern Cameroon it seems we've been stopped every 15 minutes by military checkpoint. My hand reaches automatically for the passports zipped up safely in a side pants pocket. Sure enough, a soldier swaggers up with a lazy *bonjour* slipping out of his mouth as he asks for

ID papers. I hand him Sarah's and mine. He scans them quickly and hands them back.

This time, I have nothing to hide, unlike the last time I came up from Yaoundé when I had an expired visa. I twist around a little to relieve my numb right leg when another soldier sidles up and asks for our passports again. I inform him politely that we've already been checked. He takes them, anyway. After a cursory glance, he asks for our yellow vaccination cards.

I hand him mine. Sarah has left hers in Béré. I explain that the card is not needed except at international borders. He says that this is the border of Yaoundé, so we need them. I ask him if Yaoundé has now become a separate country and is no longer part of Cameroon. He ignores me and saunters off with our passports. He crosses the road to his buddies sitting under a tree.

I am livid. This is an old Cameroonian trick to get bribe money. I'm so tired my normally weak inhibitions are completely obliterated. I shove open the window, crawl out, and march angrily across the street. We are in the middle of nowhere. The soldiers all have guns and are wearing military fatigues. What I do next isn't well thought out.

I storm up to the one holding the passports and start yelling at him in French. I tell him it's stupid and unnecessary to be always bothering people and trying to extort money. One of them says that I should start by greeting them. I snap out a sarcastic *"bonjoooouuuur!"* and continue my tirade. Job comes up to intervene.

Miraculously, they let us go without paying any bribes. I am wasted now not only physically but emotionally. I crawl back into the minivan through the open rear window. As I curl up again for the rest of the ride, I start to relive the other memorable moments of this trip...

Sarah and I are sitting on a sandy beach by the Chari River with Nellie, a volunteer nurse from Canada. This is the border between Bongor, *Tchad* and Yagoua, Cameroon. There is no bridge. Several dugout canoes are pulled up on the beach. Some *Tchadians* idle around, waiting to transport customers.

They offer to take us across for 1,000 francs each. We refuse. To cross the river in Lai, which is twice as far across, only costs 250 francs. We take our backpacks off, set them on the sand and sit down to chat. It is noon. We know we need to cross but we don't want to encourage the exploitation of *Nasara*. We periodically bargain with them till the price comes down to 500 francs per person.

Sarah is a hard-core bargainer. She refuses. We continue to sit looking at the invitingly cool water rippling past as we swelter in the midday sun. Sarah suggests a little swim to cool off. I have a brilliant idea!

"Why don't you and Nellie swim to the other side? I'll pay the 500 francs and transport the bags across in the canoe."

The girls like the idea. They start taking off their shoes and walk toward the water.

Suddenly, the *Tchadian* we've been bargaining with gets a frightened look on his face. He yells after the girls, "*Xalas!* I'll take you over for 250 francs apiece. The current is too strong. There might be hippos. Don't go!"

Sarah tries to argue with him to no avail. He doesn't want the girls to have to swim. Apparently, in the *Tchadian* culture, if something happened to one of the girls while swimming, those who had refused to take them across in the canoe would be responsible.

They have the means to help the girls cross, but if they don't and there's a problem it would be their fault. The Bible says a similar thing, "To him therefore who knows to do good, and doesn't do it, to him it is sin." (James 4:17) They couldn't live with that. They were obliged to take us across, even if for free! We pay up and cross, feeling the cool water refresh us temporarily as we drag our hands the few hundred meters to the opposite bank.

Immediately, guys on motorcycles pull up, clamoring for our business. It is seven kilometers to Yagoua. I've been told the price for a motorcycle taxi is 500 francs. I waltz up to the first one and say, "*Yagoua, 500 francs.*" He agrees but then his boss runs up and says "*750 francs.*" He refuses to give in. Sarah, as tough as ever, says, "Well, we'll just walk then!" She grabs her backpack and starts around the corner to the immigration office.

The office is in an old, abandoned carcass of a steel motor home with rickety wooden steps. Out back is a shelter made of sticks stuck in the ground with woven straw mats laid on top to provide shade.

"*As-salaam aleikum,*" I greet as I duck into the door at the top of the stairs.

"*Wa aleikum as-salaam,*" the camo-wearing immigration officer replies. I present our three passports and he signs them quickly with plenty of official-looking rubber stamps.

Meanwhile, Sarah has been reasoning with the motorcycle taxi men. They argue that gas prices have gone up. Sarah just picks up her pack and takes a few steps down the road before they laughingly call out after her "*Xalas, 500 francs.*" Sarah is a very tough customer.

The wind whips into my face, stinging my eyes and causing tears to streak across my cheeks. Bouncing up and down on the sandy roads riding casually on the back of the *moto* is a freeing experience. We pull quickly into town and board the first of many buses.

We spend the next several hours reading and drinking homemade yogurt from small plastic bags. The man next to me asks me in broken English where we are going. I tell him we're going to the Koza Adventist Hospital. He suggests getting off before we reach Maroua at a side road he'll show me.

Suddenly, after miles of no crossroads, a road veers off to the left. My new friend points and nods. We look for a bus and see nothing until we are past the turn. Then, we see a tiny minivan. He motions to me. I don't understand. He yells and the bus screeches to a halt on the side of the road. We explain our situation to the driver who grudgingly sends his assistant to the top of the bus to take our luggage down. Meanwhile, Sarah runs back the 100 meters to the crossroads to make sure the minibus doesn't leave.

Nellie and I snag our bags off the asphalt as the bus scurries away. We run awkwardly back to Sarah with our backpacks swaying back and forth. They have plenty of room and leave 30 seconds after we are on board!

Sarah and Nellie are crammed in the back next to a Cameroonian girl with an MP3 player. All the people on the bus are constantly checking their cell phones and commenting on whether or not the network is present. We're definitely not it *Tchad* anymore! All the while, we pass the familiar sights of small mud brick huts, herds of goats, and kids dressed in rags waving cheerfully as we chug by spewing out rich, black diesel smoke from our tailpipe.

Shortly after dark, we enter a darkly lit, smoky little town called Mokolo. The streets are rocky and steep, built on the side of a mountain shooting out of the surrounding desert. Small shops selling a little bit of everything are harshly lit with bare, fluorescent bulbs. The bus stops on the steep part of a hill and once again we are surrounded by *motos.*

One of the motorcyclists greets me, "*Docteur,* we haven't seen you in a while. We've been waiting for you." Since I've never been there before, they must be confusing me with Greg Shank, the surgeon at the Koza Hospital. I assume that like many *Tchadians,* these Cameroonians think all *Nasara* look alike. I remember showing *It's a Wonderful Life* once in Béré. All the kids thought that every male actor was me! "*C'est toi, n'est-ce pas, James-uh?*"

The night is cool, the stars are out, and the air is dry and dusty as only can be found in a desert night. The road to Koza is windy, rocky, and steep. Once again I am hanging on the back of a small motorcycle. I have an hour to just let my weary, wandering thoughts focus on the simple beauty and joy of living in the moment.

Arriving in Koza, I find Greg and his wife, Audrey, in the OR. A young man was stabbed by his brother multiple times. After half an hour in  a pushcart bouncing over mountain trails, he arrives at the hospital. His intestines hang out, one lung has collapsed, and he is bleeding profusely from wounds his right arm and left shoulder.

When we see him, Greg has the belly open, has sewn up the diaphragm and is controlling the bleeding in his liver. A blood transfusion is up and running and I ask how I can help. I change into scrubs, put on sterile gloves, and start cleaning out and suturing his shoulder and arm wounds. A piece of skin the size of a small plate has been sliced back off his arm. It has rolled up into a scrunchy, little mess at the medial border of the wound. After irrigating the wound and closing the muscles, I slowly stretch the skin back out and over the wound. I leave the lower part open to drain.

An hour later, we are both finished. The boy is still alive. Since Greg has no chest tubes, he has created one from a urinary catheter, which is sticking out of the patient's chest. A massive bandage on his abdomen and side, and two loosely wrapped dressings on his arm and shoulder complete the picture.

We head to Audrey's house to a tasty supper of cold beans and rice. I sleep till early next afternoon. We leave Nellie in Koza. Greg joins us for the next leg of the trip. We catch *motos* to Mokolo and the bus to Maroua. That night we sleep at the Catholic mission before catching the 7 a.m. bus to Ngaoundéré.

On that bus we meet up with Job and Wangkel from the *Tchad* Mission. We arrive in Ngaoundéré at 4 p.m.. We eat fried egg sandwiches in a hole-in-the-wall place showing English League soccer and serving the best papaya drinks ever. At 6 p.m. we board the train for Yaoundé.

I stretch out on the bunk and strip down to my shorts in anticipation of a nice long sleep. The overnight train ride should be cool and refreshing as we pass through the mountains on the way to Yaoundé. An hour and a half later we still haven't moved from the station. A man passes by outside informing us that the cargo train ahead of us has derailed. The train won't be leaving tonight. We sleep that evening at a church member's house.

The next day, we breakfast on avocado sandwiches. We are supposed to catch the noon bus for Yaoundé and we are running late. Our host tells us not to worry. She knows the owner of the bus company and has told him to wait for us as long as it takes. It's all about who you know!

Eleven hours and two buses later we find ourselves in Bertoua. We pull off the main route, around a corner, and into a small, poorly lit courtyard with several other buses. A guy comes running up yelling "Yaoundé! Yaoundé!" We are told to put our bags over on a different vehicle right next to ours. It's a tiny mini-bus. We transfer our bags quickly and silently. Several other buses drive off. Soon we look around to find the place empty except for us and a few other passengers. We've been abandoned.

I sit on a bench. Then I get hungry. I walk out with Sarah to the street. We sit on a crude wooden bench in front of a table covered with different food items. In one corner is a pile of French bread. Scattered across the table are piles of avocados, old tin plates, a cup full of random silverware, a cardboard egg crate half full of brown eggs, and a spatula. Underneath and behind is a metal can with some coals in it and a frying pan sizzling over it. The fresh smell of hot oil wafts across the cool night air.

Sarah has just bought some freshly baked French baguettes from a bakery. We order egg and avocado sandwiches. Nothing has ever hit the spot like those sandwiches. The smell of charcoal mixed with muddy, African street odor and the sounds of frying, scraping, shuffling, distant shouting and the occasional roaring of a passing diesel cannot be described, only experienced.

I pry open the window of one of the abandoned buses, crawl through and stretch out on a bench seat. Sarah wakes me at 2:30 a.m.. I cram myself into the back of a tiny minibus. We bounce around over unpaved, red-dust covered mountain roads until 10 a.m. and ten kilometers from Yaoundé when we get pulled over and asked for our vaccination cards...

2006

14 JANUARY 2006
NEAR DEATH EXPERIENCE

I'm staring at the old bathroom tile. On its smooth surface sit four drops of blood in the form of a T. On each has been placed a drop of liquid: one blue, one yellow and two clear. In the dim, fluorescent light I search diligently for signs of agglutination. It is a matter of life or death.

It started with a call from the nurse.

"*Le médecin* from Kélo has brought a patient. He wants you to see him."

I walk quickly over from the house to the hospital. It is dusk and the shadows are gathering. I hear the roar as the generator begins its nightly two-hour vigil. The fluorescent lights fight flickeringly to overcome the resistance to their illumination. I round the corner of the OR and toward the yellow light of the one-bed emergency room.

The nurse on *garde*, Hortence, points me back outside. A father sits on a crude bench holding tightly to his seven-month-old son. The man's wife sits at his side with fear, desperation, and hopelessness in her eyes. Dr. Assane from Kélo is standing by in street clothes, a departure from his usual stylish sport coat and unbuttoned, tie-less dress shirt.

Assane quickly explains that he went to his home village to visit relatives and found this kid on death's door. Since our hospital is the closest, he brought them here.

Truly, the kid is not long for this world. His eyes are rolled back. His body is limp. His respirations come in gasps. I listen to his heart, which is pounding furiously in desperate struggle for life. I look at his eyelids, white as snow. Anemia. Severe Malaria. The hospital's bread and butter.

In 2005 we saw 67 patients die of Malaria, over 90% of whom were kids two-years-old and under. Of those 67, 25 died of severe anemia requiring blood transfusions (hemoglobin less than 5). As depressing as that is, despite the desperate condition of the patients, we were able to save 75% who would've surely died otherwise.

This baby has the look of not even making it long enough to test his blood, much less get the transfusion going. The father gazes at me, pleading in his eyes. I tell the night watchman to go get Anatole.

Meanwhile, I ask Hortence to try and find an IV on the child. At least we can be ready if and when the blood arrives. The father places the limp child on the exam table. His head flops to one side as he continues to stare up, uncomprehending. His arms and legs are like jelly.

Anatole is not at home and he's taken his key with him. I sit there, helpless, watching Hortence search in vain for a vein on this tiny baby. He has lost probably at least 3/4 of his red blood cells to the Malaria parasites.

I've seen Anatole do blood typing countless times. If only I had the key, I could probably do it myself.

Adam, our newest volunteer nurse, is standing by. I ask him to go get the bag-valve-mask so we can at least help this tired baby breathe. He returns and I place the mask over the baby's nose and mouth. I start pumping in air with every effort he makes. His mom starts crying behind me.

Hortence has used up two IVs trying to find the baby's vein. Finally, Doumpa, Anatole's son, arrives with the lab key. I pass the bag-valve-mask to Adam and hurry to the lab. I open the door, flip on the light, open the armoire, find the fridge key, and pull out four bottles with droppers: A, B, AB and D. I grab two bathroom tiles, two lancets, some cotton, some alcohol prep pads, and rush back to the baby.

I prick the baby's middle finger and squeeze out a drop of blood in four different spots on the tile: three across for A, B, and AB and one underneath in the middle for D. I drop one blue drop for A, one yellow drop for B and one clear drop for AB and a different clear drop for D. I use the bottom of the vials to mix the drops in with the blood.

I rotate the tile so the liquid will move allowing me to see if small clots form (agglutination). After two minutes nothing has formed in A, B or AB but there are agglutinations in D. Baby's blood is O positive. I prick mom's finger and repeat the process. She is O positive as well. I hope I've done it right as a mistake could cause a life threatening reaction. Desperate times call for desperate measures.

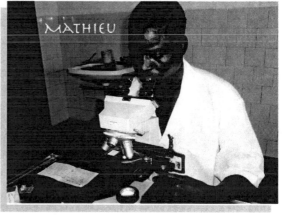

We are also out of rapid HIV tests. The only test we have takes 45 minutes to an hour. I look over at the dad. He's holding the baby as Hortence has given up trying to find an IV. He is trying to close the eyes, saying that the baby is about to die. The mom is sobbing. I make a quick decision.

One of our government lab techs, Mathieu, has just showed up. He's on strike, but I ask him a favor. He agrees and takes the mom off to draw her blood for the blood transfusion. I take the child back to the exam table. I need an IV.

Sarah has arrived and she brings me a larger IV and a 2 mL syringe. I feel the baby's femoral pulse and stick the needle in to the inside of the pulse where I know the vein should be. I pull back on the syringe looking for that quick fill of dark blood indicating I'm in the vein. I search and search. Finally, on pulling out I hit a small flash. I try to advance and it goes in. I pull out the needle and attach the IV tubing.

Mathieu has just arrived with the blood he's drawn from the mom. Adam continues to help the baby breathe. I attach the bag of blood and it drips slowly in. I breathe a sigh of relief.

After a couple minutes, Sarah points to the groin and asks if it isn't swelling. Sure enough, the IV isn't in the vein and the blood has been going in under the skin only. I ask for another IV and try the other vein. This time I find the vein easily and with the big flash I know I'm in. I attach the blood again and open it up to go in fast.

We watch a miracle take place before our eyes. First, the floppy baby's legs start to curl up. Then, he stretches his arms straight over his head as if he were Lance Armstrong celebrating yet another victory in the Tour de France. Then he pees straight up in the air, a glorious clear fountain telling us his internal organs are waking up now too. Then, his blank stare transforms into an intelligent sparkle as he looks around at the world he thought he'd left.

Three days, one more transfusion, eight IV infusions of quinine, and one grateful family later, the little boy goes home.

29 JANUARY 2006
BONGOR

I sit by the side of the road. Around me in all directions stretches the African plain. The vast, flat expanse allows one to see miles in every direction broken only by the occasional tree and smoke from a cooking fire. The single lane road stretches into infinity, swallowed up in the haze of the *harmatan* winds off the Sahara.

My neck is burned, my hands are caked with grease, and the smell of diesel clings to my plain, tan-colored Arabic robes. My mouth is parched, my lips are cracked, my nose is filled with thick, black tinged snot, and my eyes are dry.

I lean against the hood of the truck as a small crowd of kids on foot and adults on bikes stares and whispers among themselves in Arabic and some local languages.

Sarah has left to fill our water bottles in the little cluster of huts off to the left. It is 3 p.m.. We left Béré at 7:30 a.m. and Bongor at 11 a.m.. Bongor is 24 kilometers, one tollbooth, and one long day away.

I notice the problem with the truck as we come out of Bongor. The vehicle has neither power nor acceleration. As we approach the tollbooth outside of town, the car stalls. I hit the clutch, put in the brake and then pop the clutch and the truck roars back to life. A few seconds later, the engine dies again as I try to juggle braking, hitting the gas and pulling the emergency brake so we can stop and pay our toll. I try in vain to restart it. Finally, the toll guys give us a push through the gate and we try to start it that way. Nothing happens.

With my wrenches in hand, I open the hood and remove the diesel return valve bolt from the injection pump. It is filthy. I ask some of the bystanders if they have any kerosene. One guy with a shortened upper arm brings me a plastic cap full. I clean out the tiny filter with the kerosene, a match, and blowing with my own mouth. I replace the part and the car starts right up.

I'm feeling really good about myself until five kilometers later when the pickup reaches its final destination for the day. The time is 11 a.m.. We

pull up under a tiny tree providing the only shade around. A few meters ahead a path turns off to a school built out of woven mats. The kids are outside playing a game. A medium-sized man with a pot belly sidles up, his hands deep in his pants' pockets. The trousers are pulled up to his belly button with a tight white tank top tucked in.

He introduces himself in the classic *Tchadian* fashion by stating the obvious, "*Bonjour, Nasara,* you need a mechanic."

At the same moment, he yells to a passing motorcycle driven by a blue-robed Arab with curly, nappy hair and a short mustache. He immediately starts messing around with the engine by taking off the fuel filter and hand fuel pump. He says the problem is with the hand pump. I think it's the filter, which looks a little crushed by the man's efforts.

He calls someone in town. I climb on behind him on the motorcycle. We tear off down the tarmac, the wind stinging my eyes. The thought crosses my head that if the tire blows out, or we hit a goat or something that I'm dead. I grasp a five-liter jug in one hand and the old filter with hand pump attached in the other. I promptly upend the filter, spilling diesel all over my lap. The unchanging African plain whirs by in a blur as my eyes continue to tear up from the wind and dust.

We arrive in Bongor and stop at a little shop. Different sizes and shapes of glass bottles filled with a variety of fuels sit on an uneven table out front. Inside are an assortment of car parts old, new, and used piled haphazardly on shelves and all over the floor. We buy a new filter and a new pump, which is obviously a cheap imitation. We haggle out the prices and I'm not satisfied but am desperate and know I will never get the same price as a local because I'm a *Nasara*. I am surrounded by Arabic greetings. *As-salaam aleikum, al-hamdullilah,* and *mashallah* float around in the shop as I wait for our motorcycle friend to fill up the bike for our return trip.

The return is the same except I am doubly weighed down with filters and pumps, and the five-liter jug is now full of diesel.

The truck has been pushed off the road and now sits under a tree next to the school. Sarah is playing jumping games with the school kids. Three more Arabs have now joined us. They all seem to know a little about engines but not much. They alternately open and close things, pumping furiously and often on the new hand pump. One of the men gets in the cab and we try to push start the truck. Eventually, with a long push we get the car started. I sit back in the cloud of dust watching our means of transport fade into the distance down a dusty side road.

A half an hour later, Sarah and I are beginning to wonder if our truck has been hijacked. Maybe we'll never see it again. One of the other Arabs comes back on his motorcycle and takes us 100 meters up the paved road where the truck has stalled again.

Finally, at 3 p.m. the men leave for Bongor to find a mechanic. I find myself leaning against the hood waiting for Sarah to come back with water. All I can think about are the watermelons in Guelengdeng just 45 kilometers up the road. They are the best in the world, especially on a dry, hot, dusty *Tchadian* day.

I glance up and see four round green objects sitting on my side of the road just 50 feet ahead. I ask the locals hanging around what they are and to my unbelieving ears hear the word *pastèque*! I immediately buy two. I borrow a razor-sharp Arab knife from a boy standing by and slice into the red fruit. I quickly devour one of the sweetest, crispest watermelons I've ever eaten.

As the juice runs down my face and chin and drops on my diesel stained robes, Sarah comes back and partakes in the feast. She says she saw some horses back in the small village and wants to go back see if they'll let her ride them.

She arrives at the edge of the village where a marriage is being celebrated. They're in the midst of traditional spontaneous horse races up and down the dusty path in front of the wedding site. The men are hesitant to let a mere woman get on a horse as they are sure she will fall off and kill herself on their wild stallions.

She mounts expertly and challenges them to a race. They all smile condescendingly and the women turn to smile and cheer. They've never seen a woman ride in a horse race before. They're on Sarah's side.

Sarah races against two Arab men. Pale white with delicate feet, Sarah's horse has obvious Arabian blood in it. Sarah is mounted like a jockey on the high, short stirrups. In a short race, she beats the Arabs hands down, not once but twice. As she rides up to where I am waiting there is a wildness and gleam in her eyes. It reminds me again of what an amazing thing it was to have met and married a girl like her in a place like this.

The mechanic comes and promptly breaks the diesel intake valve. I had been warning them all day not to touch that as I'd broken that same part last year. I knew how fragile it was. He leaves, promising to send a tow truck.

I'm frustrated and mad by now. I go to talk to his associate who's stayed behind. I tell him we'll just stay here in the bush tonight and sleep by the truck. They can bring us the part in the morning and we'll go from there.

He calls and cancels the tow-truck. It's not until the darkness descends that I regret my decision. The associate says he'll flag down a car that'll pull us into Bongor for at most 5,000 francs. The next truck is a tiny Peugeot piled so high with baggage and people prickling out from on top of the cargo that the bumper is almost touching the ground. They stop and the turbaned chauffeur offers to tow us for 25,000 francs. After negotiation we get it down to 10,000 francs. I'm so angry with the frustration of the whole situation, I refuse.

I continue to regret my decisions until a tiny, old Toyota car pulls up equally weighted down. A tall, commanding Arab with a goatee pulls out and finally talks sense into me. He tells me we need to go to Bongor for our own safety. He says his car is too weak to pull us, though. As I discuss with the mechanic's associate, the commanding Arab comes back and says he can't leave us stranded like that. He's willing to tow us for the same price, 10,000 francs. I accept.

We attach a cord to our bumper and to the other car. There's about ten feet in between us. He says that when we see his left uncovered brake light go on we should stop, as the other lights don't work. We limp into Bongor and are deposited next to the dimly lighted grilled chicken restaurants. Our tow man comes back to tell us he's called the chief mechanic to come meet us here himself. We pay him and he leaves.

We wait. Our tall Arab comes back to say the chief mechanic is sick but he will pull us to the garage where these other guys can help us. It is the main garage in Bongor, run by the *Chinois*.

I'm not reassured as a wobbly gate made of tin roofing is slid to the side revealing what looks more like a junkyard than a garage. Two guys pull up to the shop on a *moto*. They replace the broken part, fiddle with some things, start up the car, and take it out for a test run. It does great! On the return drive, however, it starts to lose power again. They say they'll come back tomorrow at 5:30 a.m.. It's now 8:30 p.m..

I call Job in N'Djamena and he gives me the name and number of a local pastor. Maybe we can stay with him. I call but get no reply. I know he lives somewhere near the Mayor's office. The mechanic on the *moto* takes us to the Mayor's. We ask a group of Muslims lounging on some mats under a tree if they know the pastor. They point us up the road to the Adventist church.

All is dark as we pull up behind the church. I call out, "*As salaam aleikum.*" A groggy Pastor Issa emerges in shorts and an unbuttoned jacket to welcome us. He then wakes up his kids and moves them out of their mud hut so Sarah and I can sleep there. We stay up another half hour eating cold chicken and some bread Sarah has with her. Issa tells us stories of how the Béré Hospital came into existence. He recounts the adventures of early missionaries like Armin Krakolinig, who built our hospital and most of the Adventist churches in *Tchad*, including the one here in Bongor.

Sarah and I finally crash on a thin foam pad surrounded by piles of cassette tapes, simple notebooks, and clothes hanging on a string over the bed. With no mosquito net, we sleep fitfully as the Malaria vectors buzz our ears all night. At 6 a.m. Issa walks us back to the garage where we left our crippled vehicle.

The mechanics are already at work. We sit around eating beans smothered in peanut oil. Sarah has bought them outside the gate. I watch as the mechanics clean the fuel tank. They putter around adjusting and cleaning the injectors and the rest of the diesel circulation system. The *Chinois* has arrived. As chief mechanic, he helps fine tune things. While waiting for some new, clean diesel to arrive, I strike up a conversation with the *Chinois*.

It seems that while his mom is *Tchadian*, his dad is Chinese, hence the nickname *Chinois*. He is about to send off someone to the pharmacy to buy him some meds. I tell him to wait. Since I'm a doctor, maybe I can find out what's really wrong and prescribe him some better drugs. He has the classic symptoms of Malaria: joint pain, headache, and intermittent fevers. I prescribe some of the new anti-Malarial medication for which he is grateful.

The others have finished so we take out the truck for another test run. I'm in the back of the pickup with one of the mechanics while the other one drives with Sarah inside. We accelerate well and fly out of Bongor back toward Kélo. About ten kilometers out, I sit up a little  and the wind catches my glasses sending them tumbling onto the road.

I bang frantically on the roof for the driver to stop. Eventually, the driver hears me and we screech to a halt. We spend the next 45 minutes walking up and down the road looking desperately for my glasses. Without them I am blind and can't drive. We ask everyone we pass if they've seen them.

We are about to give up when a bike that had passed us a few minutes ago returns with my smashed and twisted glasses. The right lens is gone but the left one is still intact. With a little bending I make them fit my face. We leave Bongor again. While the truck stalls a few times, it easily starts back up. An hour into the trip, I have Sarah take the wheel. I'm getting a headache driving with only one lens in my glasses and keeping my right eye shut.

That evening, we finally arrive in N'Djamena, grateful to just be there. Sarah and I look at each other, wondering how we ended up in a place like *Tchad*.

07 FEBRUARY 2006
RIVER SURF

I am fatigued. The weekend has brought a brief respite. For only the second time in two weeks I have had a day without a surgery. All the government health care workers have been on strike for over a month. Even the General Hospital in the capital of N'Djamena is closed. Here in Béré, the nurses assigned by the government to our hospital have only worked six weeks since June 2005. So, we are even more understaffed than usual. Since mid-December, the surrounding hospitals have been closed.

For the last two weeks all the health centers have shut down, too. We are currently the only hospital open in the five surrounding counties. In other words, I am the only doctor for a population of approximately half a million people.

Our hospital is overflowing. We have moved into the partially completed new church in order to free up the old church for a tuberculosis ward. The 20 TB patients had been crammed into a ward made for eight. We have no beds, despite a fast discharge rate. And we have been operating like crazy. As usual, when I need a break, I head for the water.

I pull out the bag from the back of the truck and unzip it. Inside I pull out two halves of a bright blue epoxy surfboard. I place the carbon fiber tube in the center for strength and cinch the two halves together with the patented Pope Bisect integrated screw mechanisms. The board is already waxed and I head down the beach to the water.

SARAH & PEPPER

A gorgeous redhead, my wife, is waiting on the bank with her somewhat scrawny pony named Pepper. There is the definite smell of a cattle crossing and the edges are muddied by numerous hoof prints. I wade out into the foot deep water and shove my board ahead of me as I jump on, bend my back up, and feel that oh so nostalgic feeling of hands dipping in and out, gliding my stick effortlessly upstream.

I hear Sarah mount the horse and begin chasing me, water splashing furiously in the horse's wake. Yeah, there's nothing even remotely resembling a wave. But somehow, that motion up and down, pull and drip forward is comforting and relaxing. A great blue heron flaps up suddenly and awkwardly across my path as numerous other birds twitter and flit around the steep clay banks.

I cannot completely relax. I still have to keep an eye out for hippos and crocs. I finish my upstream paddle and gently coast back down with a leisurely stroke now and then. Near the put in point I call to Sarah and suddenly paddle furiously, put my hands on the board and in one motion push off, slide my feet up and am standing. Surfing? Not quite, the board shoots out from under me and off to the side. As I tumble in, I raise my arms in exultation while Sarah giggles helplessly almost falling off her horse.

23 FEBRUARY 2006
MIRACLE?

Drained. Another day. Up early. Drink a liter of water. Read the Bible on the throne. Eat breakfast. Go to staff worship. Sing something in *Nangjeré*. Read some obscure Old Testament passage. Listen to how many patients got admitted with Malaria last night. Hear how many kids died of Malaria last night. Pray.

Grab stethoscope, clipboard, and pen. Walk to the wards. Notice how much plastic, bloody cotton, and trash is lying around. Look at the dirty walls and floors. Watch them bring out the filthy round cart. Walk around. Look and see how many medications haven't been given. Yell a little. Listen to some hearts and lungs to make it look like I'm doing something.

Write prescriptions. Send people home. Send people to the lab. Change dirty dressings. Smell many things I'd rather not describe. Repeat same thing in Pediatrics. Yell at mothers and fathers for not buying the necessary meds to treat their children. Yell at them again for giving the drugs wrong.

Get high fives from chronic, cute kids who'll probably be handicapped for life because the best place they can come is here and here's not good enough. Hear about a premature baby referred for warming lights. Smirk bitterly as I remember warmers without probes and a lack of electricity. Promise to come see baby after rounds. Finish rounds.

Go see baby on front steps of clinic. Notice sun shining on tiny seven-month preemie who is blue. Watch and see no breathing. Tell mom boy is dead. For some reason, listen to heart with stethoscope. Hear heart beat. Lackadaisically pick up baby and walk over to gurney. Put baby on gurney in sun.

Call for bag-valve-mask to breathe for baby. Start breathing for baby. Ignore soon gathering crowd of locals. Too tired to care. Continue breathing. Baby starts to turn pink and grimace. Baby starts to move legs and arms. Listen to heart. Beating stronger. Keep breathing. Getting warm.

Murmurs ripple through crowd. Sweat drips onto baby. Baby opens eyes. Stop breathing for baby. Baby breathes with difficulty on own. Continue to help from time to time. Send for mom. Give pink, squirming and breathing baby into mom's arms. Tell her to sit in sun. Feel heart pounding. Warm, feel-good feeling. Go back to grind. Miracle?

Two hours later, nurse tells me...baby...is...DEAD.

09 MAY 2006
BACK IN CHAD!

After our two-month vacation spent in the USA and Denmark, we prepare to return to *Tchad*. However, a rebel attack on the capital, N'Djamena, forces us to reroute our return through Cameroon. We arrive in Yaoundé, take an 18-hour train trip up to Ngaounderé followed by a nine-hour bus ride to Maroua and a two-hour pickup truck ride up to the Koza Adventist Hospital. We spend a week working with Drs. Greg & Audrey Shank before going back to Maroua and taking a three-hour bus ride to Yagoua, a 20-minute motorcycle ride to the border, a five-minute canoe ride across the river and a three-hour ride in our truck back to Béré. The rains have already started, the desert is starting to turn green again and our staff has heroically been holding down the fort amidst strikes and local hospital closures. Samedi has performed almost 80 surgeries during our absence saving countless lives with a 100% post-op recovery rate. *Al hamdullilah!*

17 MAY 2006
ECLAMPSIA

The young woman's eyes are swollen almost completely shut. Her face is puffy and deformed. Her pregnant belly bulges out as if it wants to explode. She is unconscious. I turn to the family standing by to learn more. She has been having seizures since the morning. I check her blood pressure. It's 176/132, unbelievably high. The diagnosis is sure: eclampsia. I check the fetus' heartbeat. It's normal. Keining goes to call Samedi. Hortence has already given Diazepam. She finds the vein while I run to the pharmacy to bring back an old bag of magnesium.

As Hortence inserts a urinary catheter, I watch the magnesium drip in drop by drop. She's still having occasional seizures. Samedi arrives. We transfer her to a gurney and wheel her toward the *bloc opératoire*. I fumble with the code on the lock in the dark and finally yank it open. We creak open the doors, flip on the lights and pull the patient into the OR. A quick scrub and drape and the patient is ready: the knife is in my hand.

We pause while Samedi prays. I quickly slash down to fascia and pull apart the muscles and peritoneum to reveal the glistening lower uterine segment. I make a small incision, push in with a clamp and the amniotic fluid sprays up into the wound. Fingers in to guide the scissors, cut, cut, and a shock of wet, black hair is revealed. Hand reaches in and bends the head forward as Samedi pushes on the uterus from the top. The baby pops out and starts to gasp for air as its arms and legs jerk upward. Clamp, clamp, and cut between the two and the baby is in Sarah's hands to be dried, stimulated, and revived. A piercing cry from a newborn's healthy lungs soon pierces the air. I clamp the bleeding edges of the uterus and start suturing to close. There are no complications and the skin is soon sewed shut with a subcuticular suture. A dressing is placed, and we un-scrub to go back and sleep.

Early the next day, I'm in morning worship and a commotion starts up outside the door. Sarah goes out and soon comes back to whisper in my ear that I should go see this patient. I quietly get up and go to the exam room. A young Arab woman, wrapped in brightly colored clothes and headscarf, is lying unconscious on the bed having seizures. She is obviously pregnant.

Just like the woman yesterday, her blood pressure is also elevated at 162/130. This time, however, the baby's heartbeat is absent. She has been like this since yesterday. The same process is repeated until I get my hand in the uterus to bring out the dead baby. Samedi pushes and a limp fetus plops out. I start to clamp, clamp and cut between the two when the baby gives a faint gasp! I quickly cut and hand the baby to Sarah who begins to breathe for her with a bag-valve-mask. She finds a faint heartbeat. Samedi and I continue our work on the mother. We are soon rewarded with a small cry followed by a hearty yelp from a vigorous little girl!

21 MAY 2006
LIGHTNING

It all starts with a clear, still night. Nothing moves for fear of creating even more heat, more sweat, and less sleep. The stars are such as can be appreciated only by one who lives with no electricity in an unlit village on the African plain. The only things daring to break the stillness and silence are the ever-present, Malaria carrying Anopheles mosquitoes. They neither sleep nor slumber.

I feel something crawling down the back of my leg. I slap at it only to discover a rivulet of sweat. I drift in and out of a feverish dream. Then, it starts with a gust, a flutter of the curtains, or a rustle of leaves. A flickering on the horizon, like a fluorescent light bulb on its last legs. A muffled roar growing louder by the second leading to an explosion of curtains shooting out like billowing robes of an Arab fleeing on his camel. Somewhere in the dark a rooster scurries off with a squawk half caught in his throat.

I turn on my sweat-soaked pillow. My body begs to be touched by even a wisp of that cooling breeze. A pitter-patter starts on the tin roof. The sent of a moss-filled rainforest drifts in on winds dropping sharply in temperature. The pitch-black night starts to be interrupted by nature's strobe light.

Suddenly, all silence is drowned in thunderous applause as a million shimmering liquid bullets pound out their cadence overhead and all around. The stars are gone in a billowy mass of tumbling clouds. A constant flickering of lightning illuminates the shadows. The naked limbs of the trees perform their yoga at breakneck speed as they are thrashed about in the torrent.

An occasional flash blinds the eyes followed by the sharp crack and rumble of a bolt hitting close to home. The inside of the mosquito net becomes a spider's web filled with shadowy forms flitting back and forth across the walls and ceilings of this bomb shelter. The "rockets red glare, the bombs bursting in air" makes sleep neither possible nor desired.

The next few days bring a flood of change across the landscape of Béré. People melt away from the hospital and stream to the fields. Horses and cows appear out of nowhere attached to locally fashioned plows. Rows upon rows of freshly turned soil mark out their measured lines in between, around, and almost in the mud huts. Pigs grunt in contentment contributing to the tilling of the soil in their ceaseless search for earthworms. Other porkers lounge lazily in the mud puddles newly formed in the middle of the main road. Soon, the roads will be a thing of the past.

The rainy season has started.

22 MAY 2006
HOW NOT TO FALL OFF A HORSE

Koumakoi just cannot get on the horse. When it was just Sarah and me, it was easy. I put my foot in the stirrup and swung up easily. Then, I put my weight on the opposite stirrup and she swung up behind me. Koumakoi can't seem to understand that little technique. He comes straight at it, puts the foot in the stirrup and than grabs for me, almost pulling me off the horse. People run up to the fence from the TB ward offering all kinds of advice in *Nangjeré*. Being an exceptional athlete, Koumakoi finally somehow manages to get up behind me without ripping me from the saddle, and we're off.

It's Saturday after church. The local churches have organized a yearly get together called the *Assemblée Regionale*. Everyone has walked off to the river for a baptism, but Koumakoi wants to talk to me about something pressing.

We are on Sarah's horse, Pepper. We start in a walk. I relish the distraction of Koumakoi's story as this is my first major solo horse ride. I'd rather not think about it so the horse won't sense my fear. Soon, the hospital fades into the background. We are soon in the *Tchadian* bush. We take a small sandy path in the midst of the freshly plowed rice fields and their thin covering of green weeds. Huge, billowy cumulous clouds break up the monotony of the deep blue African sky. It is a pleasant 80 or 90 degrees. A cool breeze whips my hair back as I bounce up and down in a steady trot.

Koumakoi is relating the sad story of his best friend and his sister. This friend promised not to get involved with the sister, but now he's got her pregnant. He says he's already forgiven him but doesn't know what to. Now he can't trust his best friend and doesn't know what is best for his sister. The friend wants to marry the sister, but both sets of parents are against it. I just let him talk as I try to concentrate on balancing on the horse and not getting bounced around too much.

All the paths look the same to me, but Koumakoi knows this bush like the back of his hand. He tells me to turn here or cut across this field there or go around that bush or whatever.

The smoke of fires in the distance announces the presence of the village of Kasserei. Kasserei is close to the river where we often swim and where today's baptisms will take place.

Soon, the crevasses and small mounds of hardened clay with the tops of a tree line just visible above them, broadcasts our arrival at the river. Koumakoi bounces off. I continue on horseback down the steep bank. I feel like all I need is a Stetson and six-shooters to be right in a John Wayne movie, or maybe one of my childhood dreams. I tie the horse to a bush around a patch of grass, strip off my pants revealing swimming trunks underneath. I climb down and join Pastors Job and Atchouma in the water.

After everyone else leaves I take a short relaxing swim. Then, I pull my pants on and quickly mount Pepper. I ride the pony up the bank to the waiting Koumakoi. I was kind of hoping Koumakoi would return with the rest on foot. That way I could have a few moments to myself for a leisurely ride back. But since he's still hanging around I let him try to get up. That's my first mistake.

Using the same technique as before, he manages to pull me straight off sideways to the ground. I whip my foot out of the stirrup and manage to keep from hurting myself but the saddle is now underneath the horse. I heave and tug until it is back right side up. I remount and tell Koumakoi he better just walk.

After about 15 minutes, I start to feel bad so I dismount and let Koumakoi ride. As the cell phone tower of Béré comes into view I want to ride again, my second mistake.

I easily get in the saddle. I might be feeling a little overconfident. I have the single rein in my right hand and the rest of the rope in my left. As Sarah taught me, I make a puckering "pop" with my mouth and at the same time dig my sandaled heels into the horse's flank. On the way out, that was sufficient to start a trot. Now, Pepper jumps straight into a full gallop.

Now, for those of you accustomed to horses that would be no problem. For me, however, I couldn't get into the rhythm. No matter how I tried I was opposite of the horse. My butt was getting pounded with each bounce and I was hanging on for dear life. Amazingly, I still hadn't lost my confidence. I was actually rather enjoying the speed of racing with the wind in my face and the mud huts of Béré rapidly approaching. In fact, I was cocky enough to think that I'd just slow the horse down, get in sync and restart the gallop.

As I'm bouncing along, I start to lean back and yank on the rope tied around Pepper's muzzle. At the same time, still at full gallop, the horse moves up to go over a small earthen dike in the local rice field. These two simultaneous movements combined with my lack of experience, leads to disaster. I am totally out of control and off balance. I fall backwards and to the right as I let go of the rope.

Then things move to slow motion: Pepper is moving his front legs up and over, followed by a lifting of his hind parts in the same movement. The rope flies out of my hand and goes off still attached to the horse. My left foot swings out and up while my body leans back and right. I remember in the blink of an eye that according to the cowboy movies I shouldn't get caught and dragged in the stirrups.

I instinctively kick my right leg back, up and out to sling off the stirrup. My right arm reaches out behind me and finds sand at about the same time as my right hip and lower back. Then things speed up quickly as I crash to the ground. I roll, jump to my feet and watch the horse high tail it for home. I gather my flip-flops, and not yet feeling any pain, take off after the horse.

I watch Pepper trotting merrily away with the saddle hanging off to the side. One stirrup drags on the ground under his belly. My only thought is please let me catch him before he shows up at home revealing instantly to everyone what happened. I doggedly walk after Pepper, who happily runs off every time I get close.

I soon start to feel a burning in my arm and notice that I have road rash all over my right forearm. I can start to tell that once the adrenaline wears off my back and butt are going to be sore as well. Koumakoi comes running up and I tell him I'm OK. I continue to follow Pepper. I finally get a break when the pony follows the trail in a rectangle around a plowed field. This allows me to cut across at an angle and get in front of him.

Making sure to not look back, I start walking casually toward home. Occasionally, I'll stop and then restart walking so that Pepper starts to follow my lead. That's what he really wants: to follow. At last, he gets close enough that I grab the rope, reposition the saddle and mount back up only to discover that the right stirrup is missing.

Koumakoi, Pepper and I retrace our steps until we see two kids walking up holding the missing stirrup. I reattach it to the saddle. Needless to say, there was no galloping the rest of the way home. But, I can't wait to get back on Pepper. I've been challenged, and I'm ready.

25 MAY 2006
SPRING UP, OH BLOOD

As I walk into the wards I hope I won't throw up. I've been down with Typhoid Fever. I only got up because I can't help worrying about this one patient. I'm not sure if I've made the right diagnosis. She'd come in with pelvic pain, no period for 2 1/2 months, and no bleeding. Since our ultrasound is down, I just had the physical exam and my own intuition to go on. I decided it was an infection and started her on antibiotics while ordering tests for today.

This morning, I was feeling nauseated and had diarrhea, so I didn't to into work. However, I couldn't get it out of my head I should go check on her. I enter the female ward and turn to my right. I find the young woman sitting comfortably on the edge of her bed, smiling. I breathe a sigh of relief and walk up to her.

"*Lapia.*"

"*Lapia ei.*"

I reach for her *carnet*. Inside, I find a lab slip with red writing letting me know that the results are in. I quickly peruse the tests. There is no infection, but the pregnancy test is positive and her hemoglobin is 4.66 g/dL, less than a third of normal. My heart sinks. I ask her to lie down and I palpate her abdomen. I think it's more swollen than yesterday and is tender in both lower quadrants but is still soft. I think about doing a culdocentesis to confirm that it's an ectopic pregnancy. However, deep down I won't feel at ease even if it's negative. She needs an operation.

She is soon prepared and lying on her side for the spinal anesthesia on the OR table. The Ampicilline has been given. The blood transfusion is running in. She has two good IVs. We can start. I easily find the spinal fluid and inject 2 mL lidocaine.

Samedi, Josué, and I flip her over on her back and tilt her head down slightly. Josué attaches the pulse oximeter and automatic blood pressure cuff while Samedi and I prep the patient. We scrub, gown and glove, and drape the woman. I grab the scalpel and Samedi says a prayer. I'm ready to start.

I casually turn my head and look at the pulse oximeter. It reads 85% oxygen saturation. It should be above 90%. Her pulse is a slow 65 beats per minute. I look across the drape at the patient and my eyes are drawn to the skin on her shoulders. She is covered with hives. Her eyes look blank and I'm not sure she's breathing.

I glance at the blood pressure and it's 84/36. I start to bark orders at Josué to start bagging her. He panics. He can't find the bag-valve-mask. Then he has no idea how to use it. I stand there helplessly scrubbed and sterile, holding my impotent scalpel for a few frustrating moments.

Then I give up, break scrub and grab the mask from Josué. I place it over the girl's face and start breathing for her as the pulse oximeter starts to beep slower and slower. The alarm sounds as the red numbers keep going down and down to 40% before my bagging starts to bring it back up.

Meanwhile, I order Josué to give Dexamethazone and Adrenaline. The IV fluids and blood are running full speed. I think we have some IV Benadryl somewhere. Fortunately, Anatole pokes his head in just then and I yell for him to go get Sarah. Anatole is by far the most high-strung of our nurses and takes off like a scared rabbit.

The woman's pulse starts to pick up. Her O2 saturation is still in the 80s but holding. Sarah comes in and then goes off in search of IV Benadryl. The blood is almost all in. She is fighting my attempts to breathe for her, so I have Josué give her Valium and Ketamine to put her under.

Sarah comes back. She can't find the Benadryl. I give the bagging over to her and go to look myself. I can't find it, either. I come back. The blood pressure has almost normalized. The pulse is up to 115 beats per minute thanks to the adrenaline. The O2 sat keeps going up and down.

Samedi says he thinks the IV Benadryl might be in that little blue pouch down on the shelf behind the anesthesia machine. Sure enough, I find it just in time to hear the patient start to retch. Foul, yellow-green, thick barf comes out her nose and mouth.

I get the suction machine ready while Josué gives the Benadryl. The O2 sat starts to fall again. She needs to be intubated. I grab the kit and a size 8 breathing tube. I check the laryngoscope and it works. I put a stylet down the ET tube, tilt her head back, insert the laryngoscope and pull up. I suction out the airway and have a clear view of the vocal cords opening and closing. I position the ET tube and than quickly jam it through the cords as they open.

It slides in. I forgot to attach a syringe so Sarah quickly grabs one and blows up the cuff. I attach the bagging apparatus as her O2 sat has hit zero even though her pulse is still strong at 136 per minute. Her O2 sat slowly climbs up to the high 80s but doesn't seem to want to get normal.

Sarah takes over bagging. Feeling like we need to get this surgery done as quickly as possible, I don't take the time to rescrub but just put on new sterile gloves. I grab the scalpel again and swiftly slice through skin, fat, fascia, and muscle to the peritoneum.

I see the ominous dark look of intra-abdominal blood. I make a small nick in the peritoneum and dark purple blood shoots out. As I make the incision bigger, Sarah gives the woman a deep breath. The blood literally wells out of her belly in a tidal wave crashing to the floor. I grab suction but it's like trying to drink from a fire hydrant.

I attach the autotransfuser and slowly suck up as much blood as I can. Whatever I can collect in this apparatus can be re-given to the patient. Meanwhile, what I can't suck up, surges out of the abdomen every few seconds with each breath. The blood splashing on the floor soon makes the OR look like a war zone. Pools of blood collect and seep into all corners of the room.

> THE BLOOD SPLASHING ON THE FLOOR SOON MAKES THE O.R. LOOK LIKE A WAR ZONE

Samedi takes over the suction as I start to insert lap pad after lap pad into the never-ending reservoir of blood that is her abdomen. The only bright spot is that with the release of the abdominal tension, her breathing becomes easier and her O2 sat shoots up to 96%.

We take off 1,200 mL of blood into the autotransfuser. There is a couple liters on the floor and another liter or so soaked up in a mound of lap sponges and gauze piled on her legs. Now, we can start to make out the anatomy of the abdomen.

I give the autotransfuser to Mathieu to give back to the woman. He attaches it to a blood filter on some IV tubing. I watch the blood slowly drip back into our patient's circulation. I turn back to the operating field and I see the telltale smooth, purple mottled mass of placenta in her pelvis. She has an ectopic pregnancy on the right side of her uterus.

I reach in my hand to dissect it off the posterior peritoneum and a five-inch-long, perfectly formed fetus shoots up and out. I grab him between my fingers and toss him onto the instrument stand. The placenta part pulls up and out easily and I place one clamp across the tube where it is bleeding and the bleeding stops.

We suck and mop up the rest of the blood hiding out in the various pockets of the abdominal cavity. I tie off and remove the right tube and ovary, and we close her up.

The hives have disappeared, her blood pressure is normal and, with bagging, her oxygen saturation remains normal. The transfused blood won't flow through the right IV. We switch to the left where it runs for five minutes and then stops there too. Both Sarah and Josué are unable to find another IV so I grab a central line kit.

I betadine her groin, palpate her femoral artery, stick a large needle into her femoral vein, slide in a guide wire, pull out the needle, nick the skin with a scalpel, slide a dilator over the guide wire and slip the central line in before finally pulling out the guide wire and attaching the blood line.

After 800 of the 1,200 mL of her own blood has run back into her veins, there are two many small clots clogging up the filters. We have to give up and stop the blood transfusion. Sarah, Josué, and I have now been artificially breathing for her for over four hours.

While Samedi, Jacob, and Josué clean up the substantial mess in the OR, the girl starts to wake up. I pull out the breathing tube. We then bag her for a while more, and then wean her off oxygen. When she's breathing on her own, we wheel her out to the ward.

When I go home, I feel tired but energized. I drink some cold water, grab a bite to eat, and sit down with my guitar. The joy flows out of me as my heart and soul are poured out into the music and songs. I know I have just experienced a miracle. I know God has just used me to miraculously save a life. The chills run up my spine as the tears run down my face.

The next day, the girl is asking for something to eat. Three days later, she goes home.

25 JUNE 2006
THE LONGEST DAY

Sarah and I are on the road to Béré again. It has been a grueling and psychologically draining three days in N'Djamena. There's a reason why *Tchad* was voted the world's most corrupt country in 2005. I spent three days shuffling from bureau to bureau, from office to office, getting papers, having letters signed, arguing, bargaining, yelling, manipulating, threatening, shaming and pleading. Finally, I was so discouraged I just wanted to get on a plane and leave.

We've found a donor willing to treat the AIDS patients in our district with anti-retroviral medications. For a year and a half we've tried to get the authorization to import. Finally, the medications have arrived but I am blocked by greedy, money hungry, grasping hands all around wanting a piece of the pie. No one cares that the drugs are to be given away free. No one cares that it is to help their country. Finally, through the intervention of some friends and God, we get the medicines out of the airport warehouse and now I'm on the road back to the hospital.

We spend the night in Kélo after arriving late. Now, the sun has just come up. The air is cool. The sky is an early morning bluish gray. The atmosphere is filled with mounds of fluffy clouds stacked like pancakes. The sun shines its rays in a descending pyramid from a hole in the clouds. The road gleams red. The bush is green. The millet starts to push through the earth. The goats and pigs are tied up.

The bicycles are just hitting the road with their cargo tied on back: everything from jugs of diesel to sacks of charcoal to live animals to people. The women start the daily walk to and from the well with huge pots balanced easily on their heads. Their bodies sway with a rhythm only possible for women who have carried heavy weights on their skulls for years.

The evidence of vigor, courage, hardiness, strength, newness, and hope is all around. I feel the weight of the last week slip from me. Excitement courses through my veins as I think of what we can do now for the most marginalized of Africans, the AIDS patient.

Little do I know that this day will not end until well after midnight.

I pull into the hospital compound, run in for a quick shower, change into scrubs, and head over to the hospital for worship. It is 7:30 a.m.

By 8 a.m. the waiting room is already packed full of patients and I'm on my way to see the hospitalized ones. There is one mother that Samedi had done a C-section on who is doing well. I send her home. A young man with an intestinal obstruction also operated on by Samedi during my stay in N'Djamena is passing gas so I advance his diet. A man with an infected testicle taken out by Samedi three days ago is sent home.

I come up to a 17-year-old Arab boy. He is skin and bones except for an amazingly distended abdomen. I tap it with my fingers and it resonates like a bouncing basketball in an empty gym. I fill out the operation order sheet and send the family off to pay for surgery. We then approach Jacques, the man whose leg I had amputated a week ago. His wound is foul and filled with pus. Black, dead muscle hangs out the ends. I send him off with Samedi to the OR to be debrided.

I continue on to Pediatrics. The one-month-old we'd done a laparotomy on last week has a wound dehiscence with part of his intestine sticking out. I prepare him to go back to the OR as well. I finish with the other patients and go to see Samedi. He has Jacques on the bed, knocked out with Ketamine.

Samedi shows me that there is pus all the way up Jacques' thigh. He squeezes down and pus comes out through the stump of the amputation.

We haul him into the main operating room, tie a tourniquet around his upper thigh, and prepare him for surgery.

I pull on gloves, put on the drape, and grab a large scalpel between my fingers. Samedi prays and I slash down Jacques' mid thigh to bone. I continue cutting quickly all around 'til I cut through the main artery and vein, which I then clamp and tie off. I grab the small handsaw. Samedi retracts the muscles out of the way as I saw through the femur. I close the bottom part of the muscle flap leaving the top and entire skin wound open for dressing changes.

As we finish, our medical student, Aaron, goes out to get the gurney. He comes back quickly to say there's a women there having seizures. The nurses are desperately trying to find an IV and take her vital signs.

I pull off my gloves as Samedi, Sarah, and Aaron clean up. They put

SAMEDI

Jacques on the other gurney to take him back to his bed. I go to examine the new arrival. The woman is in her early 20s and is pregnant with her fourth child. Her blood pressure is 160/110 and she is combative. We can't find the baby's heartbeat. We give her magnesium and take her directly into surgery.

A few minutes later I pull out a baby girl. As her head pops out of the abdominal incision, she starts to gasp and her arms start to move. I suction out her nose and mouth, clamp and cut the umbilical cord, and hand her off the Sarah.

The baby is soon screaming that beautiful newborn "I'm alive and not sure I like it" wail. I close up the uterus, fascia, and skin, and go out to see a few patients while the OR team takes the patient out, cleans up, and prepares for the next patient.

The Arab boy's family hasn't yet paid, so we take in the one-month-old with the wound dehiscence. I open up the wound a little more to find the extent of the wound breakdown. Then, Samedi pushes in the intestines and holds them in while I put a nice big suture bite through skin, fascia and peritoneum and slowly bring the wound back together. The baby is so tiny that even with skin and fascia and peritoneum together the layer is only a few millimeters thick. I finish and put a sterile dressing on.

After seeing all the outpatients, I finally go home at 4:30 p.m. and eat for the first time since 6 a.m. that morning. I'm exhausted. Fortunately, the

Arab family hasn't paid yet because I'm too tired to even think of doing another operation.

At six, Samedi comes to the house to say he's going to Kélo in the morning. I get a little nervous as the Arab boy needs to be operated on and without Samedi, it'll be very difficult. No one else really has much experience with assisting on big cases. I ask Samedi if he'll go see the family with me.

They say they have sent someone to get a cow to sell in the market and they'll get us the money Saturday. Can't we just do it now? I think he needs it urgently because his belly is really bloated and he is already wasting away. I look to Samedi and he nods. We call in the team and take him to the OR.

As I stand after the prayer poised to cut I wonder what I'll find: a sigmoid volvulus? Small bowel obstruction? Tumor? Mass of worms? Nothing I imagine is close to what I find.

I cut carefully down from his rib cage to below his belly button. The skin is thin and he has no fat. Before I know it I'm in the abdomen and I see a huge, shining white mass: an immensely distended colon! I open the belly completely and find that his colon is the size of a six-foot long boa constrictor that has just had several nice big meals.

Starting from his rectum the Sigmoid stretches up all the way to his stomach and then back again to the bottom of his pelvis and then the descending colon starts which is the same size and goes up to his spleen where the football sized intestine continues over to under his liver where suddenly it gets a little smaller. His small intestines are completely flat like a pile of small tapeworms piled in the center of his otherwise massive abdominal cavity.

I have to remove his colon. It looks like the rectum is okay so I start at the sigmoid and start to clamp, cut and tie off the blood vessels. He is so malnourished that the arteries and veins are easily identified due to the absolute lack of fat. After over four hours of careful dissecting, cutting, clamping, and tying I have an over two-meter piece of colon out on the table. It is filled with air and stool must weigh well over 20 kg.

I then free up the corner of the part of transverse colon that is left and bring it down to reattach it to the rectum. It is so bizarre to look in a two-foot long abdominal incision on a now almost empty cavity. I put in a drain and close up the fascia and skin. I attach suction to the drain and watch his belly descend to a massively concave emaciated state that matches perfectly the rest of his malnourished body. We finish a little before 1 a.m.

I go home, eat some beans and rice, drink a liter of juice, take a shower, and hit the sack. I'm asleep before my head hits the pillow.

05 JULY 2006
TEARS

I can't sleep. It's still dark. A cool wind is rustling the leaves outside my window. I lie under the mosquito net with a heaviness in my eyes that screams for slumber to come. My mind is racing and my stomach is churning. I want to just roll over and fight to sleep but something deep inside is pulling me elsewhere.

I roll out under the net trying not to wake Sarah. I slip on some shorts and bang the front door open. I feel for my flip-flops with my feet and stumble through the dark across the porch and down the steps.

A faint tinge of what could be less blackness touches the eastern horizon. The stars are brilliant. There is no moon and not a single light, lamp or fire anywhere. I've learned to find my way around the compound even in the dark. I brush against some low-lying mango branches and steal cautiously toward the back gate. It's locked and I don't have the key.

I scramble over the chain link fence to the side of the cement post holding the door. As I slither over the top, I scrape my leg against the cold, rough concrete. I land with a thud on the other side jarring my spine. I dust off my hands and stand up.

With my eyes now adjusted to the dark and the continued advancement of the dawn I can barely make out the trail through the millet field out back. I walk to the middle and gaze up.

I start to cry.

As tears stream down my face my body is wracked with sobs. It's been too long and too much. The national strike. The closing of all the other hospitals. The countless surgeries. The red tape in N'Djamena. The poverty. The needs. The kids in tattered clothes. The dirt. Equipment breaking down. The government project shutting down.

The fear. The ignorance. The witchcraft. The weird traditional practices. The drums all night. The grasping. The begging. The manipulating. The young guys hungry for something better. The almost palpable longing for hope. The AIDS patient on the way to recovery stolen away from the hospital by her sister so she can die at home. The Arab boy with complications post-op who despite two surgeries lasting over eight hours ends up dying anyway.

The immensity of the task. Being in over my head all the time. Never-ending needs. But most of all, sorrow. A deep, unexplainable sorrow for the people of Béré. A longing to somehow be a part of bringing them out of darkness, fear and ignorance into who they were made to be. A cry from my heart that God will help me to love when I don't feel like it.

Through the haze of my watery eyes I spot shooting stars. To the west, far across the plain, lightning flashes. Some clouds steal up over the eastern stars. Insects are chirping. Roosters are crowing. Bats are fluttering past my ears. Guinea fowl are squawking in their nighttime perches.

Various coos, warbles, trills and hoots waft around me in a symphony that sucks the tightness out of my chest and abdomen. I relax things I didn't know were tense. I slowly become still, filled with an extraordinary Presence. I turn slowly toward the house as dawn breaks across the village.

20 JULY 2006
MOURNING

A cool east wind chills me to the bone. I've just finished praying with Sarah. For the first time in a long time I settle down to sleep without earplugs. As I snuggle next to the warmth of my wife, I drift off to the chirping of a myriad night insects. All things slowly fade off into dreamland. But, just before starting the night visions, I am reluctantly tugged back to reality by a soft tap, tap, tap on the door.

"*Médecin?*"

"*Oui?*" I groggily reply.

"It's me, Keining. One of the patients just died. The family traded a bicycle in so they can get their ox cart out of hawk. They want to take the body back to their village tonight. But I can't get the combination lock on the gate to open. I called Boniface, the gatekeeper, and he can't get it open either."

My brain zooms back out of the tranquility of my subconscious. I start to hear the wails, groans, and shrieks of a *Nangjeré* mourning ritual. I pull up the mosquito net and grab my flashlight.

"*J'arrive.*" I mumble as I search for some pants and a ragged t-shirt. I pull my clothes on, punch open the metal door, slip on some flip-flops by the slim light of my torch and pad reluctantly toward the hospital.

"Aaaaaaaahhhhhh! Ohhh, ohhhh, ohhhhhhh! Aye yi yi yi yi yi yi!" The ghoulish sounds of the dead man's family waft across the campus as if straight out of nightmare. Am I really awake? I follow Keining to the gate where the eerie, flickering glow of a kerosene lamp dimly lights up the shadows of people's arms waving and dim forms moving back and forth and rocking up and down.

I shine the flashlight on the lock. Three turns to the right, stop at 30. Turn back left past 30 and stop at 20. Back to the right till 02 and tug! The padlock falls open. I remove the chain as Keining and Boniface both click their tongues in approval in the background. They shake their heads followed by "*ça, ça, ça*" and "*kai, kai, kai*". Keining opens the gate and two shadowy forms silently slip in past us.

I look outside to where the dancing orange flame lights up a series of rolled up mats, three bicycles tightly in a row, and a couple of bundles wrapped up in cloth and tied at the top. A group of what appears to be women, as judged by the shadows from their head and body wraps, sit to the side. One woman with a bundle, probably a baby, strapped to her back is weaving back and forth. Her arms flail the air as she marches five steps forward, turns and comes five steps back in a never-ending dance of death.

> HER ARMS FLAIL THE AIR AS SHE MARCHES IN A NEVER-ENDING DANCE OF DEATH

The others are kneeling or sitting in a tight bunch with various head bobs and arm movements rhythmically accompanying the chants, wails, moans and groans in a macabre symphony of fear.

A man walks up with an agonizing yell tearing from his throat as he beats his breast. Dogs bark in chorus in the background as a cat yelps in a discordant cacophony straight from hell.

I find anger, pity and sorrow welling within me. It's so unnecessary and disheartening. The sorrow is not real. These same people left their relative sick for a week without treatment followed by three days in a coma before coming to the hospital. To pay $20 for his treatment is all but impossible. Yet, now, they will spend hundreds of dollars on entertaining and feeding the relatives and friends who will come to pay their condolences.

Everyone will gather and make a lot of noise to prove how sorrowful they are. They have to make sure that his spirit doesn't come back to haunt them for not being sad enough at his passing.

It makes me sick to sense all the fear of death, spirits, and haunting that I hear in their cries. To see and know the ignorance that keeps them captive breaks my heart. I know the One who has promised to "deliver all of them who through fear of death were...subject to bondage." (Hebrews 2:15). But it seems so overwhelming to fight against so much superstition, tradition, and fear.

I show Boniface and Keining how to work the lock. Two male relatives of the deceased emerge out of the darkness pulling the ox cart past us and out the gate. We put the chain back around as the two watchmen click and mutter their excitement at learning how the combination works. I walk back through the tall grass toward my bed. The chilling sounds of mournful *Nangjeré* fade again into the background. Soon those cries will be lost to the darkness of the African bush as it swallows up its children once again in a bottomless pit of despair.

08 AUGUST 2006
RIVER STORIES

I feel the stress flow off me as the wind blows in the open truck door. I'm on my way to the river. I hear the singing coming from the back as the young guys express their joy in the moment. The road is red and dusty. Green is starting to push up through the perpetual brown of Béré. The warm wind cools as it dries the sweat off my face.

We pass a small village where women are selling peanuts, donuts and grilled meat. The smell of smoke and cooking flesh wafts its pleasant odor across my nostrils. I wave to the kids who jump up to chase after us waving and yelling *"Nasara! Nasara!"*.

We round a corner as the road narrows. The truck passes some nomad women in brightly colored headscarves, their tiny bodies swaying gently on their donkeys' backs. A little ways ahead a small boy with a huge turban and a stick watches his cattle amble across the road. I honk my horn and a few cows turn to stare blankly at the truck while a few others start to lope across a little faster. I slow down and slowly weave my way through the bovine maze.

A few meters farther and I see the sign announcing the end of the road. An arrow points out the detour to the left that takes one to the barge. I go straight and pull up just to the edge of the cement where the bridge used to be.

There are backhoes and graders parked on the other side watching in silent contemplation their destructive handiwork. All the trees have been mowed down leaving a naked scarred earth with deep ruts and grooves. All this is supposed to somehow help them rebuild the bridge.

On the other side, cars and mini-vans are parked as people unload their merchandise to cross in tiny, hand hewn dugout canoes. Today is Saturday, market day. With the barge under repairs, there is no other way across.

I get out, take off my shirt and glasses, and tie the car key to my swimming shorts. I climb down the rough volcanic stone to the water's edge. Daniel and Ferdinand follow me while the others head downstream to a safer crossing.

In between the two buttresses of the ancient bridge, the water way is forcibly narrowed creating whitewater and rapids from its strong current. As I step in I feel the tug and lean back to keep from being swept away. I feel the sharp pumice stones encrusted with shards of oyster shells cutting into my feet. I move slowly downstream until it gets deep enough to let go and ride the rapids.

The current whips me around to the left as the whitecaps slap my face. I am borne to the left toward a 20-foot high clay bank. Roots from bushes hang over the top. One tree has fallen in head first leaning its trunk against the bank.

I twist around, give a few quick strokes with my hands and feet and grab onto the tree. I pull myself around and up, using it as a ladder to get to the top of the cliff. The wet clay slips between my toes as I try to get a grip on the bank. I make it to the top where a small crowd has gathered to watch the entertaining *Nasara*.

DOUMPA

I look down and see that Daniel and Ferdinand have entered the current and are approaching the tree swiftly. They rapidly follow me up. Downriver, Koumakoi, Doumpa and Felix are crossing in the shallows.

Sarah has just arrived on horseback. Her curly red hair blows wildly in the wind. She effortlessly trots up and wipes the sweat from her forehead. Smiling, she gives me an enthusiastic wave. The horse descends slowly down to the river to drink. Sarah then takes him for a swim.

Koumakoi joins us. Looking down at Sarah, he tells me that she needs to be careful or her horse will turn into a hippo. I laugh, thinking he's joking, but one look at his face tells me that he really believes it.

We decide to jump off three by three. Doumpa, Ferdinand and I are the first to jump. I step back and then take a few quick steps forward to launch myself out as far as I can. I wildly flail my arms and legs to amuse the crowd with the silliness of *Nasara*. As I plunge in, I feel it all the way to the tips of my sinuses as they get their ritual cleansing. I touch the sandy bottom and kick my way to the surface taking in a big gulp of refreshing air. First wiping my eyes and nose, I paddle leisurely back to shore.

I see Ferdinand has reached the bank as well. Forgetting about Doumpa, I look up to watch the others jump. They are a little hesitant and I start to egg them on. Suddenly, I hear Ferdinand behind me.

"Where's Doumpa?"

I turn and look just in time to see a pair of hands break the surface about 15 feet from me. The hands then sink back beneath the surface. As thoughts race through my brain of how I'm going to explain the drowning of his son to Anatole, I push off and quickly swim to where I saw the hands.

Ferdinand reaches the spot first and does a surface dive straight down. I arrive just in time to feel a head and arms being pushed up. I grab Doumpa as he sputters and coughs for air and I pull him to the bank. Ferdinand follows. Instead of the expected fear and sympathy, everyone, including Doumpa, starts laughing. Maybe I'm the only one who realizes how close we came to death in those swift, muddy waters.

A few weeks later, Sarah and I decide to go to the river again and this time she accompanies me in the truck. Israel, our latest nurse volunteer, follows me into the current. Sarah and Pernille, a Danish medical student, walk downstream so they can get in to the water out of view of the stares of the ever-present crowd.

Since the water has risen about five feet, Israel and I are able to enter at the top of the rapids. This time, the slaps from the waves are harsher and I'm a little out of breath when I get to the calmer water. We climb and jump just like last time and then circle around with the current as it circles the deep pit at the center of the river. It's perfect since we would be unable to swim upstream if it didn't reverse itself and bring us easily and quickly back to the rapids. We make the circuit several times then watch from the cliff as Sarah and Pernille also navigate the whitewater.

Sarah and Pernille then go to rest in the shallows by the opposite bank, near where it rises up to the bulwark of the old bridge. The water is calm there. Some old tree branches stick out of the river near shore. We pass by several times without incident on our way back to the rapids.

When Israel and I get tired of swimming we start chasing kids who have gathered to watch. Many of them are laughing, but some are truly terrified. One time, I actually catch one, but I'm afraid he'll faint from terror. His eyes are wide and he screams bloody murder while shaking his hands and shouting "Ai, Ai, Ai, baaaaooooooooooo!"

Finally, we are tired and I walk downstream to get Sarah and Pernille's clothes from where they'd left them. As I return, an excited Israel runs up to me and says, "Look, a hippo!" I look downstream just in time to see some huge nostrils break the surface.

"He was hiding down by the bank in the branches, right where we swam past all those times! Then he finally came up and then headed downstream. We were this close, man!"

Suddenly, a cry goes up from the onlookers. Sarah and Pernille are still in the water by the rapids. I yell at them to come look. They get out quickly and also see the massive hippo waddle out of the water, up the bank and into the bush.

The locals start running after him with sticks and huge rocks that they throw at him. We jump into the truck and give chase. I veer down a small path only to have the kids on top yell for me to go back, go back! I slam it into reverse and squeal back onto the main road.

"Forward, forward!" they scream. I hit the gas and we follow the crowd. I stop and climb out onto the roof. I see the hippo just 30 feet away crashing through the bushes with the boys still in hot pursuit. We follow the chase for about 15 minutes before they finally get too far away.

That night, I tell the story to Koumakoi and the rest of the young guys. He informs me that those hippos that come out of the water are really men that take on the form of the animal. Apparently, hippos are not really animals, they're men or horses that have been transformed. Whatever they are, I'm just glad this one didn't take a bite out of me, Sarah or anyone else. I'm thankful to be back home in one piece!

13 AUGUST 2006
RESURRECTION

I take the well-worn path between the house and the hospital. The rains have turned the desert into a jungle. The foliage is barely kept at bay by the constant munching of our two half-starved horses. Hortence has called me to look at a child with anemia to see if he needs a blood transfusion. I savor the cool air, slight breeze and overcast sky. Maybe it'll rain. I walk down the verandah of the OR and toward the nurse's station.

A few minutes later we are in the dimly lit cave that is Pediatrics. The tin roof windows are mostly closed to keep out the cold. As a result, the entire ward is lost in the shadows of late afternoon. After verifying that the five-year-old is stable enough not to need a risky blood transfusion, I walk back down the rows of beds.

I stop to look at the miracle baby. She is, amazingly, still alive. Her chubby body lies flaccid on the mattress, her breathing shallow but not too fast. Her eyes are rolled back and she is unconscious. Her body is hot to the touch. I grab a thermometer and insert it in the baby's anus: 38 degrees Celsius, a high fever consistent with cerebral Malaria. I prescribe an injection to lower the fever and walk back to the nurse's station with the father of the child in tow.

As the father of the child pays for the medicine I can tell he is tired and discouraged.

"It's a miracle she's still alive," I say.

"Yeah, but it's all a waste..." the dad replies leaving unsaid the obvious fact that he's sure she'll die.

As I look at the tears that well uncontrollably in his eyes the whole story of her resurrection passes quickly through my head as told to me by Sarah:

I was just making normal rounds on Pediatrics when I saw that little baby Koussekoura's IV wasn't working. They hadn't been able to find an IV in her anywhere except her external jugular. There she was, semi-conscious, with this big taped IV and tubing coming out the left side of her neck.

Israel and Pernille tried to help me get it working. We tried everything: injecting a syringe of glucose solution, wrapping the IV tubing around our fingers to press the fluid through the catheter, inserting needles in the IV bottle to let out the air, everything. This was only her 2nd day of treatment for cerebral Malaria and she needed that IV!

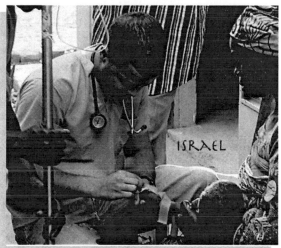

ISRAEL

Just then, I noticed that she was breathing faster. Then her hands curled up into fists, her eyes rolled back in her head and her body stiffened as she had a generalized seizure. The mom and great aunt were standing by. Before I could do anything, she stopped breathing. Israel, Pernille and I all searched for a pulse and couldn't find one; neck, wrist, groin, chest, nothing.

The women starting crying softly as the mom came to close the eyes and arrange the limbs. The baby was completely limp. The great aunt went to look for a cloth to wrap the body in. We started to comfort them.

Several minutes passed when, suddenly, the baby gave a small gasp for air, then another. Shocked I checked for a pulse and found a slow one. I started doing external cardiac massage until the heartbeat became faster. She was still unconscious but now definitely alive! Then she started seizing again and I had to give her three doses of Valium before she calmed down. She was then breathing short and fast with big pauses. I thought there was no way she'd live through the night.

It is now a day later and little, chubby Koussekoura is still alive, but the dad is convinced she won't last. It is still sketchy but something in me rises up and forces its way out.

"No, it's not a waste!" I cry, "She's alive. Our only responsibility is to do what we can while we can. Our money won't last. One day it's going to burn. But what we do with our money lasts. One day, whether she lives or dies right now, one day you'll see her again. God will reward you because you have given from your heart. You sacrificed to buy the medicines to treat your baby even though you thought she would die. Whether she lives or dies is now in God's hands because you've done all you could. That's all that's required. But if you didn't do all you could, then you would be responsible. Courage! You're doing the right thing!"

The dad walks back to his comatose daughter and I walk back to my house. I look up at the stars that have now come out and pray that God will reward that dad's love and sacrifice. I feel an unexpected warmth and peace as I walk the familiar path home.

29 AUGUST 2006
MALARIA NIGHTMARE

I'm standing awash in pools of blood and amniotic fluid. I've just slashed down deep through skin, fat, and fascia then ripped through muscle and peritoneum to find the bulging uterus. Now, I cut through well-perfused muscle causing arteries to spurt blood into the wound. A gush of amniotic fluid, thickly stained with meconium, pours onto the operating field.

I reach a hand down into the swirling pool of red mixed with split-pea-soup green to find a grossly distorted baby's head. It is too big to fit through his mom's pelvic outlet. I now pull the head up and out through an abdominal incision. I clamp and cut the umbilical cord as the blood and gunk continues to pool all around us. I then reach in and rip out the placenta, which is not normally a pretty sight, much less when covered with meconium.

> MY BODY IS WRACKED WITH CHILLS AS A COLD SWEAT BREAKS OUT ALL OVER

It's at this point that I get nauseated. One would think that what I'm in the midst of doing would be enough to nauseate anyone. But this is different. It's sudden. Clamminess. A churning of the stomach. Light headedness. Aching muscles and joints. A splitting headache. Sweat dripping despite the air-conditioned chilliness of the OR. This can only be Malaria.

Somehow I find the strength to clamp the bleeders on the uterus, suture it closed and close the skin. I feel ready to collapse at any point. I quickly help clean up the patient as the feeling of needing to vomit increases. My head is going to explode. How do you describe it unless you've experienced it? A coldness inside that reaches to the depths of who you are and strangles you.

We move the patient out to the wards and clean up the OR. I walk back in a haze, one step at a time. *You can do it, James. You're almost home.* It's 3 a.m.. In my bathroom, I open a packet of Artesunate and swallow six pills. I chase it with 800 mg of ibuprofen, a tablet of promethazine and a gram of Tylenol. I collapse in bed. My body is wracked with chills as a cold sweat breaks out all over. I pile on the blankets and crash into a deep sleep.

At 6 a.m., Hortence wakes me up. There is another woman who is having trouble delivering. Using all the willpower I have left, I pull myself out of my Malaria-induced fog, slip on my scrubs and head groggily up to the hospital. I slip on gloves and examine the woman.

The head of the baby is very deformed and high up in the pelvis. I give her a few chances to push to see if she can make the head come down. In between encouraging and waiting, I literally almost fall asleep on my feet. I feel I have nothing to give. Please, God, don't let her need a C-section.

HORTENCE

Finally, I face the inevitable, the baby won't come out. But then, deep in the recesses of my sluggish mind, I remember another option: symphysiotomy. Of course! It's only her third pregnancy and like a typical *Tchadian* woman she'll want at least five more pregnancies. This way she won't be obligated to suffer all the risks of a C-section each time. I force myself to walk to the OR and get the symphysiotomy box. I still feel like passing out or just lying down somewhere. It is sheer willpower that keeps me going.

Once back in the delivery room, I shave her pubic area, inject lidocaine, prep with Betadine, drape with sterile towels, put on sterile gloves, grab the scalpel and cut straight down to her pubic symphysis. I can feel and almost hear as the scalpel cuts through cartilage. My fingers are inside moving the foley catheter to the side so the urethra can't get damaged. I feel that it's mostly cut. I stick my finger in and feel a nice gap.

I tell Hortence and Israel to pull the legs apart and down to the side. Suddenly, there is a crack and her pelvis opens up. I quickly suture up the wound and almost immediately the baby's head drops down and appears. I suction the nose and mouth and pull the shoulders and legs out. The huge 4.2 kg baby starts yelling immediately as I clamp and cut the cord. My adrenaline wears off and I start to feel my aching body again. I'm racked with chills.

I go home and crash. I sleep for 24 straight hours almost without moving. Every part of me feels like it's been punched and pounded. I feel I can't sink in deep enough into the mattress. I alternate between soaking the sheets with foul smelling sweat, to being so cold that even wool socks, a sweatshirt, three blankets and a sheet aren't enough to keep me warm.

I huddle in the fetal position. I try to drink but everything has a metallic, bitter taste. I'm dead to the world. I wake up briefly to realize it's night and the generator's on. Sarah stands over me asking me if there's anything she can do for me. I take some more drugs, fall straight back into my self-induced coma, and wait for the morning to come.

18 SEPTEMBER 2006
MUD

Two kilometers from Béré. Two kilometers from home and a much needed shower, supper and sleep. I can almost feel the cool water against my skin washing off two days of grime and sweat. My personal odor is pungent and seeping into the seat of the Toyota Hilux as I grip the steering wheel with my last ounce of strength.

Alternating drifting white and shadowy gray clouds break the dark steel blue of the *Tchadian* night sky. A gentle pink tinges the sky as the sun makes its final descent. We've made it through the worst of the unknown and known. It's a straight shot to Béré. Sure, the road is flooded and muddy but I know this stretch and I've already been through so many roads much worse. What could go wrong?

I spot a large transport truck stuck at a diagonal angle across the road coming from Béré. There are deep water-filled ruts down the center. To the right is a bank with a motorcycle and bike path worn in it and a rice paddy further right. It looks wide enough for our truck and in a zombie-like last-minute poor decision, I take the path to the right instead of straight center. I make it almost to the other vehicle when going up a slight hump I feel the tires slip and I slide into the rice field. The truck is now angled at a 45-degree slant, the tires are spinning against wet clay and the axels are digging into the bank. We are stuck. After all we've been through to get this far and this close, we are stuck.

Despair clutches at every part of my being as the fatigue of the last four days finally hits me and I have nothing left to give. Five guys from the other stuck truck come and help. We spend three hours digging, pushing, lifting, pulling, unloading, everything to no avail. I just stand and mostly watch with a blank, hopeless look on my face. I think back over the last week and think, *"C'est pas posible."*

It all started with a simple trip to N'Djamena to drop off our Danish medical student, Pernille. The trip up was uneventful and we spent Saturday at our *Tchadian* medical student, Odei's, church. Cedric accompanied us. He's a theology student I'd met in France who had come to visit and was now on his way back to Cameroon to finish his internship. Noel, our chaplain, was also there with us. We planned to go back Sunday.

Sunday morning, I receive a telephone call from Sunmbola Paul, a Nigerian nurse who has wanted to come to work as a missionary at Béré since last February. He informs me that he finally has all his papers and is on his way. In fact, he'll arrive in Banki at the Cameroonian-Nigerian border tomorrow. I inform Pierre at the hospital that we'll be a couple days late and we make plans to go to Banki.

Monday, Sarah, Cedric, Noel and I pile into the Hilux and after running around N'Djamena accomplishing nothing for four hours we finally are at the Cameroonian border. I take in the car registration to get the necessary handwritten *OK* for the car to leave *Tchad* while Sarah goes to get our passports stamped. We hand the car's *OK* to some camo-wearing dudes under a woven mat shelter, pay the 1,500 francs bridge toll, stamp our passports on the Cameroonian side, fill up with diesel and are on our way. It's 12:30 p.m..

The road south from *Tchad* is a monotonous flat, straight route through grasslands now flooded with rain. There is the occasional mud hut village, herd of cows, goats or sheep, and tollbooth. We pass briefly through a game park that has all the appearance of a classical African safari except for the animals. We do see a couple monkeys cross the road, but that's it.

Finally, we turn off the pavement onto a bumpy, winding, puddle-filled road that leads to Banki. With four-wheel drive engaged, the passage is uneventful. We pass customs and arrive at the bridge only to find it half washed away by the rains. A pile of battered cars is on our side while a steady stream of porters loaded with all kinds of merchandise crosses the wide, shallow river on foot a little downstream. Even motorcycles manage to find a way across carried with large sticks stuck between the spokes and carried by four men.

Cedric and I decide to cross to look for Paul while Sarah and Noel guard the truck. I roll up my pant legs, gather my Arabic robes in my hand

and cross, sandals in hand. Needless to say, we are the object of much commentary as it's not everyday they get to see a tall lanky *Nasara* crossing a river wearing African attire accompanied by a short Frenchman wearing shorts.

After a kilometer walk through the typical plastic-adorned, mud-filled and cow-dung smelling streets of a sub-Saharan village we arrive at the Cameroonian immigration office where I'd told Paul to meet us.

Not finding him, we pass the time discussing the world cup and other international soccer events with the local police as time ticks away lazily in a dusty border office. We finally saunter over to the Nigerian side. Suddenly, despite the same familiar village ambiance, the language changes to English. Now, we are greeted with "How?" and "You are welcome!" instead of *"Bonjour!"* or *"As salaam aleikum!"*

No sign of Paul. We wait. We return to the truck across the river and then go back again. It's almost 6:30 p.m. and the Cameroonians are still there even though they said they close at 6 p.m.. We go back to the

Nigerian side where we find a relieved Paul who greets us enthusiastically.

After getting his passport stamped, we haggle with the motorized tricycle that is carrying his two massive, heavy bags until he agrees to take them to the river. We follow on foot. At first, we are afraid we've been had, since the tricycle is nowhere to be seen. Finally, he arrives. It is dark with just a slight gray left over from the departed sun.

I pick up a suitcase and carry it as far down the bridge as possible to where we descend into the river. Instantly, many helpful hands surround me grasping at the bag.

"Let me carry it for you, very cheap!"

"I need the work!"

"I need to feed my family!"

They start at 5,000 francs and after bargaining I get them down to 500 francs. I'm about to agree when someone to the side advises me in English "too expensive." So I grab back the suitcase and tell Paul we'll just carry them over. It's not that far.

I wade into the water. It is cold and fast. The bottom is sandy and undulating. With the darkness I am just feeling my way. Suddenly I hit a small trench created by the flow. I stumble but somehow keep from falling or losing the bag. I push on against the current tugging me, wanting to suck me under. One more spot up to my thighs for a few meters and I stagger up the bank and gratefully dump the suitcase on the dirt. I turn around to see Paul struggling with an even larger bag on his shoulder. I wade back out and give him a hand across the deeper part.

Now, it's 7 p.m. and we only have a few hours of horrible roads ahead of us before getting to the Koza Adventist Hospital. We've been told that the northern route is passable because it hasn't rained in three days. I've done this route once in the daytime and in the dry season. We'll give it a try, as it's half the distance of the other route winding around to the south.

We manage fine, crossing several rivers on cement lined dips through the waters. We finally get to a very wide one. I look at the cement markers though and it doesn't look deep. I'm in four-wheel drive, I start across but get stuck in the sand after about five meters. I jam it in four-wheel low and Cedric, Paul, Sarah and Noel get out to push. I gun it, the engine screams in protest but the sand is forced to slowly relinquish its hold and the Hilux inches forward. I don't dare stop so I keep the engine wound out and squealing until I slowly make it to the other side. The others rejoin me and Cedric is ecstatic that *finalement* he has an *aventure* to write home about!

After many more uncertain stretches and one really sketchy crossing we arrive in Koza at 9:30 p.m.. What joy to see our friends Greg, Audrey and Sarah Shank again! I crash onto a futon on the living room floor and sleep like a dead man after filling my stomach with rice and beans. I wake up late. Cedric and Noel have already gone to visit the hospital. We catch up with the Shanks and then head to Maroua.

By 1:30 p.m. we are in Maroua. With the help of Koza's accountant, Issa, we find a ton of medicines that we hadn't been able to find in *Tchad*. To find it, all we had to do is visit three different pharmacies despite a heavy downpour. We spend the night at the Baptist mission guesthouse. As I look at the pile of medicines, IV fluids and supplies, I don't feel it'll ever fit in our small pickup.

We happen to meet a Danish reporter who'd done a series of articles on Sarah and her work in Béré last year and after eating chicken together at a restaurant we gratefully get some rest. Tomorrow should be an easy few hours to Yagoua, a simple ferry crossing and one hour of good roads from Bongor to Kélo before braving the two hours of bad roads to Béré. Nothing to worry about!

Wednesday morning, we carefully pack everything and amazingly it all fits, although it's piled pretty high. I tie on the tarp, say goodbye to Cedric who's taking the early bus to Yaoundé, and Sarah, Paul, Noel and I pile in with a local pastor who'll help us make some last minute purchases.

We buy bleach, oil and fuel filters for the hospital as well as a little food and we're on our way.

We arrive in Yagoua without incident only to find that the ferry is down. The border police tell us, no *problème,* we just have to take the road to Fianga where we can cross on the Ham Bridge. The road to Fianga is unpaved, in the bush, isolated and filled with holes and water. We pass a Cameroonian police checkpoint, which lets us through without doing anything.

PAUL

Suddenly, we find ourselves at the *Tchadian* border control. They want us to pay the *formalité* to get across. They insist that Paul needs a visa. We calmly explain that Nigerians don't need visas for *Tchad* and that if we can just have the forms to fill out and a receipt we'll be happy to pay the *formalité.* After a few more attempts at coercion we are let through with strict orders to see the immigration authorities in Fianga.

We chat up the immigration officer in Fianga who is happy to practice his English on me and hear about our trip so far. After stamping all our passports for free he then informs us that a week ago, a storm washed out the Ham Bridge. We'll have to go to Gouna Gaya. After visiting with a friend, Pastor Wongkel, we hit the road for Gouna Gaya.

A couple of drunk youths in street clothes hassle us at a rain barrier but finally let us pass. A few kilometers later, we ask someone and find that they had put us on the road to Pala instead of Gouna Gaya. We turn around and I hear a noise coming from somewhere under the car. I get out and look and see nothing. It continues. It's a grinding, horrible noise. Sarah insists it's not one of the regular noises so I get out and check again.

That's when I see the right rear wheel. Almost all the nuts have come loose and the holes in the rim have been worn off. This has happened before and we just tightened them all down. This time, though, two of the bolts shear off as I try to tighten them. A third won't tighten down leaving us with only three of the six to hold the wheel on. We continue gingerly and after being detained for a while again at the same barrier we are back on the road to Gouna Gaya.

Eight kilometers from Fianga, I hear the sound again. The nuts have started to come undone. We debate what to do. We ask some locals and they say we'll never find those parts even in Fianga, only in Gouna Gaya. We take off the tire and replace it with the spare. The nuts are sheared, too. One of them refuses to go back on the bolt because the threads were crushed against the rim as it wobbled. We take one nut off each of the other three wheels to attach the fourth with the three bolts remaining. Every ten kilometers I stop to tighten the bolts.

This is the worst road I've seen yet. I leave it in low four-wheel the whole time. It is dark. We have made it through many deep, muddy puddles I never thought we'd find the end of. Now we are before another one. There is no way around. No solid bank to at least have one side gripping on. I am forced to head dead center. As I plunge in, the car sinks to the doors in a steep and sudden hole. The car bogs down but somehow never stops as I press the accelerator to the floor. The engine whines and in slow motion we come out the other side.

Several hours and many turns of the wrench on the wheel nuts later, and we finally arrive in Gouna Gaya. It is like a ghost town. There are power lines and streetlights everywhere with a large central water tower— all rarities in a *Tchadian* village—but everything is dark, lit only by a few kerosene lamps in the market place.

We are exhausted and hungry. This is my friend, Bonaparte's town so I hope to find him. His phone is off but we find his movie theater, an outdoors affair with a crowd gathered around outside chatting and eating grilled corn. His partner informs us that Bonaparte left this morning for N'Djamena. Fortunately, I know the district medical officer and he lets us crash there after a brief stop in the market for a grilled goat and bread supper.

I haven't showered all day, but fall into an immediate, exhausted sleep. The next morning, we sit around under the mango tree eating donuts and hot, sweet milk. The doctor's mechanic tells us they don't have the parts in Gouna Gaya, we need to go to Kélo.

Fortunately, the road to Kélo, while long, is pretty good. The three bolts hold and we arrive at 10 a.m. in Kélo. We pull off the road at the local mechanic's garage. There is a pile of junked cars sitting under a tree next to a crowd of grease covered youths tinkering with this and that engine.

They take off the wheel and discover the brake pads are basically non-existent. After many attempts with the wrong sized parts, they finally have both back brakes replaced but have found only one replacement bolt. We are forced to hit the road to Béré now with only four bolts still in that one back tire. Since yesterday, I've eaten only some pastries, bananas, grilled goat, boiled eggs, donuts and milk. It is 4 p.m. when we finally finish at the mechanic's and hit the familiar road to Béré.

The only really bad stretch is where the hippos live. The road is completely under water for about the length of a football field. Fortunately, the road is firm and the water isn't deep. I follow a motorcyclist who's half-driving, half walking his bike across. We then cross the ferry leaving us only four miles from Béré. There is one bad stretch that we cross easily and then I'm only a mile from home when...

As I stand by the car that keeps sinking deeper and deeper into the rice paddy I am suddenly overwhelmed. All I want is for this nightmare to end. A motorcycle starts to pass and then stops to ask who the driver of the truck is. Obviously, he has no idea what he's doing. He should have done like this or like that...blah, blah, blah. I feel a gripping anger well up within. He has no idea what I've just been through and how many dangers I've navigated successfully in this stupid truck. He has no idea how tired, dirty and hungry I am. Fortunately for him, he decides to drive away before I do something I'd regret.

Sarah heads off running to Béré to find some of the youth and staff who can come help us with more manpower. After a half an hour they start to show up. It's so good to see familiar faces and while it's embarrassing to be stuck this close to home, it's also a blessing. Still, with the extra help, we are no closer to getting out.

Finally, a Land Cruiser pulls up with some other missionaries, Rich and Anne. Rich attaches a towrope and guns his engine. After a few moans and groans, the Hilux slowly is pulled out of the watery grip of the muddy rice field. We load half of our stuff into their truck and the rest into ours. The volunteers pile in and I hit the gas. The car doesn't move! After a quick feeling of desperation and hopelessness, I ask the guys to pile out and push. Within seconds the truck moves forward and across to dry road!

Five minutes later, I'm back home. A hot shower has never felt so good!

24 SEPTEMBER 2006
DER

I'm walking back from the hospital. I've just finished late Sunday morning rounds and plan on doing some emails or computer work. I see André standing by the gate. I waltz up and ask him what's going on. He's dressed in a light blue and white full jogging suit like he's about to warm up for some match.

"We're going to Der to visit Daniel. We haven't seen him in awhile and we heard he was deathly sick. Pierre, Keining and I are going as soon as Keining gets here."

Daniel is one of the teachers at our school. I instantly am impressed I should go. The words of my late brother, David, come to mind: "do what's important, not what's urgent." I decide this is important.

I put on my swimming suit and a t-shirt and grab the keys for the truck. Pierre, André, Doumpa and Keining pile in. We head across Béré till we find a narrow, sandy track out of town heading more or less west. We go until we hit water.

"It only gets worse," warns Keining. "We'll be up to our knees at least. Everything is flooded this year."

There's no room to turn around, but I try anyway and immediately get stuck in the thick mud of the adjacent rice field. The guys easily push me out. I guess I'll just have to back out when we return. Little do I know how hard that will prove to be. We tumble out and I lock up.

The day is beautiful. The sky is blue like a Pacific atoll on a calm day. Billowy white clouds add character making the sky seem infinite, yet so close. The sun brings out the warm greens of the vast fields of tall, orderly rice waving in the gentle breeze in neat, but not perfect rows. The water is warm under my feet while the sandy bottom almost makes me believe I could be near the ocean. I feel I should hear the crash of waves at any time.

SMALL FISH AND TADPOLES SWIM IN SCHOOLS AROUND OUR LEGS

Small fish and tadpoles swim in schools around our legs and through the rice fields. Tiny, delicate dragonflies with fluorescent green heads and fluorescent blue tails flit across the surface of the water-covered trail. Larger, ugly dragonflies ply the air between the heads of rice. Dark, bug-like animals scoot with coordinated flaps of their legs across the sandy bottom.

Small birds chirp and dart from patches of scrub bushes on slightly elevated islands in between the flooded fields. They are the bright red or yellow colored millet eaters. The sand gives way to a black silt. It is very slick. I almost fall several times. We head out into the rice fields where at least walking on the grasses makes it less likely we'll slip.

The water gets deeper. I find myself wading up to my thighs. The path takes a bend around an island and I finally see the village. The huts poke their thatch-roofed heads above the tall clusters of millet and between the mango trees. Smoke rises from several cooking fires. I reach a dry path and put my shoes back on.

Keining, Doumpa and I wait up for André and Pierre. We march together through the village until we find Daniel's house on the other side. It has been blown down in the last rain. We finally catch up with him at his mother-in-law's. Things have been going from bad to worse for Daniel.

Daniel greets us and tells us the whole story. Apparently, he became dizzy and weak while out working in the fields. He couldn't move his legs and arms because they just cramped up. He thought he was going to die.

All his family and friends came by but refused to pray for him because he's been going to the Adventist Church. "Pronounce the name of the Evangelical Church of Chad or we won't pray for you," they said. So he did. He was very confused though. Why would Christians not pray for each other just because they were from a different denomination? I wonder the same thing.

At the Béré Adventist Hospital we pray for all our patients whether they are Adventist, Evangelical, Muslim, Animist, Atheist, Pagan, or

PIERRE

whatever. His two daughters are sick now, too. So we convince him to come back with us. I put the four-year-old on my shoulders and wade back through the water until it gets shallower and shallower. We arrive back at the truck. The round trip has been 4 kilometers through the mud and water.

After waiting again for André and Pierre, I back the truck up. There is no problem until we almost get to the dry sand. Suddenly, the engine revs and the car slows down as the right front tire sinks in.

I get out to look and see that apparently the hard sand is only about a foot thick under which is a liquid soup of mud. We work for an hour or so without even the slightest movement of the truck. I call Rich, the same friend with a Land Cruiser who pulled me out of the mud last week. I can't get a hold of him. I try Sarah, nothing.

André finally calls another friend who agrees to go search for Rich. Keining heads off on foot since it's getting dark. He needs to start the generator at the hospital and begin his shift as night watchman. We are about to leave the truck ourselves when we see a motorcycle followed by a Land Cruiser. They've come!

Rich comes to check things out on foot. He then returns to the Land Cruiser to turn it around so he can back up to out truck. Unfortunately, he ignores the rule he'd taught me last time he pulled me out. He drives into a rice field to turn around. Now he's stuck too!

Someone heads off to a nearby evangelical church to round up manpower. We wait around getting eaten alive by mosquitoes the size of small vultures. It's night and the beauty of the day has fast faded. I'm starting to get frustrated. Then, I remember that I felt impressed to come, that this was important and that I can choose how I'll react to any given situation.

Instead of getting mad, Rich and I go a little ways apart and talk. Apparently, he's had a horrible weekend and this just tops it off. But, he's amazingly upbeat. I am able to share with him some of my hard times from the past week. I realize that this bad situation has given us both a chance to debrief that we wouldn't have had otherwise. We pray together and then the crowd arrives.

With the arms, legs and backs of 21 people, the Land Cruiser is fairly easily pushed back onto the road. Rich doesn't want to risk getting closer to the truck to pull us out so he goes to where the road is solid. Then, with a lot more effort but no less enthusiasm, the 21 *Tchadians* lift the back of the truck out of the holes onto more solid ground. I gun the engine for all it's worth as the men push the truck out of its front tire pits.

I get about 100 feet when the left side of the truck sinks again into the mush. This time the 21-man force just pushes the truck to the right, out of the hole and onto the path. I keep the pedal to the metal until I'm back on solid ground.

What a relief! But I don't think I want to drive again, at least not until the rainy season is over!

26 SEPTEMBER 2006
DEMONS

A young girl with Malaria comes in with seizures. She has received three doses of IV quinine by the time I get to examine her the next morning. She says that someone is always hitting her and that's why she jumps and starts all the time and has her seizures. I instantly sense that this is demonic possession or harassment. I ask her if I can pray for her and she agrees. As I do, she calms down a little. The next day, I learn that her father tried to bring in a witch doctor the night before to cure her. Fortunately, our night duty nurse refused.

I walk up to her bed and she is kind of tossing and turning, looking wildly about, confused. I examine her, find nothing otherwise abnormal and ask again if she wants me to pray. She refuses. Mathieu, one of our lab techs, who speaks her dialect starts bugging her to let me pray. She asks how come I say she can't see the *marabout* now when yesterday I said she could. So, she doesn't want me to pray for her. Mathieu insists as do her relatives. She finally consents and I kneel and pray. She calms down some but I sense there is still a lot of resistance. I call for Noel, the chaplain and he spends time with her and her family, counseling them on how she can be freed from this harassment if she lets the one true God come into her life.

I decide to fast. That morning for worship, Noel read Matthew 10 where the disciples can't cast out a demon because they didn't fast and pray. I've never been big on going without food. I find it hard and I've never gotten the point. But, I decide to give it a try.

That evening, after work, instead of eating with the others, I go to Sarah's and my side of the duplex and plop down with the guitar. After pounding out a few songs, I read some from the Bible and crash on the couch to meditate and relax. It's about 6:30 p.m. and Hortence knocks on the door.

"That girl is shouting and singing at the top of her lungs and annoying all the other patients. I tried giving her a shot of Valium but it didn't touch her."

As I walk over, I stare off into the bright, starry sky of Béré. "Maybe this is what it's all about; what will you do, God?" The mud squishes under my sandals and there's a cool breeze. Mango leaves soften the sharp glow of the bright fluorescent lights on the hospital buildings. As I approach the wards, I hear the chanting and crying of the young girl.

I walk up, kneel down and tell her that this time she doesn't have a choice. Since she's bothering others, I'm going to pray for her whether she wants it or not. As I start to pray in French I feel complete peace and patience. I continue. Hortence and the family as well as some other patients' family members gather around and bow their heads. I pray for forgiveness for whatever she's done, for freedom from the harassment and the attacks of the demons and for freedom so she can choose God if she wants. Words just flow.

Slowly the sounds die down. I have my hands folded near her head. I feel her head roll into my hands and her body relax. Like a child in mama's lap, I sense peace come into her. I finish my prayer and she is sleeping like a baby. She sleeps all night long and goes home the next day after further counseling from Noel.

I've just finished a newsletter for the hospital talking about Malaria prevention, what happens when we die, who the new volunteers are and why we took such a crazy trip through Cameroon. I simply want to print it. I turn on the printer. Nothing. I check the transformer, which works. I try another transformer just in case. Zilch. Hmmmmm, I guess I'll have to go to André's office and use the other printer.

Sarah comes in and asks me to recharge her I-Pod. I turn on the other computer and it starts beeping. I push down F2 and it stops. The computer starts up, but then the mouse flips around and doesn't let me highlight or click on what I want. I keep opening programs I didn't click on and can't seem to get it to work. I fiddle around and get more and more frustrated. Every time I reboot, the same beeping starts and now no matter what button I push, if I hold it in it makes it start but with the same weird mouse behavior. I am mad by now. After 30 minutes of messing around I can't figure it out. The computer's brand new and not connected to the Internet, so there can't be a virus. Finally, I just shut it down and go over to André's office to print.

I turn on the printer and the ink cartridges start zipping back and forth. No matter how many times I hit cancel or open up the printer to check and pull out and reinsert the cartridges nothing helps. Then, it hits me; this is too many weird things in one night. It must be demons harassing me. I almost laugh at this point to see how easily I've been distracted, frustrated and angered at the smallest things. I bow my head and pray. I turn the printer off and

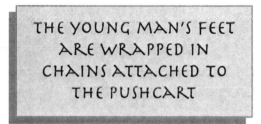

THE YOUNG MAN'S FEET ARE WRAPPED IN CHAINS ATTACHED TO THE PUSHCART

back on again and it works perfectly. I print out the newsletters, which are extremely well received by the community.

The young man's feet are wrapped in chains attached to the pushcart he is imprisoned in. His hands are tightly bound with ropes already cutting into his wrists. He is strong, handsome and has a leering smile on his face. He converses easily in perfect French.

He is well educated. Then he starts talking nonsense. The words are French, but they are random and scattered. I feel overwhelmed. Not another demoniac. I am too tired. I quickly explain to the family what I think is going on and tell them we'll have the chaplain see them. I go get Noel who spends the morning with them.

That night, I am again called. This time it is David, the nurse.

"That young man in the pushcart is writhing and chanting and disturbing everyone. I gave him two shots of Valium...nothing."

I go again. This time, I don't feel ready. I feel impatient and tired. The path is dark. I light it up with my flashlight until I get under the shelter of the clinic. Even that light is out, mirroring the darkness I feel in me. I whisper silently, "Forgive me, God, give me strength, I'm weak."

I go to the verandah of the wards where the young man is still chained in his pushcart. He is fairly calm. I ask the family to wheel him off to the side by the operating block.

I squat down by the rails of the pushcart, lean my hands over almost touching his shoulders and start praying. This time it's more difficult. The words stick in my throat. The French just won't come out. He starts crying and wailing. He spits in my face. I get more and more focused. For some reason, I'm not even close to mad. I feel pity for him. He is chained in more ways then one. Slowly, it gets quieter. Finally, I stop. He is asleep somehow, his neck hanging back awkwardly over the opposite rail. The family puts a pillow under but still refuses to unchain him. They are wise. It lasts until 4 a.m. when he starts up again.

At 7:30 a.m. it is my turn to read for worship. We are in Mark, the chapter that talks about the two men possessed with demons, bound with chains that they broke, who are freed by Jesus who then sends the demons into a herd of nearby pigs. I hear chains rattling in the background as our patient reminds us of his presence. It is so appropriate and I ask for all present to pray for him. Noel takes him on again. From time to time I hear singing from under the tree where he's resting.

The next day, his chains and ropes are off. He is eating under the tree between the lab and the surgical suite. He waves and thanks me. He says he's going home and points with a smile at the Bible he's now carrying.

23 OCTOBER 2006
RAMADAN

My horse, Bob, seems very tired. I have such a love-hate relationship with him. One day he seems like he's the best horse around and the next, I wonder if I shouldn't sell him. Ever since he was injured, he just hasn't been the same. Sarah's horse, Pepper, chased him around until he tried to jump over a six-foot fence. He dislocated his knee and broke part of his pelvis. After several months, Bob miraculously recovered. Now that both horses are castrated, they get along fine, but the damage has been done.

Sarah and Israel are far ahead. They are both riding bareback on Pepper who has boundless energy. Bob can't even walk straight. Every once in a while, when I get too far behind, I make him trot to catch up. Bob doesn't like it. Pepper has to be held back to keep from galloping the whole time. Bob won't even do a slow trot.

But the day is beautiful. We are headed out to an Arab village to celebrate the end of Ramadan, the Muslim month-long fast. The sun is out, the sky is a deep blue with billowy white clouds, and there is a cool breeze. Our sandy path takes us through endless fields of high, waving, green rice divided by rows of tall grasses swaying in the wind. There is still water on much of the path but the water table is descending rapidly as the rains have mostly come to an end.

The horses eat like pigs and are constantly turning their heads to the sides to sweep, gather and tear off luscious heads of rice. They are in perpetual search of food and never cease to eat even at night. They are insatiable!

We pass through the *Nangjeré* section of the village accompanied by the usual cries of *"Nasara! Nasara!"* wrung from the throats of a thousand kids. Soon we enter more open fields. The Arab part of town is not really a village but rather a few small huts scattered around a huge central cattle enclosure. The *Nangjeré* are farmers and the Arabs are herdsmen. The cows are all out to pasture now. We wind through some huts until Ahmat comes running to meet us.

We commence with the ritualistic Arabic greetings:

"As salaam aleikum."
"Wa aleikum as salaam."
"Kikef?"
"Afé."
"Afé tayybin?"
"Afé, bel afé?"
"Al hamdullilah!"
"Mashallah!"
"Kullo afé?"
"Mashallah!"
"Al hamdullilah!"

AHMAT

Ahmat leads us through the village to his small mud brick hut. The fired mud brick hut is where his mom lives. To the side, there is a round nomad tent. Wood bent over in curves sheathed in cow skins covers a low, three-foot high door in one side.

Inside is a bed made of curved, twisted sticks with a cotton mattress covered by layers of ornate Arabic rugs. The dirt floor is meticulously swept and to the side there are piles and piles of cheap, metal pots with brightly painted designs wrapped around the top. Outside is a half fence of woven reed mats. A large wooden mortar and pestle for pounding millet into flour stands to the left. A long, pointed Arab knife in a leather sheath hangs inside the door next to a long machete.

Ahmat takes us to a shelter outside the door of his mom's hut. It is made of four large, twisted branches have been stuck in the ground with cross pieces covered with mats. Woven reed mats topped with Arabic rugs cover the ground. We are invited in as the round of Arabic greetings repeats itself, not for the last time.

As we lounge on the mats, Ahmat's wife brings us tea and some *beignets*, flour donuts cooked in peanut oil. Our day is spent like this, greeting people who come to welcome us, drinking tea from time to time, eating small things here and there.

Sarah goes into Ahmat's mom's hut. Israel and I stay outside. The chief of the village comes and sits with us. A visiting Arab who'd been treated at our hospital strikes up a conversation about why Muslims shouldn't drink alcohol. He feels he should quit drinking if he wants to be a good Muslim. I ask him if he can imagine standing before Allah on judgment day with a glass of millet wine in his hand. He looks horrified and then laughs as the truth sinks in.

At 3 p.m. we head over to the cattle enclosure where they have cleared off some brush to make a place for the horse races. Of course, Sarah is hyped up to enter. We are some of the first to arrive. There are already a couple of Arabs mounted on horses decked out in brightly colored ribbons around the neck and along the sides. The horses are prancing as they are whipped with short pieces of rope. They all have metal bits in their mouths and are in constant motion as their rides try to control them.

I can imagine their thoughts as they see Sarah ride up. She's only a woman on an old castrated horse with a rope around its nose. The son of an elder in the village offers to race Sarah to start off the ceremonies. His father had been treated several weeks in our hospital for an abscess on his hand.

Sarah pulls up next to him and they take off together in a slow walk to the end of the cleared off patch. There is quite a contrast. Sarah's horse is calm and easily controlled while the Arab is constantly tugging at the reins and whipping his horse to keep him in line. The horse is bursting with energy and there is no doubt that he will win.

Finally, they are just specks on the horizon about 300 meters away. Suddenly, they both jerk their horses around and they take off at a tremendous gallop. They are moving so fast that they rapidly regain size in a blur of legs and frothing mouths. Sarah's competitor is standing up in the stirrups not moving at all but seeming to glide toward us as his horse releases all his pent up energy.

Sarah has a white veil tied as a scarf around the top of her head that is streaming behind her with her long curly red hair. The speed of the horses is actually frightening as they quickly approach without slowing down in the slightest. Finally, both riders tug back on the reins and reluctantly, fighting all the way, the horses are brought to a halt as the crowd scatters wondering if they might get trampled.

To the embarrassment of the Arab men and to the women's delight, Sarah has won!

The races continue until sundown, interrupted from time to time by herds of cattle coming in for the night. Crowds of little boys wearing new Arabic robes and crowds of girls wearing new dresses and headscarves dance around in circles to the side. Fires are started in the cattle pen to ward off insects. Sarah races a few more times and then we go back to Ahmat's.

He is HIV-positive and was treated for two months in the hospital for TB. He continues to come to visit the hospital from time to time as he made a lot of friends among the staff. He's the one who helped us get our two horses, Pepper and Bob. When Sarah showed him part of a film, he was very impressed that *Isa al Masih* spoke Arabic. Before the feast, he came three mornings in a row to remind us to come, and bring the film.

So, we set up a sheet over the side of the shelter, hook up the generator to the projector and show the film. Most of them don't understand standard Arabic and their reactions are kind of funny. When they see donkeys, goats, cows, horses, and other things they recognize, the kids get excited and shout out the names. When they see some apples, they shout out "Mangos!" When they see old white people it seems to be the most hilarious thing they've ever seen. White people look so funny to them.

At the end, I ask Ahmat if he understood. In their village they speak *Tchadian* Arabic and the movie was in standard Arabic. Ahmat says he understood everything. As I lie under the stars that night before falling asleep, little do I know that this is the last time I will see Ahmat. Where is he now? Only Allah knows.

03 NOVEMBER 2006
PUS SURPRISE

I can feel my heart start to beat a little faster in anticipation. My mouth starts to water and I hope I don't drool. The suspense is killing me! Every time I see someone with some kind of rag draped over a body part or waddling in like a sore cowboy after a long ride wearing nothing but a wrap draped around the waist, I can't help but wonder, what gross thing am I going to get to cut open or take out next?

Friday, it's an eight-year-old boy from Kélo. The father brings him in his arms. The right leg is draped in an army green rag that was probably a shirt at one point. The air gets a little thicker and I'm glad for the virus-induced mucus plugging my nasal passages. I quickly pull out the strip of paper to cover the exam table. The rag is hanging wet and limp. As soon as the boy is put down I regret having brought him into my office as the paper is starting to soak up whatever foul liquid is oozing from whatever it is under that bandage. I hurriedly pick him back up myself and take him outside to the gurney where I gingerly lift up the cloth to reveal...

Saturday night, it's a quiet shake from my wife. Sarah's on night duty and I am feeling drugged from fatigue. The last two weeks we've been doing two to three surgeries a day and it's taking it out of me. She's saying something about a teenager who has no lung sounds on one side. I seriously can't wake up. I'm trying but it's like I took a sleeping pill. I mumble something about sticking a needle in over the rib and seeing if there's liquid or air making the lung collapse. I tell her if there's air to come get me, if liquid than I'll see him in the morning. I wake up early Sunday morning wondering what I'll find as I walk over to the hospital in the coolness and stillness of an early African morning...

Monday, two guys waddle into my office wearing only skirts. They've both come from far away. I can hardly contain my excitement as I ask them to lie down on the exam table and fumble with the knot attaching the cloth skirt to their waist. As I slowly un-wrap it and take a look, I find just what I was expecting...

Tuesday, I operate on a woman who'd come in the Thursday before. She had a cloth wrapped around her mid-abdomen. She'd been sick for a month with pus draining from a small hole (fistula) in her belly button. As I am poised with my scalpel after the pre-op prayer, I wonder what I'll find inside. I quickly slice down from her belly button to her pelvis. To my surprise, I find...

Wednesday, Sarah comes running up to me with an amazed grin on her face. "James, you have to see this guy's arm. It's three times the usual size."

I walk into the clinic and see an elderly man with whitening hair and beard on his rugged face lying moaning on a stretcher on the floor. His left arm is wrapped in a rag that probably used to be white. From the tips of his fingers to the middle of his upper arm, I can see nothing. The upper arm to the shoulder is swollen to three times the size of the other arm. As I grab some gloves and bend over to unwrap it and take a look I have a feeling I might find...

One of the glorious benefits of working in a bush hospital is the phenomenon of pus surprise. No matter how often I see it, no matter how often I suspect it, no matter how often I have to really search for it, I always find it. Seek and ye shall find is my motto for tropical pus explorers. It is usually deeper than you think, but it's always there. But why this rush when I suspect it or the anticipation when I sense it's there hidden under some rag? Maybe I'm weird, but few things bring instant gratification like liberating some imprisoned pus.

The boy's leg is a fungating, purulent mass surrounding his entire lower leg with the exception of his foot, which is swollen and edematous. I take him to surgery, wrap a blood pressure cuff around his upper thigh and slice down to his tibia. I then cut up his tibia taking off his patellar tendon from the bone. That opens up his knee joint where I cut through the ligaments and menisci exposing his patellar space. There is barely a drop of blood anywhere thanks to the tourniquet. I divide and tie his vessels and cut through his sciatic nerve. I then slice down leaving some muscle for the flap. Israel lifts off the leg under the drape while I attach the patellar tendon to the posterior cruciate ligament. I then suture the flap closed and put a dressing and acc wrap on. While I didn't get to directly liberate pus, I did get to cut it off.

Three days later he's already up on crutches moving around on his own. Sarah has been giving him books to read and crayons to draw and he is quite smart and a talented artist. He talks almost nonstop without fear. The only time he expressed any reserve was after I took the dressing off and was going to replace the bandage. In a tiny, timid voice he begged, "please, not too tight, it hurts."

As I enter the OR, Sarah has already prepared the young man for his chest tube. I infiltrate around the ribs between his nipple and his armpit. I slice down to muscle and then poke up and over the rib with a curved clamp. I feel the pop. I see the stream of liquid pus squirt up. I am almost floored by the pungent force of the odor that escapes with the pus geyser.

I smell plenty of body fluids and odors in my work but this one I can barely take. It's not that I feel nauseated, I just can't breathe. I try to hold my breath as I grab the large bore chest tube with the clamp and 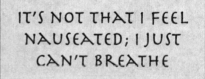 push it in over the rib and into the pleural space. I then attach the drainage chamber and suture the tube in place. I have never fixed and wrapped a chest tube in place faster in my life. As soon as I finish hooking the wrap around the boy's chest, I lunge outside for a breath of fresh air. The operating theater isn't the same for days, despite our best efforts at deodorizing.

Unfortunately, as I follow the fistula down from the woman's umbilicus I find it leads to the bladder, which is filled with a friable tumor. I scrape out as much as I can. This is a very advanced cancer that I can do nothing about. I'm forced to close up and give the family the bad news. Sometimes the surprise is a bad surprise, especially when there's something besides pus.

I lift off the rags from the man's arm. The whole arm is three times the usual size. The skin on the back of his hand is like the bladder from a basketball that is half-filled with water. It pokes in and bounces out as if there's nothing but liquid inside. His skin is peeling off in many places and in others is like wet cornmeal that crumbles off when rubbed. He has blisters in spots and holes leaking pus in a few spots.

We sedate the man, pump up a blood pressure cuff to act as a tourniquet and I incise down the back of his wrist. Yellow and red liquid seeps out. I extend the incision toward his shoulder with scissors. The skin is thin and like rubber with nothing attached underneath all the way to the elbow. There is just a little yellow jelly-like substance that melts away with pressure like a jellyfish caught on the beach on a hot summer day. I find what used to be muscle and fat. It's now just a fibrous mass the consistency of sponge cake, which dissolves into pus when my fingers dig into it searching for the limits of the infection.

I pull up mats of this spongy pus revealing anatomy I haven't seen since cadaver lab in Gross Anatomy my first year of medical school. All the superficial veins are intact and clotted off. A fine net of superficial nerves remains draped over the veins. All the tendons are exposed on the back of the hand. The skin is left intact only on his fingers. The rest of the skin is rotten and has to be removed. When I finish, the wound extends from the base of the fingers to above the elbow and half way around the circumference of the arm on both sides. The other side of the arm, while swollen, doesn't appear to be necrotic or pus-filled.

We wrap up the arm in diluted bleach soaked lap sponges and hold the dressing in place with an ACE wrap before letting off the tourniquet. There is some brisk bleeding near the elbow that I compress while sending Siméon to get a sand bag. A family member soon comes with a piece of cloth filled with a few kilos of sand that helps stop the bleeding. We wheel the man out to his bed.

29 DECEMBER 2006
DARKNESS AGAIN

One minute I'm eating my Danish tuna pasta salad garnished with circles of fresh green pepper and the next I can't even see my hand in front of my face. Silence abruptly descends as the motor driving the generator is shut off. With the increasing silence, the cries of the bereaved increase as well. The wails, shrieks and moans have become all too common, yet it still cuts deeply into my psyche with its piercing hopelessness. This time, it's coming from behind our house

It must be our neighbors. It has to be the family of Allawaye, the father of "Naked Boy" and "One Armed Boy." We've given our little neighbors self-explanatory names, although "Naked Boy" has recently transformed himself into "T-shirt and Sometimes Pants Boy." Allawaye's third wife's little one-year-old was recently hospitalized for meningitis.

We treated the infant with a full course of IV Chloramphenicol. At discharge, the fontanel was normal, there was no fever and the child was breastfeeding and otherwise healthy. Three days later, the child came back seizing and with a tense fontanel. The *H. flu* bacteria infecting his little cerebral spinal fluid was resistant. We had no good other alternative but did what we could.

Last night, David came to talk to me. "Allawaye's wife came to the gate with the child insisting on going home. I told them to wait until morning."

This morning, I enter the pediatric ward and see Allawaye with two of his wives, including the mother of the child with meningitis. The mother looks down the whole time and has a scowl on her face. The baby is breastfeeding, an improvement from two days ago when I was forced to put in a feeding tube. The fontanel has become less tense.

DAVID

I start to explain to Allawaye that while the baby is still sick and could die, there are some positive signs. Just then the other wife pipes up with a low, vicious voice and an evil glare. The nurse translates. She insists on going home. The child isn't better. Our treatments haven't worked. It's time to consult the witch doctor.

I make her leave and continue to explain to Allawaye why I think the child should stay in the hospital. He seems to understand and agrees to finish treatment. The mother of the child continues to act like we're trying to torture her child by asking him to stay. I offer to pray for the child and they accept. I'm desperate for God to prove that it's not some witchcraft that is making the child sick. I ask that he continue to heal the child.

We've done our best but with the limit in our arsenal of antibiotics we need a miracle. Now, in the crying, wailing and yelling coming from next door I'm afraid God has once again not intervened.

Friday, a boy came in with a leg wound treated for 18 days at the Kélo Hospital. All I see is a fungating mass encompassing his entire lower leg between the knee and ankle. The foot is swollen and the eight year old is in obvious pain. We take him immediately to surgery.

His leg is doubled up in contractures from weeks of not moving. I prop up the leg with rolled up towels after giving him his spinal anesthetic. He is naturally afraid and curious at the same time. I feel his eyes on my every movement. I put on my sterile gloves and attach sterile towels around the legs leaving just the knee exposed. I'm about ready to start, but then Israel asks if I'm going to let the boy watch. I look over and see him still staring at me in wonder tinged with anxiety.

I ask for a sterile drape as well so that the surgical site can be hidden from the boy's view. Israel pumps up the blood pressure cuff around his thigh and I pray before starting.

I imagine in my head the two flaps I want to create and then slice down to bone across the anterior tibia. I retract up the skin flap with forceps and free up the bone cutting off the patellar tendon from its attachment. I then enter the knee joint and cut across the menisci and the ligaments. There is no blood thanks to the tourniquet.

The only things holding the leg on now are the blood vessels, the sciatic nerve and the posterior muscles. I dissect a little around the vessels, clamp and tie them off, and cutting them loose along with the nerve. I then slice inferiorly to leave a muscle flap and have Israel pull off the leg from under the drape. He tosses it in the trash, as I sew up the two flaps and wrap an Ace bandage around the wound.

As I'm about to leave the OR after surgery, I pause over the trashcan. It's in the middle of the floor filled with plastic IV bottles, tubing, tape, gauze, plastic drapes and an upside down, normal looking foot sticking straight out. It looks like someone has been dumped in the garbage upside down.

It reminds me of a story Samedi told me. In the early '90s, they did a ton of amputations and dumped the body parts in a pit behind the hospital. One day, after a rain, a woman came running into the compound screaming that someone had drowned in a pit outside. All she saw was a foot sticking out and was sure there had to be a body attached somewhere in the water.

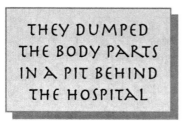

THEY DUMPED THE BODY PARTS IN A PIT BEHIND THE HOSPITAL

I get the same feeling now as I stare down at the bottom of the boy's foot so recently attached to a living body.

The next morning, one of our new nurses, Siméon had to listen to this boy talk and talk all day long. He wouldn't keep quiet and told Siméon how his leg got infected. His dad sent his mom away shortly after he was born and married another woman. According to the boy, the new wife is a sorceress who transforms herself into a cat. A few months ago, she became a cat and bit the boy's leg, which "poisoned" it. That's why the leg didn't heal and had to be cut off.

To the boy, it was a natural phenomenon. These stories are not uncommon. Most people think that diseases are caused by witchcraft, "poisoning," or *sorcelerie*. Therefore, usually some sort of traditional treatment has been tried before they are brought to the hospital. Often, when they do come, the illness is very advanced. Then, the hospital is blamed when the patient dies.

I sit in the darkness listening to my neighbors trying to appease the spirit of the departed child. I feel frustrated and hopeless. How can one fight against not only the forces of physical disease in a resource poor setting, but against the forces of ignorance and the forces of darkness? It seems sometimes that they want the person to die to prove that they were right. They want to show us that it was really witchcraft and that our medicines are useless.

SIMEON

I've seen people go out of their way to discourage a patient and tell them they're going to die. All this after I've spent so much time trying to get them to be encouraging and hopeful. Then, when the person finally does die, largely in part to the psychological attacks of their family, they go out of their way to brag.

They say, "I told you so. I knew they would die, but you kept insisting they had a chance. See, I was right and you were wrong." Nothing that I've experienced here is nearly as discouraging as this.

I light a kerosene lamp to bring a little light to the darkness of my room and pull out a well-worn book. Finally, I find what I'm looking for, right next to the Bible's most famous verse: "This is the judgment, that the light has come into the world, and men loved the darkness rather than the light; for their works were evil." (John 3:19)

I can now understand a little of God's dilemma. As shown humorously in the movie *Bruce Almighty,* God can't "mess with free will." In other words, Satan has an advantage: he can use fear, force, superstition, manipulation, coercion, and brutality but God can't. Because I've aligned myself on God's side, I can't use those things either.

As much as I'd like to take some parents and wring their necks, I can't. I want them to realize they need to bring their kids to the hospital when they first become sick rather then when they're on death's door. But I can't force them. I have to try and persuade them.

It's true. Men and women really do love the darkness rather than the light. It's so frustrating realizing there's nothing one can do about it except continue to fight. Even if it seems like a losing battle, I have to continue to fight against the darkness of ignorance, tradition and superstition. Why? Because who knows, maybe one or two will see the light and come out of the darkness.

EPILOGUE

As of the end of this book, I'd been in Africa for three years with Sarah and we'd been married for two of those. We continue to work in the Republic of *Tchad*.

Samedi was sent off to nursing school since he doesn't even have a high school diploma. Everything he's learned, he's learned on the job.

Anatole continues to run the lab and wear old, worn out baseball caps.

David left to work for a government hospital in the north on the edge of the Sahara.

Nathan returned to the US and is currently the Administrator of the Haiti Adventist Hospital in Port-au-Prince.

Dimanche moved to N'Djamena with her husband and child.

Degaulle still insists on trying to sing in English.

Koumakoi is studying in Yaoundé, Cameroon.

Doumpa is training to be a nurse in N'Djamena.

Israel works as a nurse in the Southern California.

Jennie returned to Tennessee to work in an ER.

Gueltir is still the principal of the Béré Adventist School.

Lona moved to eastern *Tchad* near the border with Darfur in Sudan and took Fambé with him.

Rahama has retired and lives within a few blocks of the hospital. Her husband recently died.

Pierre still works as the cashier, sometimes with his shirt on.

Ahmat disappeared into the wilds of the Sahel.

TO BE CONTINUED...

GLOSSARY

ANTI-RETROVIRAL (ARV): medication to treat HIV/AIDS by slowing down the multiplication of the virus. To be most effective, three different ARV medications are taken simultaneously. ARVs can control AIDS but not cure it

AS-SALAAM ALEIKUM: Traditional Muslim greeting, Arabic for "Peace be unto you." The standard response is *"Wa aleikum as-salaam"*

ASCITES: liquid in the abdominal cavity, usually from cirrhosis, (scarring) of the liver or cancer; in the developing world is often caused by tuberculosis

BÉRÉ: village of approximately 15,000 in southern *Tchad* where the Béré Adventist Hospital is located

BÉRÉ ADVENTIST HOSPITAL: District hospital in *Tchad's* health care system founded by the Seventh-day Adventist Church in the late 1970's where the stories in this book take place

BETADINE: Povidine Iodine, a brown disinfectant used to prepare skin for surgical procedures

BOUILLIE: traditional *Tchadian* porridge made of flour, rice, sugar, peanut paste and lime

BREECH: The position of a fetus in the uterus, butt first, feet and head following; carries a higher risk for complications during delivery

CADEAU: Gift in French, often the first word a *Nasara* hears on arriving in *Tchad*, usually accompanied by *donnez-moi* (give me). The only French many children know.

CARNET: French word for small book. Portable medical record in the health care system of *Tchad;* usually made out of a school notebook cut in half

CHARI: Main river in *Tchad*, joins with the Logone River at N'Djamena and empties into Lake Chad.

C-SECTION: Short for Cesarean section, a common obstetrical operation where the surgeon opens up the uterus through the abdominal wall to deliver the baby as rapidly and safely as possible. Reserved for complicated labor and delivery.

DEBRIDEMENT, TO DEBRIDE: Surgical term for cutting away dead tissue in an infected wound to speed up healing or arrest the advancement of the infection

DOCTEUR CHOUKOU: Under qualified person passing himself off as a medical doctor, often a nurse or someone with a Red Cross certificate, they usually practice out of their own homes or make house calls, common in *Tchad*

ECTOPIC PREGNANCY: Pregnancy outside of the normal location in the uterus

PLASMODIUM FALCIPARUM: most virulent strain of Malaria responsible for most of the deaths and severe complications of this global pandemic, also the most common and most drug-resistant species of Malaria

FRANC CFA: Money used in *Tchad* and throughout francophone Central Africa, 500 FCFA is equivalent to approximately one US dollar.

FULANI: Nomadic cattle herders ranging across most of western, sub-Saharan Africa, almost 100% Muslim

GARDE: French word for nurse, doctor or other health care worker on overnight duty or call at the hospital

GENDARME: regional police in a French-based government

INSHALLAH: Arabic, if Allah wills or wishes, when Allah wills

IV: Intravenous, inside the vein, how to get medications and fluids directly into a person's blood circulation

JALLABIYA: Arabic word for long, loose-fitting robe with long sleeves and matching pants, the most common garment worn by Muslim men in *Tchad*

KETAMINE: anesthetic medication providing a dissociative effect allowing the patient to be operated on without pain, yet without losing his airway, breathing or gag reflexes; not used much in developed countries due to emergence reactions which can cause vivid nightmares and hallucinations

LAPIA: Greeting in *Nangjeré*, the local dialect of Béré; literally "health"

MASHALLAH: Arabic, whatever Allah wills

MECONIUM: Newborn's first stool; if the meconium comes out before birth, it is a sign that the fetus is stressed

MÉDECIN: Medical doctor in French

NANGJERÉ: The local language spoken in the health district of Béré

NASARA: *Tchadian* Arabic for foreigner, used especially for white foreigners. Not a derogatory term.

N'DJAMENA: Capital of the Republic of *Tchad*, formerly known as Fort Lamy

OSTEOMYELITIS: infection of the bone, common in developing countries

OR: Operating room where major surgeries are performed in as sterile an environment as possible

OTOSCOPE: Medical instrument used to illuminate and magnify when examining the ear canal and nasal passages

RAMADAN: Muslim month-long yearly fast from sunrise to sunset; one of the five pillars of the Islamic faith; the end is celebrated with a feast: *Id al-Fitr*

SACAND: Small, plastic covered water pot with a spout used by *Tchadians* for ablutions before the five daily Muslim prayers; also used before meals for hand washing

SOUK: Arabic market

SYMPHISIOTOMY: Obstetrical procedure where the surgeon cuts through the cartilage holding the front of the pelvis together. This effectively widens the pelvic outlet permitting a large baby to be born through a small pelvis

TCHAD: Official spelling of the country of Chad in French

TCHADIAN ARABIC: Second official language of *Tchad*; related to classical Arabic, but a recognized different language. The trade and market language in *Tchad*.

UNDP: United Nations Development Project

VESSICO-VAGINAL FISTULA: Hole between the vagina and bladder leading to urinary incontinence, usually from a difficult delivery or a complication of a pelvic surgery, often leads to isolation and abandonment in the developing world

XALAS! : Arabic. Enough! Okay! All right! At last! Finally! Done!

ABOUT THE AUTHOR

James Appel, MD graduated from the Loma Linda University School of Medicine in 2000 and then completed a three year residency in Family Practice at the Ventura County Medical Center in California. He spent seven years as the only doctor at the Béré Adventist Hospital directly responsible for the health care of over 150,000 Chadians. He is also the Chad country director for the NGO Adventist Health International which runs over 20 hospitals in Africa and the rest of the developing world. When he's not saving lives in Africa he likes to surf, eat Mexican food, and drive his orange VW Vanagon.